THE WILD MISSISSIPPI

For the Mississippi River and the life it supports

Photo and illustration credits appear on page 323.

Timber Press
Workman Publishing
Hachette Book Group, Inc.
1290 Avenue of the Americas
New York, New York 10104

timberpress.com

Timber Press is an imprint of Workman Publishing, a division of Hachette Book Group, Inc. The Timber Press name and logo are registered trademarks of Hachette Book Group, Inc.

Printed in China on responsibly sourced paper
Text design by Vincent James
Cover design by Leigh Thomas

The publisher is not responsible for websites (or their content) that are not owned by the publisher.

The Hachette Speakers Bureau provides a wide range of authors for speaking events. To find out more, go to hachettespeakersbureau.com or email hachettespeakers@hbgusa.com.

ISBN 978-1-64326-179-9

A catalog record for this book is available from the Library of Congress.

THE
WILD
MISSISSIPPI

A STATE-BY-STATE GUIDE TO THE
RIVER'S NATURAL WONDERS

Dean Klinkenberg

TIMBER PRESS
PORTLAND, OREGON

CONTENTS

PREFACE

I GOT MY INTRODUCTION to the world of the Mississippi River as a college student in the 1980s. I lived in La Crosse, Wisconsin, in the famed Driftless Area, with fishing enthusiasts, hunters, and river rats as my neighbors. I spent a lot of time near the river. I hiked up and around the bluffs and biked to the river's edge to watch the river flow. Time along the river calmed me. I felt connected to a bigger world. I was hooked.

I still spend a lot of time along the river today and never tire of it. The river offers something new every day. I've watched beavers chewing on sticks and bald eagles snatch fish out of the river. I stood twenty feet from a bobcat before it slipped into a marsh. In Minnesota, I watched a porcupine on the side of the road enjoying a snack. From northern Minnesota to the Gulf of Mexico, I have immersed myself in the river's waters. Every sunset soothes my mind. Every morning on a sandbar renews my spirit.

The river we call Mississippi is a remarkable place, a life-giving and life-sustaining force that runs through the heart of the United States. Its name is from the Algonquin-speaking Native Americans who lived in the river's headwaters region. The earliest known written use of the name is from a letter written by Father Claude-Jean Allouez, a missionary spreading the Christian gospel to Native Americans along the Fox River in central Wisconsin. In 1667, Allouez wrote: "THESE are people [the Mascouten People] dwelling to the West of this place, toward the great river named Messipi. They are forty or fifty leagues from this place, in a country of prairies, rich in all kinds of game."

It's likely that French trappers had heard the name even before Allouez. In 1681, Estienne Michallete created a map on which he refers to the river as "*Mitchisipi ou Grande Riviere.*" By the 1700s, Mississippi was the name most commonly used by cartographers. The Algonquin words that gave us the river's name—*Messi-sipi*—do not mean "great river" but something more like "long river," according to the Ojibwe language experts I've consulted.

Indigenous communities lined the entire river, of course, and each had their own name for it. The Cheyenne People were apparently not starry-eyed romantics about the river; they called it *Má'xe-é'ometaa'a* (Big Greasy River). Interestingly, the Missouri River was *É'ometáá'e* (Greasy River, just without the superlative); they also knew a *É'komó'eo'hé'e* (Greasy Grass River).

The Pawnee called the river *Kickaátit.* The southern Lenape, who encountered the Mississippi after being forced from the east coast, may have called it *Namesi Sipu* (Fish River), although they used the same term for some other rivers. The Arapaho used the word *Beesniicíe*, whereas the Wyandot (Wendat) word was reportedly *Yandawezue.* You get the point. Lots of names. But all these names also reveal that this river has been central to our lives for a long time.

The author canoeing the Mississippi River in northern Minnesota.

Whatever we call it, the Mississippi is a special place. The river's north-south route has enabled the long-term survival of many species of plant and animal life. When the climate cooled, they migrated south. As the climate warmed, they extended their range north. The river's world provides space for life to emerge, grow into adulthood, mate, and provide sustenance to others in death.

When you look at the Mississippi, it's hard not to focus on all that water. The Mississippi, though, is far more than moving water. It's a complex system (even a complex of systems) that has evolved over millennia. Water from the main channel connects to wetlands along its reach. Trees grow in dense clusters along the river and along the land that rises away from it. Grasslands occupy niches in the Mississippi's world. And hundreds of species of animals depend on this interconnected system for their survival—from tiny zooplankton to massive alligator gar, from delicate silky asters to ancient bald cypress, from mayflies to damselflies, from songbirds just passing through to resident bald eagles. All depend on the world of the Mississippi for space to raise their children and to sustain them through their lives.

I'm going to guide you into the river's world. For the sake of convenience, I've divided the topics into main channel habitats, wetlands, prairies, and forests, but these divisions exist mostly in our heads. In the river's world, everything connects. Birds need mayflies, which need wetlands; paddlefish need zooplankton, and both need the flowing waters of a big river; least terns need sandbars. Boundaries are ephemeral. Today's cypress swamp can be tomorrow's marsh. Prairies become forests.

I'm sure some people find mountain scenery more appealing than the Mississippi. I get it. Mountains may inspire people to great heights (just not me!), but the Mississippi invites us to slow down. There are places along the river that offer jaw-dropping beauty, but most of the beauty in the river's world is more subtle.

I first visited the Mississippi headwaters in the middle of winter. From the parking lot at Itasca State Park, I snowshoed to the edge of the lake and took a selfie. I had the entire spot to myself. I continued through the forest and got lost in the quiet, then retreated to a cabin where I warmed up with hot chocolate. In spring, I've hiked through floodplain forests painted with wildflowers and filled with the music of songbirds. I've savored fall mornings when cooler air dips into the Mississippi valley and wisps of fog rise from the water like spirits, framed by the oranges, reds, and yellows of trees preparing for their winter slumber.

All this and so much more keeps me coming back, in different seasons, at different times of day. I hope this book inspires you to do the same, to visit the Mississippi time and again, and experience its varied moods, to get to know the life that depends on it, to listen to the river and take your time while you're there.

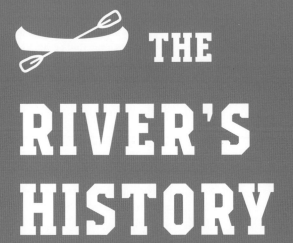

THE
RIVER'S
HISTORY

THE BIRTH AND LIFE OF A RIVER

THREE HUNDRED MILLION years ago, practically yesterday, the Earth's land masses collided and formed the supercontinent Pangea. The great tectonic plates beneath the land masses pushed up, over, and under each other, which forced the land to rise. Along the margins of the areas where the plates collided, mountains rose, one of which was the Ouachita-Appalachian Mountain range.

As Pangea split up a hundred million years later—just thirty million years after the emergence of dinosaurs—one of the fault lines was along the Ouachita-Appalachian Mountains. As the land masses drifted apart, the emerging gaps filled with water. The gap south of the Ouachita-Appalachian Mountains grew into the coral-ringed Gulf of Mexico.

For tens of millions of years, those mountains blocked most water in North America from flowing into the Gulf of Mexico. Most rivers flowed to Canada and the Boreal Sea. Only the few rivers that flowed south of the range emptied directly into the Gulf—but big changes were coming.

About one hundred million years ago, the Farallon and Kula tectonic plates slipped under the North American plate, causing a portion of west-central North America to sink. The lower elevations gradually filled with water (sea level was rising, too), which formed the Western Interior Seaway, a body of water that eventually grew long enough to link the Boreal Sea with the Gulf of Mexico.

Rivers flowing from the western side of the Appalachians no longer merged with streams that flowed to the Boreal Sea, but emptied into the Western Interior Seaway, as did some rivers west of the seaway. The ancestral Tennessee-Alabama River flowed through the southern section of the continent and was the largest river that connected with the Gulf of Mexico. Geysers dotted the landscape. Dinosaurs roamed.

Thirty million years later, sea levels dropped, and the Western Interior Seaway slowly drained. Around the same time, a sixty-two-mile gap had opened between the Ouachita Mountains and the Appalachian Mountains. Much of the land below the gap had sunk well below adjacent areas, so water crept into it from the Gulf of Mexico and covered the low-lying areas for the next sixty million years.

By seventy million years ago, the land above the subterranean Reelfoot Rift in the central United States had dropped in elevation. The areas that had sunk then captured water and allowed it to flow south, where it merged with the waters of the Gulf of Mexico around Cairo, Illinois. The Mississippi River was born.

During its infancy, waters from the northern and central Appalachian Mountains fed the Mississippi. The ancestral Tennessee-Alabama River flowed from the southern Appalachians to the Gulf of Mexico.

Out west, water from west-central North America drained into the ancestral Brazos, Colorado, and Arkansas Rivers, which eventually emptied directly into the Gulf of Mexico. An ancestral Rio Grande River drained a small portion of the southwestern United States.

Just a few million years after the Mississippi River began to flow, a huge meteor struck Earth in the Gulf of Mexico and wiped out much of the planet's life, including the dinosaurs. By sixty million years ago—about when the Rocky Mountains had reached their highest point—the Mississippi River had grown to, perhaps, 1,200 miles long and drained much of central North America.

By fifty-six million years ago, the Platte and Arkansas Rivers had rerouted so that they flowed into the Mississippi River at the northern end of the Mississippi Embayment. This was the first time the Mississippi River received water and sediment from western North America.

By thirty million years ago, the Tennessee River had shifted north and merged with the ancestral Ohio River, which eventually merged with the Mississippi at the northern end of the Mississippi Embayment. The Platte River shifted north and east for a few million years before rejoining the Mississippi basin. Farther south, the Arkansas and Red Rivers shifted their course to drain into the Mississippi River at the southern end of the Mississippi Embayment.

The Mississippi grew into an enormous river. By five million years ago, it was carrying up to eight times as much water as the Lower Mississippi River carries today. The Mississippi's headwaters may have extended into southern Canada.

Three million years ago, sea level was about eighty feet higher than it is today. The Mississippi and Ohio Rivers merged around Helena, Arkansas. Just a blink of geologic time later, everything changed again when the planet cooled and massive sheets of ice slowly covered much of the Upper Mississippi valley.

WATER TO ICE

Two and one-half million years ago, the climate cooled and water turned to ice. As the water froze, it grew into towers of ice that slowly spread across the land and seas. The first major advance of glaciers into the central United States began about one million years ago. For hundreds of thousands of years, ice sheets reached deep into the Mississippi valley, retreated for a while, then returned. During peak cold periods, ice covered as much as 30 percent of the planet. Millions of square miles of permafrost formed in the areas next to the glaciers. In North America, a permafrost belt about one hundred miles wide developed around the margins of the glaciers. Sea levels dropped up to three hundred feet as the glaciers trapped moisture.

The giant Laurentide Ice Sheet spanned millions of square miles in North America and soared more than a mile high in places, covering most of Canada and, occasionally, creeping as far south as the Middle Mississippi valley. As the glaciers advanced, they leveled hills and the ground compacted and sank under their enormous weight. Parts of the Upper Mississippi valley disappeared under ice.

The glaciers rearranged the flow of water around the continent. Ice redirected the flow of the ancestral Ohio River and gave birth to the Missouri River we know today. The glaciers forced changes in where the Mississippi River flowed, too, sometimes pushing the channel east or west.

Along the Lower Mississippi, the river forged a wide floodplain covered with sand and sediment scraped up by the advancing glaciers and carried by the river. As the ice sucked up more and more water, the Lower Mississippi's flow decreased while the sediment load increased, and the river developed a braided channel, multiple small channels that flowed around thick island complexes. Once the glacial meltwater flow diminished, the volume of water in the Mississippi decreased. The current slowed and the braided channel transformed into one that meandered across the land. Beginning about 250,000 years ago, winds blowing over the floodplain picked up fine-grained particles from the river's floodplain and, over tens of thousands of years, built the loess hills upon which Memphis, Vicksburg, and Natchez would be built.

About eighty-five thousand years ago, just before the onset of the Wisconsin Glacial Episode, the last major advance of ice in North America, a portion of the Mississippi River broke through the Bell City–Oran Gap in southern Missouri's Crowley's Ridge and followed a path through the Eastern Lowlands where it formed a new confluence with the Ohio River. Twenty-five thousand years ago, the Mississippi permanently abandoned its channel through the Western Lowlands and settled fully into the Eastern Lowlands, where it would flow for the next thirteen thousand years.

ICE TO WATER

Twenty thousand years ago, the glaciers in North America reached their peak penetration into the Mississippi valley. When the glaciers reached their maximum extent, the drainage basin for the Mississippi River was immense, reaching all the way to Hudson Bay.

The climate soon warmed again, and ice slowly turned to liquid. The weather was sometimes warmer and sometimes cooler, so the pace of melting varied. In northwest Minnesota, a piece of the ice sheet called the Des Moines lobe expanded briefly before it melted away. In its wake, it left behind the Big Stone Moraine, a tall ridge built up on the side of the ice from debris that the glacier had pushed to its edge. As the glaciers melted, the moraine formed a dam. The water behind Big Stone Moraine grew into a massive lake known as Glacial Lake Agassiz.

The water rose until it reached the top of the moraine, then, thirteen thousand years ago, it spilled over near Browns Valley, Minnesota, and carved a path through the Traverse Gap. Torrents of water raced down a channel of the Minnesota River to Saint Paul and continued to flow for hundreds of miles south. This was Glacial River Warren.

Glacial River Warren transported melted ice for five hundred years, slowed for a thousand years, then picked up steam again and flowed for another seven hundred years. The torrents of water carved deep into the land from Browns Valley to St. Louis.

Farther south, the Mississippi River changed course again around Cape Girardeau. Instead of turning southwest for twenty miles through the Eastern Lowlands before turning back toward Commerce, Missouri, the river—possibly aided by changes in the land wrought by earthquakes along the New Madrid fault—diverted south through dense bedrock hundreds of millions of years old and cut a narrow gorge known as the Thebes Gap. Forty-four miles south of Thebes Gap, the Mississippi River formed a new confluence with the Ohio River.

The waters of Glacial River Warren filled the Mississippi's preglacial valley at Saint

Paul. The current washed away two hundred feet of soil and sediment from the bottom of the valley until it reached limestone bedrock. As the water dug out all that sediment, the elevation changed between parts of the channel around Saint Paul, which formed River Warren Falls, the ancestor of today's St. Anthony Falls in Minneapolis.

South of Saint Paul, River Warren followed a preglacial Mississippi River channel. The water flowed south until Pine Bend, where it turned to the east and followed an old channel near where the Minnesota and Mississippi Rivers merged before the Ice Age. Farther east, the water merged with more meltwater coming down the St. Croix River, and the channel shifted to the south.

By ten thousand years ago—not long after the formation of the Great Lakes—the continental United States was free of glacial ice. After the glaciers retreated north, the most northern channel of the Mississippi River emerged in Minnesota above Saint Paul.

Nine thousand years ago, the meltwaters feeding Glacial River Warren reduced dramatically. As the volume of water reduced to a fraction of what it had been, the current slowed and returned sediment to the base of the wide valley. Tributaries cut steep paths to reach the Mississippi River. At Saint Paul, for example, the channel was as much as 150 feet deeper than it is today. Tributaries built fan deltas that sloped to meet the Mississippi, and those deltas pushed the Mississippi's channel around. The Vermilion River near Hastings pushed the current to the northeast. The Chippewa River Delta

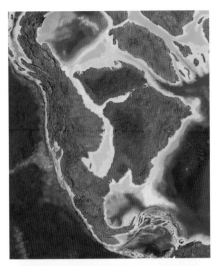
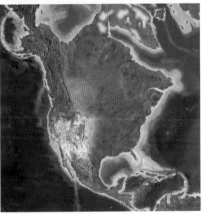

TOP TO BOTTOM:
• *North America 70 million years ago, when the Mississippi River was born*
• *5 million years ago*
• *12–15 thousand years ago, at the end of the Wisconsin Glacial Episode*

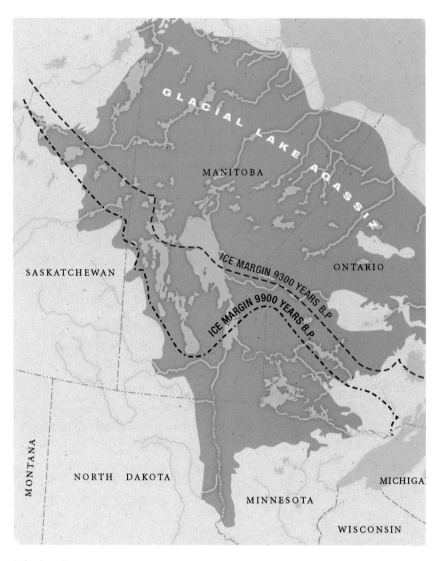

Lake Agassiz

formed a natural dam that created Lake Pepin, which may have backed up as far as Saint Paul a few thousand years ago.

By seven thousand years ago, the Mississippi River that we know today—or at least knew in the nineteenth century—had taken form: a braided channel on the upper river that flows around multiple islands and a meandering river farther south.

THE FUTURE

Change is the rule in the natural world, even if much of that change happens well beyond a human time scale. The land rises and falls. Temperatures change. Rivers alter course and grow and shrink in response to conditions around them.

The Mississippi River is not immune to change. It's likely, for example, that the Mississippi River will grow bigger in the future, although I won't be here to witness it. Much of the land in southern Canada is still rising. Glaciers are heavy, so as they form and spread across the land, their weight pushes the land down. When a glacier melts, the land it previously covered rises. Southern Canada has been uplifting since the retreat of the Laurentide Ice Sheet and could rise another four hundred feet over the next few thousand years. When that happens, the rise will probably direct more water into the Mississippi basin and turn the Mississippi into a bigger river again.

GEOLOGIC FEATURES OF THE RIVER TODAY

The Mississippi is much more than water moving down a channel toward the sea. From its headwaters in northern Minnesota to the Gulf of Mexico, the river responds and changes to the world around it. Sudden elevation changes create rapids or waterfalls. Other streams merge with the Mississippi, creating a bigger river. The river cuts through rolling hills, carving a dramatic valley in the process. Those hills give way to flat floodplains, which are sometimes dense with stands of trees and, other times, lined with manicured rows of corn. Let's look at the major geologic features that still define the Mississippi today.

St. Anthony Falls today

Owahmenah/St. Anthony Falls

The cataract at downtown Minneapolis is the remnant of a massive waterfall known as River Warren Falls. The Dakota People called the falls Owahmenah (falling waters), whereas neighboring Ojibwe named it Kakabikah (severed rock). We know it today by the name it was given by Father Louis Hennepin in 1680, St. Anthony Falls.

The falls trace their roots to the end of the last ice age as glacial meltwaters filled the Minnesota and Mississippi valleys. What a remarkable sight they must have been when they formed: water cascading down 175 feet—about the same as Niagara Falls—and stretching one-half mile wide. Glacial River Warren flowed over hard Platteville limestone that rested atop sandstone. As the water flowed, it seeped through cracks in the limestone and eroded the underlying sandstone. Over time, a ledge of limestone hung farther and farther out over the eroded sandstone until gravity pulled down

unsupported chunks. As these chunks of limestone cracked and fell, the falls migrated upstream at an average pace of four feet per year.

When the falls reached the confluence of the Minnesota and Mississippi Rivers, they split. One branch retreated up the Minnesota River until it hit an old river channel about two miles from the confluence and petered out. The other branch continued up the Mississippi River, leaving behind the only gorge along the Mississippi's course.

Businesses near the falls—sawmills, mostly—relied on the falls to generate hydropower for their factories, so the continued erosion was problematic. In 1869, an attempt to stabilize the falls led to a near catastrophic collapse. After a few years of failed attempts to fix the damage, the US Army Corps of Engineers poured a concrete cap over the falls to prevent further erosion, which is still in place today.

The Mississippi River in the Driftless Area, from Lansing, Iowa's Mount Hosmer

The Driftless Area

Much of Minnesota was shaped by what the glaciers did, but there's one area that is shaped by what they didn't do: they didn't flatten the land. The Driftless Area covers twenty-four thousand square miles in Minnesota, Wisconsin, Iowa, and Illinois that were not touched by the last round of glaciers. The area has none of the rocky, gravelly debris, called drift, left behind by glaciers, hence the name. Rolling hills, steep valleys, and a variety of ecosystems, some of them quite rare, define the Driftless Area. This landscape contrasts markedly with the hundreds of miles of agricultural lands all around it. The topography isn't ideal for city-building, so most of the communities in the Driftless Area are rather small.

The Mississippi River cuts through the heart of the Driftless Area, carving a dramatic valley framed by tall limestone bluffs. Tributary streams with clear, cold water disappear into the Mississippi at the ends of steep valleys that some folks (mostly in Wisconsin) call coulees. Many of these streams provide ideal habitat for trout but are also prone to unpredictable bouts of flash flooding.

As the glaciers melted, unfathomable amounts of water raced down the Mississippi River, carving a deep path through the limestone and sandstone bedrock of the Driftless Area. All that glacial meltwater carried tons of silt, sand, and gravel that eventually settled to the bottom of the valley as the water flow slowed. The river valley today—framed by bluffs that rise five hundred feet or more above the river—sits on top of sediment that is three hundred feet deep.

The Missouri River near its confluence with the Mississippi

The Missouri River

Running for 2,522 miles, the Missouri River is not only the longest tributary of the Mississippi, it is the longest river in North America. From its presumed source at Brower's Spring in the Centennial Mountains in Montana, it flows through six states and much of the Great Plains. If we define the Missouri River as the body of water that emerges from the Rocky Mountains and that flows east and south, eventually emptying its waters into the Gulf of Mexico, there wasn't really a Missouri River before the Ice Age began more than two million years ago.

For millions of years, water from the northern Great Plains and Rocky Mountains drained east and north into Canada and the Boreal Sea. Much of the Missouri River's course today, from Great Falls to Kansas City, formed along the edge of glaciers, some of it through old channels of preglacial rivers and other parts in new channels that were cut by meltwaters as the glaciers retreated. The river's narrow valleys were, for the most part, cut after the glaciers left, whereas the wider valleys formed in preglacial times. In North Dakota, for example, the Missouri River flows through some valleys that are six to twelve miles wide and that typically flow west to east; these are preglacial river channels. In contrast, the Missouri flows through valleys that are less than two miles wide and that typically flow north to south; these are the more recent channels.

The Chain of Rocks

The Chain of Rocks

The last set of rapids on the Mississippi cuts across the river just north of St. Louis. During the end of the last glacial period, the Mississippi, Missouri, and Illinois Rivers carried vast amounts of water from melting glaciers. Around St. Louis, the Mississippi's channel shifted west over areas of exposed bedrock. When the river is relatively low, the bedrock creates a series of rapids. Barges can't navigate over rapids, so the US Army Corps of Engineers built an 8.4-mile canal to bypass the rapids. It opened in 1953. On the river side, the Corps built a low-water dam from bank to bank, so the rapids we see today are actually water running over the concrete dam, not bedrock.

The Ohio River near its confluence with the Mississippi at Cairo, Illinois

The Ohio River

The Ohio River—the name came to us from the Seneca People—zigzags for 981 miles from Pittsburgh, Pennsylvania, to the Mississippi River (a distance of 546 miles as the crow flies) at Cairo, Illinois. Today, we identify the start of the Ohio River at the place where the Allegheny and Monongahela Rivers merge, but the Lenni Lenape (Delaware) and Haudenosaunee (Iroquois) Peoples carried the name "Ohio" up the Allegheny valley.

The Ohio is pretty young for a river. Some segments may be only one hundred thousand years old (such as the channel that passes Cincinnati). Before the Ice Age, the Teays River carried water from much of central and eastern North America east and north to the ocean. When the first sheet of ice crept south, the Nebraskan, it wiped out most of the Teays River but gave birth to the Ohio, a stream that flowed along the edges of the ice. Subsequent pulses of ice continued to shape and reshape the area around the nascent Ohio River, but by 130,000 years ago, the Ohio had more or less settled into its current channel. As the Ohio's channel shifted, so has the river's confluence with the Mississippi. The current confluence of the two rivers is only about 9,500 years old.

Although the Ohio River isn't as long as the Mississippi, it carries more water at their confluence, about 50 percent more than the Upper Mississippi does. The ecology of the Ohio has suffered tremendously from pollution dumped in it from the big cities and industries along its banks as well as from a series of locks and dams built to aid navigation, but some habitat restoration efforts are underway.

The Mississippi Embayment

About ninety-five million years ago, part of south-central North America passed over a hot spot deep in Earth's crust. Magma oozed toward the surface along existing fault lines in the crust. The heat and pressure bent the ground upward. Over the next ten million years, the land rose as high as 9,800 feet in places. Wind and water gradually eroded the uplifted land until it was roughly level with the surrounding land again. After ten million years, the hot spot rotated away and the land cooled. As the land cooled, it sank until it settled as much as 1.6 miles below sea level, which created a sixty-two-mile gap between the Ouachita and Appalachian Mountains.

The gap between the mountains and its lower elevation created space for a river—the ancestral Mississippi—to enter and flow through. Water also crept up and into the gap, covering the low-lying areas for parts of the next sixty million years as sea levels rose and fell. Scientists call this area the Mississippi Embayment. Layers of soil tell the story of the geologic history of the Embayment: sand, silt, and clay deposited thirty-five to fifty-five million years ago; sand and gravel three to five million years ago, and blankets of fine loess blown into place during the Ice Age.

The Mississippi Embayment

The Delta

The land at the end of the river, the area from roughly Baton Rouge, Louisiana, to the Gulf of Mexico, didn't exist as land until the Mississippi River built it, grain by grain, over seven thousand years. The delta plain in Louisiana spreads about 150 miles wide and 150 miles deep. Fan-shaped deposits from the Mississippi spread over even more of the floor of the Gulf of Mexico.

During those seven thousand years, the Mississippi has shifted the channel it follows to the sea five times. The areas where the channel meets the sea formed new lobes of land with each shift. The Mississippi River long ago moved away from four lobes (Lafourche, Maringouin, St. Bernard, and Teche), but two are active today: the Plaquemines-Balize lobe is today's bird's-foot delta, and another lobe is active at the end of the Atchafalaya River.

Each time the river jumped to a new channel, the sea became the dominant force shaping the borderlands. Some of the land in the old lobe dried up, eroded, and sank. Along the margin of land and sea, wind and water sculpted some areas into sandy points that eroded into barrier isltands.

The Mississippi will jump channels again. The Plaquemines-Balize lobe is reaching the end of its land-building cycle. Only a mass of concrete called the Old River Control Structure has stopped it from jumping to the Atchafalaya River in our lifetime.

Other Major Tributaries

The Mississippi River basin today covers 1.25 million square miles across thirty-two states and a small part of two Canadian provinces. Hundreds of rivers feed directly or indirectly into the Mississippi River. Here are some of the longer rivers:

- Arkansas (1,469 miles long)
- Des Moines (525 miles long)
- Wisconsin (430 miles long)
- Minnesota (370 miles long)
- Iowa (323 miles long)
- Rock (299 miles long)
- Illinois (273 miles long)
- Yazoo (190 miles long)
- Chippewa (183 miles long)
- St. Croix (169 miles long)

OPPOSITE: *The Mississippi's birds-foot delta*

HUMAN HISTORY

THIRTEEN THOUSAND YEARS ago, small groups of people lived in communities along the Gulf of Mexico at the mouth of the Mississippi River. The shallow, brackish waters of the delta teemed with fish and oysters that were easy to harvest. Farther upriver, Clovis-era people moved into Missouri around the same time. They hunted megafauna such as mastodons, but their diet was diverse and included a lot of the food that remained staples of Indigenous Peoples' cuisine for centuries.

Twelve thousand years ago, after the glaciers had retreated from the Upper Mississippi River valley, people migrated into Minnesota and Wisconsin. They adapted to a landscape in transition. The land was coming alive after millennia being buried under massive sheets of ice, and new ecosystems were emerging. Lichens slowly turned rock into dirt. Birds dropped seeds they carried from other places. Those seeds took root in the bare, gravelly soil and sprouted into green plants. At times, the Mississippi was a massive, raging river full of meltwater, an impenetrable barrier. At other times, the

meltwaters receded, and the Mississippi shrank to a fraction of its previous size.

Early residents of the Mississippi River valley traveled in small groups of a couple dozen people—extended families, probably—often accompanied by pet dogs. Vast lakes and rivers roaring with frigid water sometimes blocked travel routes. Emerging spruce-fir boreal forests supported limited plant and animal life, so food could be hard to find. The megafauna they hunted for food and hides would soon disappear. Still, they managed.

By nine thousand years ago, the continental ice was a distant memory. The climate had warmed and rains came less frequently. Prairies and savannas spread as boreal forests retreated. The flow of the Mississippi slowed as it carried less water. Some people moved into the Mississippi bottomlands, where they used stone tools to grind, chop, and cut. The Mississippi valley was rich in stone, especially in western Wisconsin, where people harvested rock, such as Cochrane chert, from ridgetops

In northern Minnesota, family groups spent summers in the grasslands. As the days grew shorter, people moved to areas around Lake Itasca and hunted bison with stone-tipped spears. After butchering the animals, they smoked and dried the meat, then scraped and tanned the hides. People celebrated their hunting success with a feast, then returned to their winter homes in nearby caves or forests. In spring, they returned to Lake Itasca to catch fish and turtles, then moved back to the grasslands for summer.

Some of their contemporaries farther south lived on the grassy plains and savannas of Arkansas and near the oak and hickory forests of the Lower Mississippi valley. They lived off abundant whitetail deer rather than bison and collected nuts and berries from the

LEFT: *Cochrane chert* / **ABOVE:** *A dugout canoe*

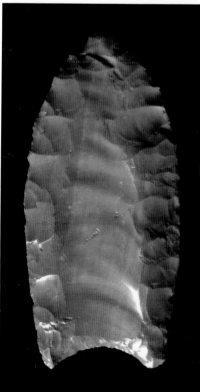

forests. They were among the first to shape stone into an adze, a useful tool for sculpting wood. It's likely that they used the adzes to carve dugout canoes to travel on the area's streams, probably even on the Mississippi.

By five thousand years ago, many people along the Middle and Lower Mississippi had shifted from living off the forest to living off the bounty of big rivers and their floodplains. They had taken the initial steps to domesticate plants. They learned first to manage plants in the family Cucurbitaceae (which includes cucumber, honey melon, pumpkin, and squash), whose seeds may have reached North America by floating across the Atlantic Ocean from Africa. People also soon domesticated chenopod, erect knotweed, marsh elder, maygrass, and sunflower.

Indigenous communities also actively managed the natural world to improve food production. Burning prairie grasses made hunting bison easier, but those fires also promoted diversity among plant communities. Indigenous People in northern forests used fire to clear dead trees to reduce the risk of catastrophic blazes, and to encourage the growth of plants they liked, such as blueberries. Along the southern reaches of the Mississippi, Indigenous Peoples managed forests to maximize the productivity of fruit- and nut-bearing trees.

MOUND BUILDERS

Indigenous People in North America have built monumental earthworks for thousands of years, especially near big rivers such as the Mississippi. The earliest known structures in the Mississippi valley were built at a place called Watson Brake in present-day Louisiana. Work on the mounds began 5,500 years ago and continued for the next five centuries. Those early inhabitants built their first mound nearly a millennium before the first pyramid rose in Egypt and five hundred years before tribes in England moved slabs of rocks into a circle to create Stonehenge.

Watson Brake sits on a slight rise near the Ouachita River eighty miles west of the Mississippi. The site includes eleven mounds arranged in an oval pattern, each connected by a low ridge. The early architects aligned the mounds with the summer and winter solstices, maybe to draw people together to mark important seasonal transitions and for ceremonial or religious worship.

Construction required a lot of effort and skill to organize labor and materials, something that anthropologists once assumed hunter-gatherer cultures couldn't do. But they did. There are thirteen known mound sites in Louisiana and Mississippi that date

to the same period, although they were probably built independently.

In subsequent generations, people in the area developed impressive trade networks, much of it facilitated by travel on the Mississippi River. Copper reached the Mississippi valley from upper Michigan, some of which was used to create elaborate personal ornaments. Seashells flowed in from the coast, flint from North Dakota, and obsidian from Wyoming. Besides growing trade networks, people increasingly milled grains and nuts for food and developed formal rituals to bury their dead.

The next known earthworks were built about 3,700 years ago at a place known as Poverty Point, today, a UNESCO World Heritage Site. The site is 15 miles west of the Mississippi River atop Macon Ridge, 130 miles of elongated high ground that snakes through swamps and forests that the Mississippi River flooded seasonally. The community at Poverty Point occupied just a few square miles, but its influence spread throughout the Lower Mississippi valley and the Southeast.

The earliest structures at Poverty Point included a mound and a plaza covered with several large circular structures. Two hundred years later, the people of Poverty Point radically reshaped the site. They abandoned the first mound and cleared and covered the plaza. They built a new mound, then a series of six semi-elliptical terraces. Shortly after that, the people of Poverty Point built an enormous structure called Mound A—the second largest earthen structure in North America. Only Monks Mound at Cahokia is larger.

The people of Poverty Point completed the ambitious reconstruction rapidly—they built the terraces in a single generation. Even more remarkable, they probably completed Mound A in just ninety days, a feat that

Watson Brake Mounds

North Mounds

South Mounds

A "Gentry Mound"

Louisiana

0 m   9m
Height above Ground

250 Meter

Mounds at Watson Brake

Poverty Point, Louisiana

would have required perhaps four thousand people to complete.

To build those structures, the people of Poverty Point had to organize, feed, and house a large labor force. Although there's no evidence that they grew their own food, they probably didn't need to. The surrounding area was abundant with life. The waters teemed with fish, which they caught with nets and seines weighed down with stone weights, an invention that improved the quantity of fish they could catch and that likely created a food surplus.

Why would a group of people who lived off what they could hunt and collect come together en masse to build mounds and terraces? Although we may never know the answer to that question, in recent years, one idea has gained traction: that Poverty Point was a site for collective worship—a place of pilgrimage that attracted the reverent.

After two hundred years of gathering at Poverty Point, the people abandoned it. Again, we don't know why, although its decline may have been driven by changes in climate. Some three thousand years ago, the region became wetter and cooler. The Gulf Coast was probably hit by more frequent and severe hurricanes. An increase in flood intensity and duration would have disrupted trade networks and may have made it harder to collect food. People may have just decided that life in the floodplain was no longer tenable, so they migrated out to prairies and savannas to start a new way of living.

ADENA-HOPEWELL TRADITION

Along the upper part of the Mississippi River, three thousand years ago, people built seasonal communities in its rich bottomlands where they lived during the warmer months. As the weather cooled, they dispersed into smaller groups and moved to the uplands where deer were abundant. As they returned to the same places every year, some communities grew. They produced pottery to store food and water and carved stone pipes for the first time (and traded some of them). They also reshaped the landscape in remarkable ways

Three Bear Mounds, part of the Marching Bear Group at Effigy Mounds National Monument

to build structures that reflected their views of life, death, and the afterlife.

The earliest mounds in the Middle and Upper Mississippi basin were built along the Ohio River by people of the Adena-Hopewell tradition. (There's a similar cultural group south of the Ohio River that archaeologists have labeled the Marksville tradition.) Between 2,400 and 1,600 years ago, they built some amazing structures in south-central Ohio, including a stunning serpent mound that coils nearly 1,400 feet across the top of a hill.

The influence of the Adena-Hopewell culture extended into the Upper Mississippi valley, where people built mounds shaped like animals. There are many spectacular examples. At Effigy Mounds National Monument in Iowa, dozens of animal-shaped mounds line the bluff tops overlooking the Mississippi River. Native Americans built most of them between 1,400 and 850 years ago. Birds are a common theme, but they shaped some mounds like turtles and bison, and there's a spectacular series of ten bears that appear to march across the landscape.

About one thousand years ago, another sea change was in the works, one that would reshape life for people along the Mississippi River and far beyond. It would result in some of the largest pre-European earthworks in North America and a population explosion that created one of the continent's great cities.

MISSISSIPPIAN CULTURE RISES

The American Bottom, the wide floodplain sculpted over millennia by the collision of three turbulent and sediment-rich big rivers—the Missouri, Mississippi, and Illinois—sprawls over 175 square miles of Illinois along the Mississippi River from Alton to Chester. It was an ideal spot to build North America's first great city, a place whose rise was so stunning, so profound, that its culture—what archaeologists have labeled Mississippian—would spread around North America and shape how people lived long after its founders were gone.

Cahokia emerged in an area with a long history of human habitation, but the city did not emerge slowly and progressively. A thousand years ago, a thousand people lived in the area. Fifty years later, that community was razed and a new city rose in its place, a process that archaeologist Timothy Pauketat has labeled Cahokia's "big bang."

Cahokia's transformative growth was not an accident. The city's leaders carefully planned the city's core, including the central plaza and some mounds, and built it all during a single construction boom about 950 years ago. At its peak, Cahokia was home to, perhaps, ten thousand people, with thirty thousand to forty thousand people living in nearby communities, including East St. Louis and St. Louis. Immigrants streamed into Cahokia from central Arkansas, the Red River valley, southern Indiana, and the Illinois River valley. We aren't entirely sure why so many people migrated to Cahokia, but it's possible that stories drew them. Cahokia may have emerged as a ritual center (or "theater state" as some archaeologists have called it) where people heard stories about creation and the heroes that helped shape their daily life.

A few key factors helped propel the city's rapid ascent. A warmer, wetter climate began about 1,200 years ago (the Medieval Warm Period), which improved conditions for agriculture, corn especially. The people in Cahokia also had relatively easy access to virtually all the resources they needed to build and maintain a large city.

The Ozark Mountains to the southwest provided chert for arrowheads, hoes, and other tools. From the prairies to the north and west, people hunted big game and harvested grasses for their buildings. Forests to the east provided a bounty of berries, game, and nuts, plus hardwood trees for tools, fuel, and building materials. From the bottomlands, people collected salt, edible plants (like cattails), and tall trees for dugout canoes. The river itself yielded a bounty of fish and waterfowl. What the Mississippians lacked nearby, they traded for. They got copper from the upper Great Lakes, seashells from the Gulf Coast, and mica from Appalachia.

Rivers were central to the lives of Cahokians. Apart from the food they provided, the rivers offered a reliable means of getting around. Cahokia Creek, which is barely a trickle today, once provided a water connection to the Mississippi River. Mississippians navigated the rivers in dugout canoes that were built in different sizes and for different purposes. They carved most of them from a single tree, most commonly bald cypress, cottonwood, or poplar.

Cahokians were also cognizant of their location in the Mississippi River's floodplain and the surrounding wetlands and creeks. They built plazas and walkways so their surfaces sloped to direct water into canals and holding ponds. These engineering measures kept the city protected from most floods.

Artistic rendering of Cahokia

Metropolitan Cahokia

Cahokia's planners laid out the city core in a diamond shape over five square miles of wetlands and creeks. They concentrated Cahokia's most important monuments and neighborhoods in the city center, which was also where Cahokians built monumental Monks Mound and a large plaza for public events such as games of chunkey as well as markets and festivals. They built mounds and the passageways to connect them that aligned precisely with important solar, lunar, and other celestial events.

Other neighborhoods radiated out from the center, each anchored by a smaller plaza of its own. Cahokians built houses by excavating a rectangular trench for the outer walls, a uniquely Mississippian style. Walkways connected neighborhoods.

They built major satellite villages at today's East St. Louis (fifty mounds) and St. Louis (twenty-six mounds). With Cahokia, these sites make up three of the five largest known Mississippian sites in North America. Besides the major population centers, a network of rural villages surrounded the principal city, many serving specialized roles to support the communities, such as growing particular crops and weaving cloth.

One of these outlying sites may have helped spark the city's rapid growth, a site known as the Emerald Acropolis. The earliest constructions at the site date to a thousand years ago, but Cahokians completely rebuilt the entire acropolis about fifty years later, coincident with Cahokia's big bang. The new acropolis included sweat lodges, council houses, temporary housing for pilgrims, and new shrines.

For the thousands of farmers living outside the city of Cahokia, the acropolis may have held particular significance. Keeping so many people fed was an enormous job. Corn was an important crop, but not the only domesticated plant. Cahokia's farmers—most of whom were women—continued to cultivate native seeds such as chenopod, erect knotweed, marsh elder, maygrass, and sunflower, as their ancestors had. Paying their respect to the Earth Mother at places like the Emerald Acropolis would have been an important ritual, and one meant to ensure bountiful harvests.

Monks Mound at Cahokia Mounds State Historic Site

By 750 years ago, Cahokia had declined, although there's no obvious reason for this. There is no evidence of a major precipitating event like an epidemic, invasion, or natural disaster. It's possible that the city's population just grew too big and, so, exhausted the resources in the area. Or, maybe the masses tired of sacrificing everything (including their lives) for the benefit of a few elites. Ultimately, it looks like people just moved away gradually.

While Cahokia emptied, Mississippian people didn't disappear. Mississippian communities thrived in other places, especially in the Southeast where monumental building continued at places such as Moundville (Alabama) and Winterville (Mississippi). Indigenous Peoples in the Great Plains, including the Osage (Wazhazhe), Omaha (Umonhon), Crow (Apsáalooke), and Pawnee (Chaticks si chaticks), maintained some cultural practices that were rooted in Mississippian traditions.

Oneota People were contemporaries with Mississippians but, although Mississippian culture had some influence on them, the Oneota were not Mississippian. They had their own distinctive cultural traits. They built communities without platform mounds, for example, and their societies were more egalitarian and not organized around hereditary leaders. They were also skilled farmers. The Oneota were probably ancestors of Kansa, Ho-Chunk (Winnebago), Missouri, Oto, and Iowa (Báxoje) People.

The Oneota built some of their earliest settlements along the Mississippi River near Red Wing, Minnesota, and later settled near the present-day Wisconsin communities of Brice Prairie, Trempealeau, and La Crosse. They spread throughout the Upper Midwest, though, with many distinct settlements from Lake Michigan to the Missouri River. These disparate communities had regular interactions with each other. Rivers connected them. There were still Oneota communities when Europeans upended their world.

EUROPEAN INVASION

In the sixteenth century, the Oneota People spread across the Upper Midwest. Meanwhile, in Louisiana, people from a group that archaeologists call the Plaquemine tradition (who had some Mississippian traits) prospered in communities near the confluence of the Yazoo and Mississippi Rivers. South of the Ohio River, descendants of Cahokia lived in densely populated towns in floodplain forests.

The bottomlands of the Mississippi were ideal places to live. The sandy soil was easy to dig into and was rich in nutrients. Regular flooding replenished those nutrients, but high ground along natural levees kept the villages dry, except during years of exceptionally high water. The streams were abundant with fish, and the forests overflowed with nuts and fruit. A network of bayous, rivers, and streams connected villages. The names of some of these places come to us from the journals of men in Hernando de Soto's invading army: Aminoya, Anilco, Aquijo, Casqui, Guachoya, Pacaha, Quigualtam, Quiguate, Quizquiz, Taguanate.

When Hernando de Soto assembled a large force in Spain in the mid-1530s, he had his eyes set on North America. He wasn't driven by curiosity or the desire to discover what lay on the other side of the Atlantic Ocean. De Soto was an ambitious man leading an army of Christian warriors. He wanted to conquer La Florida—the Spanish name for North America—and get rich.

In May 1539, De Soto's army reached the Florida coast with nine ships and a crew of several hundred, including at least six women, several Black men (some free and some enslaved), and a few enslaved white men. De Soto didn't pay anyone up front. They all expected to profit at the end of the trip by claiming a share of the wealth accumulated by the army.

For the next two years, De Soto and his army fought and plundered their way across the Southeast. In May 1841, the army reached the Mississippi River near present-day Memphis, where they found dozens of densely populated, well-stocked communities—at least thirty, just around the confluence of the Arkansas and Mississippi Rivers. They were Mississippian people, descendants of Cahokia, and it's likely that more people lived in that area in the 1540s than do today.

When De Soto's army reached the Mississippi River, they were short on supplies and demoralized after repeated attacks from Indigenous communities. De Soto increasingly worried about defections. After restocking with supplies they stole from two Quizquiz villages, the army encamped near the Mississippi on May 21, where they built boats to cross the river.

Canoes of Quigualtam

1539–1543, Lawrence A. Clayton, Vernon James Knight Jr., and Edward C. Moore, eds.

As the remnants of De Soto's army fled down the Mississippi River toward the Gulf of Mexico on July 4, 1543, a fleet of large canoes confronted them. These were the People of Quigualtam. As their fleet of a hundred canoes closed in on the Spaniards, the Mississippians' fleet dazzled with a dizzying array of colors; individual canoes were often painted a single color:

. . . inside and out, even to the oars . . . not only the canoes, but also the oarsmen and their oars, and the soldiers, down to the plumes and skeins of thread that they wore wound about their foreheads as a headdress, and even their bows and arrows, were all tinted with this one color, without the admixture of any other. As they came in such numbers and with so many different colors, and maintained such good order and arrangement, and as the river was very wide and they could spread out in every direction without disturbing their order, they presented a most beautiful sight to the eye.

They sang and paddled in unison.

. . . rowing evenly and in time, those Indians have made up various songs with different tunes, quick or slow, according to their speed or slowness in rowing. The themes of these songs are the exploits their ancestors or other foreign captains have performed in war, with whose memory and recollection they are incited to battle and to triumph and victory therein.
—*The De Soto Chronicles: The Expedition of Hernando de Soto to North America in*

A month later, they crossed the Mississippi in the dead of night. The river was high, the current rapid and full of floating debris. Still, they managed to shuttle everyone safely to the other side by daybreak. After the crossing, De Soto gained a tactical advantage by exploiting existing rivalries between Indigenous communities. He inflamed tensions between groups and instigated fights that pit communities against each other so they couldn't organize to fight the invading Spaniards.

De Soto's army captured supplies, then marched west along the Arkansas River. After surviving a bitterly cold winter and failing to discover the hoped-for riches, they retreated to the Mississippi River and occupied a village called Guachoya. De Soto grew distraught. At that point, he probably realized that his dreams of finding stashes of gold and other riches were slipping away. His health faded, too. He grew increasingly weak and died on May 21, 1542. Worried that De Soto's death would embolden the people of Guachoya, the Spanish kept it secret and sunk De Soto's body in the deep waters of the Mississippi.

Luís de Moscoso assumed command of the remaining army and led it west again, hoping to unite with Spanish forces in Mexico. They marched overland into Texas but had to return to the Mississippi River when supplies grew scarce again. They occupied a village on the Mississippi called Aminoya, where they spent much of winter constructing seven bergantines—open, flat-bottomed boats they could row with oars or power with a sail.

On July 2, 1543, the remaining Spanish army of three hundred soldiers rowed into the Mississippi and toward Spanish-occupied Mexico. They left behind most of the five hundred people from Indigenous communities they had enslaved. As they traveled downriver, fleets of canoes confronted them, some holding up to ninety men: thirty paddling on each side and another thirty in the middle. The fighting was intense, but Indigenous forces would inevitably pull back when they reached the boundary of their territory. The Spanish army reached the Gulf of Mexico after two weeks of dodging and surviving attacks, then, after a brief rest, sailed on to unite with Spanish forces in Mexico in early September.

The invasion was a disaster for the Spanish army as well as for the Indigenous People they encountered. Fewer than half of the Spanish soldiers survived, and many of the survivors ended up completely broke. The De Soto–led invasion altered life permanently for Indigenous communities in the Southeast. The Spanish killed thousands directly. Thousands more probably died from starvation after Spanish forces stole their supplies. The invaders introduced diseases that would decimate Indigenous communities for generations. De Soto's raid destabilized Indigenous communities and kicked off two centuries of conflict and accommodation as Indigenous People searched for ways to expel the colonial powers or find ways to minimize harm to their communities.

A NEW WORLD

Just fifty years after De Soto's invasion of North America, almost all the villages along the Middle Mississippi River were gone, abandoned after terrible losses from war and starvation. Survivors likely left their villages to search for stability and safety somewhere new.

Newly introduced diseases also took a heavy toll on Indigenous communities, which had no immunity to the virulent infections common in Europe and Asia for fifteen thousand years, such as diphtheria, measles, mumps, smallpox, and typhoid. A single wave of smallpox could kill one-third of an Indigenous community's people. Later waves were even deadlier.

The first documented disease outbreak in North America began in the 1630s among the Haudenosaunee People in New England, which was followed by a series of additional outbreaks through the rest of the century. By 1700, an astonishing 95 percent of Haudenosaunee had died. From the late-seventeenth to the early eighteenth century, imported diseases killed at least a quarter of the Indigenous communities in the east and Southeast. The epidemics sparked chaos, panic, and despair.

Disease wasn't the only force that undermined Indigenous communities, however. Between 1492 and 1880, European colonial powers enslaved several million people from Indigenous communities in the Americas. Although Indigenous communities in North America had a history of capturing people from other communities and keeping them against their will, that practice operated in a different cultural context. For some communities, it functioned as an exchange, as compensation from a rival group for killing someone from their community. Tribes sometimes treated captives brutally (or killed them), but other times they adopted them into the community as replacements for the people they had lost.

When Europeans arrived, though, the Indigenous people they enslaved became a commodity, and demand exploded. Spanish colonial forces first enslaved Indigenous People in the Caribbean and South and Central America. Christopher Columbus's first business transaction involved selling 550 Taíno People into slavery in Europe. All European colonial powers took part actively in the slave trade, enslaving more than three hundred thousand Native Americans, many of whom they sent to work on agricultural plantations or in mines where most died.

Some Indigenous communities took part in the slave trade, too, initially as guides and middlemen, but later by attacking other Indigenous communities and selling captives to European dealers for weapons and other goods. As slave raids spread throughout North America, they brought European diseases to new communities. Indigenous communities along the coasts and in the Southwest suffered the greatest losses from the combined threats of disease and enslavement, but the devastation reverberated throughout North America.

Disease and raids dislocated Indigenous People, which triggered mass migration and a reorganization of communities and identities in North America. Refugees of many communities retreated to new homes in Ohio, Michigan, Indiana, and Illinois, where they guarded against raids from the Haudenosaunee to the east. Meanwhile, Indigenous communities west of the Mississippi fiercely guarded against incursions into their territory.

FRENCH COLONIAL PERIOD

Indigenous communities along the Upper Mississippi River had their initial contacts with Europeans late in the seventeenth century when French traders who were eager to develop a trade in animal hides showed up. French traders desired beaver pelts, but they couldn't get them on their own. They built relationships with Native Americans who had deep roots in the Upper Mississippi valley, primarily with Ojibwe (Chippewa) and Dakota (Sioux) communities.

The Ojibwe have lived in southeastern Canada and along the Upper Mississippi River for hundreds of years. They were skilled navigators of area streams. Their primary craft for getting around was a canoe, typically made from birch bark.

Dakota People have also lived along the Upper Mississippi River for hundreds of years. In northern Minnesota, Dakota life centered on Mde Wakan (Spirit Lake, but known today as Mille Lacs). The Dakota impressed early French traders with their skills using a bow and arrow. Pierre-Charles Le Sueur once witnessed a Dakota man shoot a bird out of the air.

Ojibwe and Dakota communities negotiated an arrangement with French traders in which the Native Americans hunted and prepared hides, then traded them for European goods such as cloth, guns, and iron tools. The trade transformed Indigenous economies. Many Indigenous communities increasingly relied on trade with Europeans over traditional self-sufficiency. Although Native Americans could live without European goods, they found those products desirable and grew accustomed to living with them.

The Ojibwe established themselves at the center of the fur trade. Their economy grew, as did their population and the territory they controlled. They adapted socially and culturally by carving out new roles in the community for people who worked the fur trade (beaver trappers, for example).

Cross-cultural interactions grew. Ojibwe women frequently married fur traders, which is why, today, one-third of Ojibwe People in Minnesota have French surnames. Fur traders picked up place names that the Ojibwe used and many of those names ended up on maps drawn by Europeans (including the Ojibwe words that became "Mississippi"). For more than fifty years, Ojibwe and Dakota communities prospered as partners. Intertribal marriage was relatively common, and prominent leaders in both tribes often were of mixed Ojibwe-Dakota ancestry.

The good times ended when the French government tried to gain more control of the fur trade in the 1720s. Those efforts triggered decades of conflict between rival British and French interests and Indigenous communities allied with one side or the other. The peace between Ojibwe and Dakota Peoples was one casualty of this government interference. Tensions increased until 1736, when it erupted into open conflict that would last for several decades. Although some Dakota had been moving south and west before the conflict, the battles with the Ojibwe pushed the Dakota completely out of northern Minnesota.

By 1700, the social disruption experienced by Indigenous communities in the east and Southeast had extended into the Mississippi valley. The Sauk and Meskwaki Peoples had migrated from the east coast to territory just south of Dakota lands (around today's Quad Cities). A confederation of communities known as the Illiniwek lived across the Mississippi from them, many along the Illinois River. South of the Sauk and Meskwaki, Wazhazhe (Osage) People lived around the Missouri River confluence. Quapaws built homes along the Arkansas River. Taensa and Tunica People lived near the Yazoo River, as did the Natchez, who were probably descendants of the Mississippian community known as Quigualtam.

Communities of Choctaw and Chickasaw Peoples settled in the Southeast, especially in Alabama, Georgia, and Tennessee, but they also established some communities near the Mississippi River. By 1700, Choctaws had grown into a regional power, although they probably did not exist as a group when De Soto invaded. Their numbers grew as they integrated people from communities decimated by disease and slave raids.

In Louisiana, Chawasha, Chitimacha, Washa, and Yanki-Chito lived near each other and around Bayou Lafourche and Bayou Terrebonne. They had been in the area a long time and probably spoke a similar language. Communities of Bayougoula, Biloxi, Houma, Pascagoula, and many others lived nearby.

In 1729, Natchez People and their allies (including the Yazoo) grew frustrated with the French and tried to kick them out. The French (with the help of the Quapaw, Choctaw, and other Native American allies) defeated the Natchez, and then French leaders ordered their extermination. A few Natchez survivors escaped to safety in Chickasaw communities, but the French wiped out their home along the Mississippi River.

France gave up most of its territory and influence in North America in 1763 after losing the Seven Years' War (known as the French and Indian War in North America) to Britain. France ceded governance of the Louisiana Territory to Spain, which generally respected the autonomy of Indigenous communities.

After the creation of the United States, Indigenous communities along the Mississippi River faced increasing pressure from Euro-Americans moving into their territory. Diseases continued to take a toll, too. In 1782, smallpox raced through Minnesota, killing perhaps 60 percent of Ojibwe and Dakota Peoples. Indigenous economies suffered with the decline of the fur trade. Americans set up trading networks with Indigenous communities that worked on credit, so when the fur economy collapsed and Indigenous People couldn't repay the loans, many of those Indigenous communities settled their debts by selling land rights and moving to reservations.

Robert Fulton

THE AMERICAN RIVER

As Euro-Americans forced Indigenous People from the Mississippi valley, they built new cities. In the early and mid-eighteenth century, French traders and priests established communities at Prairie du Chien (Wisconsin) and along the Middle Mississippi below St. Louis (Cahokia, Kaskaskia, Ste. Genevieve, Prairie du Rocher).

When Robert Fulton perfected a functional steam engine for boats, he believed the technology would be ideal for the Mississippi River. He was right. Steamboats altered commerce dramatically in the United States and brought waves of European immigrants to the middle of the continent to inhabit lands ceded by Indigenous communities.

New Orleans, founded in 1718 by Jean-Baptiste Le Moyne de Bienville, grew into the first big city on the Mississippi River. Pierre Laclède established St. Louis in 1763 on a low bluff just downstream of the Missouri River. Galena, Illinois, boomed with lead mining beginning in the 1820s. A decade later, after US forces defeated Black Hawk and his band of Meskwaki and Sauk freedom fighters, three cities grew around the Rock Island Rapids: Davenport, Moline, and Rock Island. Just before the Civil War, two cities grew into regional powerhouses near the confluence of the Minnesota and Mississippi Rivers—Saint Paul and Minneapolis.

By the mid-nineteenth century, the Mississippi valley was booming economically and new residents flooded into river cities. New Orleans grew from 17,000 inhabitants in 1810 to 170,000 in 1860. St. Louis's population exploded from 5,000 in 1830 to 160,000 in 1860. Minneapolis went from 5,800 residents in 1860 to 200,000 in 1900.

Steamboats connected Mississippi River towns and moved products and people around. Along the Lower Mississippi, cotton was king. Plantations fueled by enslaved laborers lined the Mississippi River from Louisiana to Missouri. Cotton filled the decks of steamboats, along with goods

imported from around the world. As the cotton industry boomed, demand for land increased. Indigenous People in the Southeast had adapted to life under the American system and had developed successful farms and ranches, but the American government forced them to leave so Americans could convert the land into cotton plantations. Thousands died during the Trail of Tears as one hundred thousand Cherokee, Choctaw, Chickasaw, Creek, and Seminole People marched to an unknown future west of the Mississippi River.

Upriver, manufacturing took root. John Deere built a factory to manufacture plows in Moline, and the area—then known as the Tri-Cities—became a world leader in the manufacture of farm machinery. Minneapolis became a center of milling, especially for grain, as companies such as Pillsbury built mills along the Mississippi River.

After the Civil War, Frederick Weyerhaeuser and others founded companies that clear-cut the dense northern forests of Wisconsin and Minnesota and turned the trees into consumer products. Immense rafts of cut trees floated down the Mississippi River to sawmills and factories from Minneapolis to St. Louis. Big factories turned those logs into flooring, walls, and doors.

Along the Lower Mississippi—in the delta region, especially—people moved into the swamps and forests farther away from the river and drained and cleared them. In a generation, farmers turned the Mississippi Delta's swamps and forests into cotton fields. After the Civil War, sharecroppers replaced enslaved laborers, which wasn't an improvement for most folks.

TOP: *Cotton in Mississippi* / BOTTOM: *Buttons cut from mussel shells*

By the turn of the twentieth century, iron ore mining was booming in the northern reaches of the Mississippi valley. St. Louis had become a major producer of shoes and beer. Cotton continued to dominate the economy of the Lower Mississippi. After John Frederick Boepple opened a factory to turn mussel shells into buttons, Muscatine, Iowa, grew into a button manufacturing powerhouse. Bettendorf produced railroad boxcars.

These booming industries required a lot of workers, so many companies turned to new immigrants who needed work right away and who were willing to work for low wages. Germans flooded Mississippi River towns in the first half of the nineteenth century, along with Irish immigrants. Belgians settled in Moline. Swedes and Norwegians flocked to Minnesota. Italians moved to St. Louis and other river towns. Finns, Czechs,

OPPOSITE, FROM TOP TO BOTTOM: *A nineteenth-century steamboat • Factories along the St. Louis riverfront • A log raft on the Mississippi River*

Schweibert Park, Rock Island, Illinois

and Slovaks worked the iron mines of northern Minnesota. Poles settled into the mix in Winona, as did Dutch immigrants in Fulton, Illinois. Chinese immigrants moved into southern towns. When World War I created labor shortages, industrialists recruited workers from Mexico and African Americans from the South.

Shipping on the Mississippi River dropped dramatically after the Civil War as railroads replaced steamboats. Railroads had several advantages. Steamboat traffic often halted in winter or when the river was too low. Railroads could operate all year. In addition, trains could connect communities that weren't on a navigable river, which was most of the country.

In the twentieth century, agriculture in the Midwest shifted from small family farms to large corporations, and farmers increasingly relied on corn and soybean crops. After decades of unsuccessfully lobbying the federal government to transform the Mississippi River into a more reliable shipping canal, farmers and Midwest businesses got their wish in the 1930s. At the height of the Depression, the US Congress approved a massive public works project that employed thousands of people to build a series of locks and dams on the Upper Mississippi River.

The dams made bulk shipping on the Mississippi profitable again, especially since the federal government paid for the cost of building and maintaining the system. For the next several decades, barges carried large quantities of corn and soybeans for export, coal to riverside power plants, and chemicals. By the 1980s, though, the volume of goods shipped on the Mississippi River began a steady decline. Although we still ship a large proportion of corn and soybeans on the Mississippi River today, the cost to taxpayers is high and remaking the Mississippi for bulk shipping has caused considerable damage to the river's world.

When the Midwest industrial economy declined, river towns demolished the hulking remains of riverside factories and replaced them with parks and trails. As industry retreated from the Mississippi, people moved in to reclaim the space. Riverfronts once dominated by massive factories are now home to green spaces and new residential buildings. After decades of ignoring the Mississippi, Americans are getting reacquainted with the Great River.

THE
RIVER'S
WORLD

LIFE IN THE
CHANNEL

THE WATER MOVES swiftly underneath my kayak, carrying me toward the Gulf even when I'm not doing much paddling. The river is running high, just around flood stage at Louisiana, Missouri, so the water stretches from bank to bank. Below me, tens of thousands of cubic feet of water tumble and spin in a mostly downstream direction. Now and then, an object on the bottom of the river sends the water flowing straight up to the surface where it flows out evenly from the center, a boil. Pulling my paddle through the water feels like running with the wind at my back.

At the end of this paddle, an abrupt change in the elevation of the river bottom sends the water spinning into a circle that rotates in a direction that is opposite to the flow of the channel. This is an eddy, and it's right in front of the boat ramp I'm trying to reach to exit the river. I ease the kayak into the eddy's current and let it turn me upriver, briefly, then toward shore. And then I'm frozen in place by the current of the eddy pushing from one direction and the force of the main channel pulling from another. I ease my paddle back into the water and, with a couple of

vigorous strokes, push my kayak out of stasis and to the ramp, back to land.

I was paddling one small stretch of the main channel of the Mississippi River, a few miles of the 2,350-mile-long artery that flows from the lungs of North America, the great Northwoods, to the beating heart of the planet, the sea. In between, the Mississippi's main channel carves a deep, winding groove into the land, twisting and turning on a relentless journey from a quiet lake to the vastness of the Gulf of Mexico, where its waters merge into infinity.

The Mississippi's official course begins at Lake Itasca, a four-hour drive north of Minneapolis. At the headwaters, a sign indicates the river flows 2,552 miles to the Gulf. If you consult the US Army Corps of Engineers, the river's managers, they insist the river runs 2,350 miles. Pick your favorite number. Rivers are dynamic. They cut new channels and wander around, although the Corps is doing its best to keep the Mississippi from doing so.

The Mississippi changes its character as it flows south. The headwaters section runs close to five hundred miles from Lake Itasca to the Twin Cities, where it is modest in size—and sometimes marshy—and runs through some sparsely populated areas. Several dams block the flow of the channel, including one constructed by a beaver. The Upper Mississippi begins at the Twin Cities and marks the beginning of the distinct valley framed by tall bluffs as well as the part of the river we have altered highly to accommodate barges.

The Middle Mississippi flows between the confluence of the Missouri and Ohio Rivers and marks a transition from the river impounded by dams to a bigger, free-flowing river. The Lower Mississippi begins where the Ohio and Mississippi join and runs to the Gulf of Mexico. Along the river, but especially in the lower reaches, a few smaller channels carry some of the Mississippi's flow away from

TOP: *Paddling on the main channel of the Mississippi River* / **BOTTOM:** *The Mississippi River in the headwaters*

the main channel. These are called distributaries. The Corps closed off most of them as part of their mission to control the river for navigation and flood prevention, but one large distributary remains: the Atchafalaya River.

Someday, the Atchafalaya will take over the flow of the Mississippi. It currently absorbs about 30 percent of the Mississippi's waters, but that's by design, an engineering decision made to correct a previous engineering mistake. In the nineteenth century, river engineers cut off a meander at Turnbull's Bend in Louisiana to speed travel. Before the cut, the Red River contributed water to the Mississippi at the north end of the meander, while the Atchafalaya took

TOP: *The Mississippi River in Minneapolis* / **BOTTOM:** *Mississippi River bluffs*

Old River Control Structure, Louisiana

some water out of the Mississippi at the south end, although not that much water moved in either direction because massive logjams blocked the flows of the Red and Atchafalaya Rivers. The north end eventually silted in and we cleared the logjams, and the straighter, faster path sent more water from the Mississippi into the Atchafalaya. So much water diverted down the Atchafalaya, in fact, that river engineers and folks in New Orleans got worried. Very worried.

The path down the Atchafalaya offered a shorter and steeper route to the Gulf, so everyone understood the Mississippi would, if left to its own devices, shift most of its flow to the Atchafalaya, which would turn New Orleans and Baton Rouge into landlocked cities with diminishing access to freshwater. Their solution was a big dam known as the Low Sill Structure and Overbank Structure, which was supposed to keep the Mississippi from jumping channels. The structures were completed in 1962 to keep 70 percent of the

Mississippi's water in its channel and to send the other 30 percent down the Atchafalaya. A flood in 1973, not even one of the biggest, nearly collapsed the structures by undercutting them. The engineers responded by adding more and bigger bits of concrete, the Auxiliary Structure. Together, these masses of concrete, collectively called the Old River Control Structure, keep the Mississippi's main channel in place. For now.

MEASURING THE MISSISSIPPI

The opening where the Mississippi's waters trickle out of Lake Itasca sits 1,475 feet above sea level. The river drops 833 feet in elevation in its first 660 miles as it passes through Minnesota. From Cairo, Illinois,

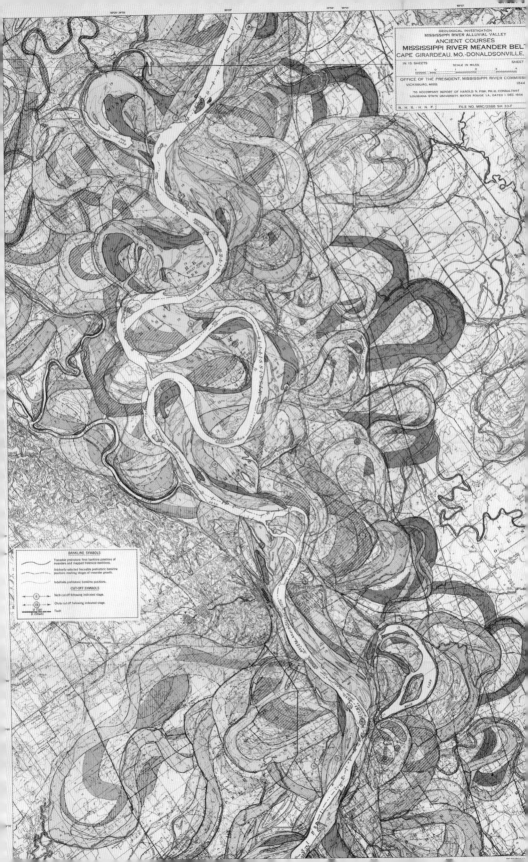

GEOLOGICAL INVESTIGATION
MISSISSIPPI RIVER ALLUVIAL VALLEY
ANCIENT COURSES
MISSISSIPPI RIVER MEANDER BELT
CAPE GIRARDEAU, MO.-DONALDSONVILLE,

IN 15 SHEETS   SHEET

SCALE IN MILES

OFFICE OF THE PRESIDENT, MISSISSIPPI RIVER COMMISSION
VICKSBURG, MISS.   1944

TO ACCOMPANY REPORT OF HAROLD N. FISK, PH.D., CONSULTANT
LOUISIANA STATE UNIVERSITY, BATON ROUGE, LA., DATED 1 DEC 1944

R. H. S. H. N. F.   FILE NO. MRC/2500 SH 33-F

to the Gulf of Mexico—nearly a thousand miles—the river drops a mere 315 feet in elevation to reach the sea. The water moves toward the Gulf at varying speeds. In the headwaters region, it ambles toward the sea at about a mile per hour, but at New Orleans, the current runs about three times as fast. When the river is high, the current can zip along at five or six miles per hour.

When the elevation flattens out, the flow of water slows and the channel digs out lazy loops known as meanders that snake their way across the landscape. Surface waters rush to the outer loop of the meander and eat away at the bank while the slower currents inside the loop drop sediment. Over time, the loops get bigger and bigger. Eventually, the river finds a quicker way around and cuts a path across that narrow section of land known as the neck of the meander. Over the past few thousand years, meanders have come and gone along the Lower Mississippi, but they have left their mark on the land.

As the old portion of the channel gets cut off from the river's flow, the remains turn into a slack water area called an oxbow lake. The two Horseshoe Lakes in Illinois are oxbow lakes, as are many lakes and swamps farther south. The regular cutoffs have made life difficult for communities along the river. Vicksburg lost its river port in 1876 after the river succeeded in doing what General Ulysses S. Grant and the Union army had failed to do: cut across the neck of De Soto Peninsula and reroute the river's flow. In 1903, after twenty-five years of work by the federal government, the Yazoo River Diversion Project opened, which restored Vicksburg's water connection to the Mississippi.

Not every cutoff happens naturally. The US Army Corps of Engineers cut through the necks of some meanders to make navigating the river easier for big boats and to speed high water toward the Gulf as a method of flood control. From 1929 to 1942, the Corps engineered sixteen cutoffs along the Lower Mississippi that shaved 152 miles of length off the main channel. The results have been mixed. The river is a dynamic force, so it has adjusted in ways that cutoff advocates didn't expect. For example, some areas where the Corps executed a cutoff now experience more frequent shoaling and have to be dredged more often. In general, it seems the artificial cutoffs (and subsequent efforts to restrict where the channel flows) created a less stable river that is searching for a new equilibrium, a dynamic we are still reckoning with.

The volume of water in the river grows exponentially from an average of six cubic feet per second (cfs) at Lake Itasca (one cubic foot of water is 7,489 gallons, or 28,349 liters) to 12,000 cfs at Saint Paul. After merging with the Missouri River, the Mississippi grows to 186,000 cfs at St. Louis. Farther south, the Mississippi's waters grow much deeper after taking in the flow of big rivers such as the Ohio, the Arkansas, the White, and the Yazoo, so it grows to an average flow of nearly 700,000 cfs at Vicksburg. Just downriver, some of the water gets diverted down the Atchafalaya River, then further spreads out as the river enters the bird's-foot delta south of New Orleans. These are all average flows from a few decades' worth of recordkeeping. During floods, the volume of water in the Mississippi's channel can be hard to comprehend. In 1993, a million cfs of water passed by St. Louis at the flood's peak. A barrel—forty-two gallons—is another way to measure the quantity of water. In 1993, enough water passed St. Louis to fill 178,000

OPPOSITE: *Map of old meanders created by Harold Fisk*

TOP: *Lake Pepin* / **ABOVE:** *A whirlpool in the Lower Mississippi River*

barrels *every second*. In 1927, three times as much flowed down the Lower Mississippi as at St. Louis in 1993.

A good way to start an argument is to ask a group of river rats to identify the widest part of the river's channel. The folks around Clinton, Iowa, insist it's just upriver of downtown. Others argue for Lake Pepin. Both have a point. Upriver of Clinton, the water stretches three miles from bank to bank because of the navigation dam. The channel through Lake Pepin—a natural widening in the channel—is two and one-half miles wide, which would have been much wider than the river above Clinton before the dam was built. Both, though, have to take a back seat to the area where the river passes through Lake Winnibigoshish in northern Minnesota, which is eleven miles wide.

The width of the river channel is just one measure of the river's expanse, of course. Ultimately, what matters most is the wide expanse of North America that sends its waters into the Mississippi: 1.25 million square miles, which is 41 percent of the lower forty-eight, the third largest watershed in the world. Rain that falls from New York to Montana and from parts of southern Canada to Louisiana ends up in the main channel of the Mississippi.

IN THE WATER

Standing on a bank of the river, the water we see flowing past us on the surface is what we think of when folks talk about the main channel. That surface, though, is just the top part of a multilayered world, one that has far more richness than just moving water.

Rivers are dynamic: water levels rise and fall; temperature changes; some parts have current, whereas others don't. The chemical composition of the river's water can vary, too. The water is harder (containing higher concentrations of dissolved calcium and magnesium) when the river runs over limestone, but it'll be softer when passing through peat beds. Alkalinity and concentrations of oxygen can also vary depending on depth, sediment loads, and temperature. The river naturally carries nitrogen, but today it carries too much of it because of fertilizer runoff from factory farms.

Rivers move not only water, but also sediment. When the current runs fast, such

as during times of high water, the flow can carry bigger, heavier stuff—gravel, stones, and bigger particles of sand. When the flow slows, those bigger bits drop out onto the stream bed. We know the Mississippi as Big Muddy, because of its reputation for turbid water, but that reputation is only partially earned. In 1839, Captain Frederick Marryat wrote that the Upper Mississippi River was a "beautiful clear blue stream, intersected with verdant islands."

Everything changed after the Missouri River merged with the Mississippi, though, as Captain Basil Hall made clear in his book *Travels in North America, in the Years 1827 and 1828, volume II*:

"The most striking circumstance observable at this confluence, is the difference in the colour and purity of the two rivers. The Missouri is nearly as thick as peas soup, of a dirty, muddy, whitish colour; while the Mississippi, above the confluence, is of a clear light blue, not unlike that of the deep sea, or the Rhone at Geneva . . . . It seemed as if the dirty Missouri had insinuated itself under the clear Mississippi; for we saw it boiling up at a hundred different places. First a small curdling, white spot, not bigger than a man's hand, made its appearance near the surface. This rapidly swelled and boiled about, till in a few seconds it suddenly became as large as a steamboat, spreading itself on all: in gigantic eddies, or whirlpools, in a manner that I hardly know how to describe, but which was amazingly striking. At other places, the two currents ran along side by side, without the least intermixture—like oil and water. But this separation never continued long, and the contaminating Missouri soon conquered the beautiful Mississippi;—indeed the stain is never got rid of for one moment during the twelve hundred miles that the united stream runs over before it falls into the Gulf of Mexico."

The Upper Mississippi, today, is not the clear, blue stream described in the nineteenth century. Right after the Civil War, the US Congress's "Survey of the Upper Mississippi River" noted that:

"The ploughing of the prairie, felling of forests, erection of mills, and other causes have already begun to disturb the former state of things. The water is no longer as clear and dark as it used to be, and more sand accumulates in the stream."

The steamboats that plied the Mississippi River in the nineteenth century burned wood to fuel their boilers. Most of that wood came from trees in forests along the river, so as steamboat travel increased, much of the forest along the river disappeared. The loss of floodplain forests destabilized shorelines, so even more sediment washed into the river.

Before we started engineering the Mississippi for our convenience, the river had rapids in several places: Grand Rapids (Pokegama Rapids), Little Falls, Sauk Rapids, the Rock Rapids near the Quad Cities, the Des Moines Rapids between Montrose and Keokuk (Iowa), and the Chain of Rocks near St. Louis. The Mississippi has (had, truthfully) just one waterfall, a place that the Dakota People knew as Owahmenah, but that Father Louis Hennepin renamed St. Anthony Falls.

In 1869, Minneapolis industrialists attempted to stabilize the falls but they nearly wiped them out instead. After a few failed attempts and over a million dollars spent, the Army Corps of Engineers figured out that a concrete apron over the falls was the best option, which is what we see today. Someday, the falls will revert to a natural state. When they do, they will continue their retreat up the remaining 1,200 feet of limestone cap, then disappear into a series of rapids.

These forces, all that moving water, distribute and redistribute nutrients—the building blocks of life—along its path. It nurtures the diversity of plant and animal life in the river's world.

RIVER BOTTOM

In the headwaters region, the Mississippi runs over gravel and stone left behind by glaciers. For most of its course, though, the Upper Mississippi flows over a thin and dynamic layer of clay, silt, loam, and sand that sits atop a couple hundred feet of glacial outwash that piled up in the few thousand years after glacial meltwaters ceased flowing. In a few places, bits of bedrock poke through, but in most places you'd have to dig through a lot of sand and silt to reach it. The Lower Mississippi has a similar bottom, composed mostly of sand particles of different sizes mixed with some gravel and, occasionally, clay. The closer the river gets to the Gulf, the finer the sand particles are that dominate the structure of the river bottom.

Some areas on the bottom offer relatively stable footing, places where sand or clay are packed hard, where bedrock pokes through, or mussel shells line the bottom. Occasionally, boulders and logs get lodged in the bottom and stay put. In other places, the bottom is constantly rearranging itself. Sand flats and sand dunes form and disappear as the current flows around them.

In the early 1980s, river ecologist Ken Lubinski dived under the winter ice multiple times to survey the river bottom. On one of his first dives, Lubinski rested quietly for nearly ten minutes to observe the world around him. (He was quiet so long that the crew on the support boat radioed him

Exposed Mississippi River back channel bottom near St. Louis

to make sure he was okay.) He watched as sand dunes shifted with the current, much like they do on a windy day in a desert. As he rested on the bottom, he heard only the sounds of his breathing and the water flowing around him. When it was time to move, he crawled forward on his hands and knees facing into the current. As he explored the bottom and communicated with the rest of the team on the surface, he felt like "an astronaut talking to Mission Control."

He and his diving partners realized that the makeup of the river's bottom varied quite a lot, even in small areas. Fine sand and silt sat next to pebbles and gravel, which gave way to beds of mussels. Scientists once believed that the world at the bottom of the river was barren and lifeless, a desert submerged in deep water. They were wrong. The bottom of the river teems with life that thrives in a surprising range of microhabitats.

Communities of algae, detritus, and microbes known as periphyton covered almost every available surface area (logs, rocks, shells). Dense pockets of caddis fly cases stuck to many surfaces. Mussels formed long rows. Flathead catfish slid into stable areas for their winter slumber. Shovelnose sturgeon buried themselves partially in sand flats. Small fish found cover in ripples in the sand.

Periods of low water expose pieces of the river's bottom. Backwater channels turn into bridges between islands and the mainland. Wide sandbars that resemble the Sahara open up. Gravel bars emerge where one can find fossils and lithified mud, millennia-old clumps of dirt that have hardened into stone. These are great times to walk on the bottom of the river—no scuba gear needed!

Limestone bluffs at La Crosse, Wisconsin

Mussels

Mussels are bivalves (mollusks with two shells), and the Mississippi River provides homes for dozens of species of them. The shells among species can be quite different (color, texture, bumps, etc.). The rings on the shells reveal the mussel's age, much like tree rings. They may look small, but mussels pack a lot of complexity into their small bodies, including gills, sexual organs, siphons to inhale and exhale water, muscles, and simple circulatory and nervous systems.

When it's time to reproduce, males shoot out sperm that females suck in with a siphon. Larvae then develop in the gills for days or months (depending on the species), then Mom expels the glochidia, which must find a vertebrate host to stay alive, usually a fish. The glochidia attach to the fish's gills to get the nutrition they need, but they don't harm the host. When they have finished growing into juveniles, they drop off and—fingers crossed!—land in a suitable spot on the bottom where they can grow into adults. Some mussels need a specific fish host, whereas others are less picky.

Mussels that need a specific host have developed a means to attract the right fish. The plain pocketbook mussel, for example, grows a mantle that looks like a minnow that it uses to lure a host. Mussels are quite sensitive to changes in water quality and habitat, so they can alert us to problematic changes in the river's world.

AROUND THE EDGES

As rivers rise and fall, especially sediment-rich rivers, they deposit sand and silt along their banks. These deposits reach their highest point close to the river, then gradually slope away from it. Along the Lower Mississippi, the higher ground of these natural levees provided ideal places to build communities, as high water rarely submerged them. The original settlement of New Orleans (where the French Quarter is today) is built on a natural levee. These ridges are just one boundary marked by the river.

In the headwaters region, the Mississippi follows a path through forests, marshes, and prairies, but there are few hills to define a valley. At Minneapolis, the river enters its only gorge, a narrow space with high cliffs on both sides that formed as St. Anthony Falls retreated upriver.

At Saint Paul, the Mississippi first enters a wide valley framed by tall bluffs, the deep path carved by glacial meltwaters millennia ago. The valley along the upper river is as narrow as one and one-quarter miles at Prescott and as wide as six miles at Trempealeau. The tallest bluffs tower over the river around Great River Bluffs State Park near Dakota, Minnesota; they reach nearly six hundred feet above the floodplain.

The rock-faced bluffs present a timeline of geologic history. Layers of limestone—the hardened remains of ancient sea creatures—alternate with compacted crystals of quartz and sandstone. As water ate away at the underlayers of sandstone, limestone blocks hung precariously over the edge until gravity sent them tumbling toward the river. In many places along the upper river—in the Driftless Area, around St. Louis—karst topography dominates. The limestone in

Trail through the loess hills of Mississippi

these areas dissolves rather easily when it rains, which scours depressions that turn into sinkholes or form caves.

The rocky bluffs reach their end just past Cape Girardeau and the floodplain of the Mississippi stretches much wider, from thirty to ninety miles across from Cairo, Illinois, all the way to the Gulf of Mexico. South of the Ohio River, another series of hills—broken up occasionally by the Wolf and Yazoo Rivers—rises along the east bank of the Mississippi. From Hickman, Kentucky, to Baton Rouge, Louisiana, winds blew silt into piles beginning in the Pleistocene epoch, which accumulated on top of gravel and rocks left behind by the Mississippi.

Water cut a path through rock to carve the Upper Mississippi valley, but wind built up the hills along the Lower Mississippi.

The four Chickasaw Bluffs in west Tennessee rise as high as three hundred feet above the river. Just as flowing rivers cut deep paths through the bluffs of the Driftless Area, runoff from rainstorms dissects the loess bluffs with precision, sometimes weakening them to the point of avalanche-style collapses.

Just east of the Mississippi in southern Missouri and northern Arkansas, Crowley's Ridge runs nearly two hundred miles long and rises as high as 250 feet above the floodplain, broken up occasionally by rivers such as the St. Francis. The ridge isn't built on bedrock but on clay, gravel, and sand topped with loess soil. Ten miles wide at its northern end, it narrows to five miles wide by the time it reaches Helena, and only one mile wide near Harrisburg, Arkansas. Upland forests line the ridge in some places; agricultural fields in others. The ridge marks an ancient boundary between the Ohio and Mississippi Rivers.

ANIMAL LIFE

Most of the animals in the river have adapted to moving water. Some life in the river, in fact, is so specialized that it can survive only in moving water. Many species of mussels, for example, depend on passing fish to carry their babies to nurseries where they will grow into adults.

Some life stays put on the bottom: algae, insect larvae, mosses, worms. Some drift with the current: bacteria, fungi, plankton, some invertebrates. Others float on the surface, such as duckweed, water beetles, and water striders. And many others swim well enough to go wherever they please. The north-south orientation of the river has made it easier for many species to survive long spans of time. If the climate got too cold, they moved south. When it warmed again, they headed north.

Much of the life in the Mississippi depends on recycled food for survival. Dead plants and animals fall into the river, which are consumed by insects and crustaceans, which are eaten by fish, which feed animals farther up the food chain. The river continually receives and disposes of nutrients. This process works only if there's enough dissolved oxygen in the water. If oxygen is too low, detritus settles into river sediment where it gets stashed and, therefore, doesn't feed anything.

The Mississippi River is a rich, productive world. Historically, the Upper Mississippi was so productive it could support seven hundred pounds of fish per acre (of many species), about thirty-five times as many fish per acre as the crystal clear lakes of Canada and northern Minnesota.

Paddlefish

Shovelnose sturgeon

FISH

THE ANCIENT ONES

Several species of fish that live in the Mississippi have been on this planet for a very long time. American paddlefish trace their roots back 125 million years. They are very distant cousins of catfish and are more genetically similar to humans than they are to sharks. They live only in large rivers and the lakes and the streams connected to them, which means they are now mostly found only in the Mississippi basin. Their cousins in the Yangtze River, the Chinese paddlefish, are extinct.

Paddlefish are unlike most river fish. They can live for decades, as long as forty years. They don't have scales and are, essentially, boneless. The only true bone in their body is their jaw; cartilage holds the rest of the body together. They are big fish, up to seven feet long and weighing up to two hundred pounds, although paddlefish today rarely exceed six feet and a hundred pounds. Their bodies resemble sharks, except up front.

The paddlefish's long snout may account for one-third of its total length. They are filter feeders and that long snout helps them find food. Tiny sensors connected to their brain line the surface of the paddle. They can detect small changes in electrical fields, which help paddlefish find food, even in total darkness. When they are hungry, they sweep the paddle around to create turbulence. This floats small creatures that had been hiding on the river's bottom. Paddlefish then swim through the cloud and filter out what they don't like, in order to get to the good stuff (insects, plankton, small crustaceans).

Paddlefish are late bloomers compared with other fish. Females typically can't spawn until they are nearly ten years old (and sometimes older), and even then might produce eggs only once every two or three years. They spawn only when environmental conditions are just right, which includes water high enough to cover the gravel bars they prefer for spawning and water temperatures between 55 and 60 degrees Fahrenheit. After they spread their eggs around the river bottom, the adults leave them to fend for themselves. In about a week, they will hatch and float to areas where they can feed on zooplankton.

Their numbers are now low in parts of the Mississippi valley because of habitat loss caused by the construction of dams and levees and by overfishing (their eggs

Bowfin

Alligator gar

are harvested and sold as caviar). If you are fishing in Minnesota and Wisconsin, they are off-limits.

Paddlefish belong to the order Acipenseriformes, along with their cousins, sturgeon, which have been around for at least 136 million years. Shovelnose sturgeon (sometimes called hackleback) favor the main channel of big rivers. They prefer a faster current and a sandy bottom, which is where they get their food (mostly larvae of flies and caddis flies).

Lake sturgeon grow slowly and mature late. They are much bigger than shovelnose sturgeon (up to eight feet long versus under three feet) and live a lot longer (females can live 150 years; shovelnose sturgeon live about 20 years). Like paddlefish, lake sturgeon mature slowly and may go a few years between periods of active spawning. In any year, only 10 to 20 percent of lake sturgeon are actively spawning. They also need clean water and a river bottom with little silt, which is why they often move into smaller streams to reproduce.

Pallid sturgeon fit between the two in terms of size and age. They can grow to five feet long and live forty years or more. North American sturgeon are in a precarious place today. Most species are endangered, but pallid and lake sturgeon are more severely threatened than shovelnose sturgeon. Human engineering along the big rivers is

the primary culprit, which has wiped out much of the habitat they need to reproduce. Both paddlefish and sturgeon traveled widely in the Mississippi and Missouri Rivers before we built dams there.

Bowfin (also called dogfish, or—for some unknown reason—John A. Grindle) are the last known species in the order of fish called Amiiformes that goes back 250 million years. They were once very common. Bowfin average twenty inches long but can grow to twice that size. They can get the oxygen they need from water by breathing through their gills, but they can also breathe air for a while. In waters with low oxygen content, they will stick their heads above water and take in air through their mouths. Because of this, they can even survive several hours out of water. They are aggressive predators that lurk quietly, then strike quickly, ensnaring prey—other fish, typically—with their rows of scary-sharp teeth.

Gar are close cousins of bowfin, with roots that also go back more than two hundred million years. There are several species, but long-nosed gar are common in the Mississippi River. They have a long snout, like paddlefish, but with one important difference: teeth line theirs. When gar capture prey, they whip their heads from side to side until it is secure in their grip, then they swallow it head first. Their skin is extremely tough, about as hard as enamel on human teeth.

Catfish

Sheepshead

Like bowfin, gar can breathe through their gills while swimming, or poke their heads above water for a gulp of air.

Alligator gar are the largest variety—and they can be enormous! The largest alligator gar ever caught measured nearly 8½ feet long and weighed 327 pounds. They inhabit the Lower Mississippi River, oxbow lakes, and some streams in the South, Texas, especially. Although they look scary, they pose no threat to humans (unless you eat their eggs—they are poisonous). They feed on other fish primarily—including invasive carp—and, sometimes, waterfowl and small mammals. Alligator gar populations have been declining for decades, but efforts are now underway in some places to help them recover.

CATFISH

If there's a single fish most associated with the Mississippi, it would have to be the catfish. There are many species around the world, but in the Mississippi's world, you'll find blue, channel, and flathead catfish. They are top predators in the waters of the Mississippi and are mostly carnivorous.

Channel catfish are the most abundant and the smallest of the three types. They prefer moving water. Ten pounds is a respectable weight, although they occasionally reach

upwards of fifty. They grow during winter, feasting on snails and crayfish. Bigger channel cats will also eat sunfish and other small fish, which they consume by sucking them in through a wide mouth.

Like most catfish, they have well-developed senses of smell and taste. In fact, they have chemical receptors on their bodies that act like taste buds—their entire body is practically a swimming tongue. Their "whiskers" are called barbels, and they always grow in pairs. They have rather small eyes, mostly because they don't need acute vision. They rely on all those chemical sensors in their skin and their barbels to find food.

Flathead catfish (also called mudcats) are the second largest species of catfish in North America and the largest in the Upper Mississippi. They average two to four feet long but can reach five; it's not usual for them to approach a hundred pounds.

Blue catfish are the largest North American catfish. Typically, they span three to four feet but can reach over five feet. The largest one caught weighed in at 143 pounds. They prefer the deeper, faster waters of big rivers, so we rarely see them in the Upper Mississippi. They are also migratory; as the water gets colder, they move south. They can tolerate water with some salinity, so they sometimes wander near the mouth of the Mississippi.

SHEEPSHEAD

Sheepshead are one of the most abundant fish in the Mississippi. They are sometimes called freshwater drum, thunder pumper, or white perch and there are some fun regional variations in their names: in the Ohio valley, you'll also hear them called grunter, while along the Lower Mississippi, folks may call them croakers or grunts. In Louisiana, they are sometimes called gaspergou, or goo. Most of these names come from the rather unique sound these fish make. When they open and close their swim bladder, they emit a noise that sounds like someone banging on a drum.

Sheepshead are native to the Upper Mississippi and its bigger tributaries and range from northern Canada to Central America. They are a close relative of the red drum (also known as Louisiana redfish), which you may have enjoyed blackened. They do well in a variety of current speeds and depths and aren't picky eaters—happy to snack on leeches, plankton, even smaller fish.

It takes up to five years for them to reach sexual maturity, and they grow upward of two feet long. Females lay up to five hundred thousand eggs at a time, which must make it tricky to come up with names for all those offspring every year. They can live for forty or more years. The otoliths of sheepshead—the stone-like structure behind their brain—sometimes end up as jewelry. All they need is a good polish, something many Native Americans figured out long ago.

Sheepshead also lend a critical helping hand to many species of mussel. Larval mussels (glochidia) of some species only attach themselves to the gills of sheepshead, where they will stay until they are big enough to drop off and build a home of their own. They don't harm the fish while they are hitching a ride.

MANY OTHER FISH

A few years back, biologists took a census of the fish population in twelve-acre Miller Lake near La Crosse, Wisconsin. They counted more than forty-five thousand fish, including fourteen thousand bluegills, three hundred largemouth bass, and lots of perch, crappies, and bullheads (another type of catfish). This is probably pretty typical for the fish population in a Mississippi River backwaters habitat, and they represent just one segment of the life supported by the Mississippi. Bluegill and crappie, in particular, need habitats like Miller Lake to survive under winter's ice, places where the water is deep enough, warm enough, and maintains enough dissolved oxygen and light to sustain them.

Sauger, which are related to walleye, are common in the Lower Mississippi, whereas walleye are more common up north. Smallmouth bass thrive in the river's current. Sunfish hang out in the backwaters. Eel-like silver lampreys attach themselves to other fish and suck out their blood.

Shipjack herring rely on open rivers to complete their life cycles, so they are uncommon now along the Upper Mississippi because of the navigation dams.

In the late 1800s, many species of native fish were declining as the US population was growing, so, in 1871, the US Commission of Fish and Fisheries, and many state governments, began efforts to introduce more game fish into rivers, including the Mississippi. Over the next decade, government biologists planted several new species of fish into the Mississippi, including shad and salmon, which didn't do well, and carp, which did (and still do).

Carp was a staple in Asian and northern European diets, so biologists introduced common carp into American waters to meet the demand. The fish had no trouble adapting, but they quickly developed a foul reputation among some folks for their tendency to turn clear waters murky and crowd out native fish. Because they lived around polluted areas, many people thought of them as trash fish. Most of this is overstated. Common carp impact smaller bodies of water, it's true, but they haven't had a negative effect on the Mississippi. They also tolerate pollution and low oxygen levels better than most native fish, which is why they do okay in impaired waters. They don't cause the impairment but can live in it.

Other species of carp that entered the Mississippi recently, though, are more problematic. Bighead and silver carp were both imported to the United States in the 1970s to control weeds and algae in fish farms, then some escaped into the waters of the Mississippi. They are doing well in some parts of the river—too well, in fact. Along the Illinois River and in the Mississippi upstream and downstream of the Illinois, they are abundant. They have a habit of jumping out of the water when disturbed, which has attracted a lot of attention (and YouTube stardom).

They don't have a stomach, so they eat nearly all the time, and they can get enormous, which means they cause quite a sting when one smacks into you on the river (take my word for it). They are often observed in huge numbers in some areas, which has led many to worry that they are outcompeting native fish and degrading habitats, which may be true. On the other hand, recent studies suggest they are more common in streams that are already impaired, so, ultimately, the best strategy for keeping them under control may be to keep our streams and lakes healthy.

INVERTEBRATES

Besides fish, invertebrates also do well in the river's main channel, including insects, mussels, and tubifex worms, a favorite food for pet fish. The Mississippi supports abundant and diverse species of macro-invertebrates, little organisms that lack a backbone but are visible to the naked eye. This group includes clams, crayfish, crustaceans, leeches, many insects, mussels, scuds, snails, sow bugs, worms, and freshwater sponges. Many of these creatures find space in the nooks and crannies of the river, in sand, mud, and on the surface of rocks.

Benthos are organisms that live on or in the bottom of bodies of water. In the Mississippi, this includes freshwater shrimp, mussels, worms, and many types of flies, including mayflies. Some of them do remarkable things in their lives. The larvae of caddis flies dig elongated shelters, then weigh down the sides with stones to keep them in place. Some of them depend on flowing water to eat, as they can eat only what passes by them.

Mayflies are survivors. They've been around for tens of millions of years and live all over the world. In North America alone, there are more than six hundred species. They live the overwhelming majority of their lives as nymphs burrowed in the river's bottom, using their tiny legs and tusks to dig a U-shaped home in the silty bottom. They eat only when they are nymphs; adult mayflies have no mouth or digestive system. When they mature, they float to the surface, throw off their skins, and take flight with millions of their companions, then find a comfortable place to rest for a few hours while they molt, which sets up a buffet for birds of many species. After they molt, they take to the air again but with more skill. Females zoom

Mayflies

Bald eagle

among the males and they mate as they fly. Soon after, the males tire and fall to the ground or water. Females, though, fly miles away until they are nearly spent, then drop thousands of eggs in the water, which sink slowly to the bottom, and two weeks later, they hatch and the life cycle begins again.

Although it's easy to get irritated during the few hours that adult mayflies cover every surface near the river, they are vital parts of the river's life cycle. They feed on decaying organic matter and are eaten by organisms from walleyes to diving ducks to eagles. Mayflies and other benthos all depend on clean water to survive. They can't survive in water polluted with sewage. Before the Clean Water Act forced tighter regulation on sewage discharge, benthos were uncommon above Lake Pepin and in other parts of the Mississippi because of sewage pollution. Biologist Calvin Fremling wrote that "Sampling mayflies can be compared to taking a blood sample and using it as a measure of the well-being of the entire body."

Many other animals, of course, thrive because of the main channel, including several species of birds—bald eagles, especially. Bald eagles are big birds, with wingspans up to seven feet long. They build equally impressive nests, up to ten feet wide and weighing a couple of tons. You can't miss them. Bald eagles don't have their distinctive white head feathers until they are four or five years old. When they choose a mate, they usually remain coupled until one of them dies, and nest in the same area every year.

For many Native Americans, bald eagles held important spiritual symbolism. Many believed eagles possessed healing powers and carried messages from humans to the Creator. Many tribes forbade hunting or eating eagles. We nearly drove bald eagles—our beloved national symbol—to extinction thanks to our indiscriminate use of DDT and thoughtless hunting, but their strong comeback is a powerful symbol of what we can accomplish to restore a balance between humans and the natural world. Today, bald eagles are a common sight along the Mississippi, from the forests of northern Minnesota to the swamps of Louisiana. They are especially common in winter along parts of the Upper Mississippi, where they take advantage of open water below the dams to feed. In colder years, it's common to see dozens of bald eagles in one small area.

These animals, from the smallest invertebrates to giant alligator gar, play their part in the complex world that is the Mississippi River and are vital strands in the river's rich and abundant web of life.

Algal bloom in the Mississippi backwaters

CHALLENGES

Life in the river's main channel remains abundant and diverse, but faces several challenges. Although we have dramatically reduced pollution from the dumping of raw sewage into the river, fertilizer runoff from large farms is polluting the Mississippi with excess phosphorous and nitrogen, sometimes causing dangerous algal blooms. Every year, these chemicals accumulate in the Gulf of Mexico where they stimulate explosive algae growth that consumes all the oxygen in thousands of square miles and makes it impossible for other marine life to live there, what we know as the Dead Zone. Years of talking about it and voluntary measures to control runoff have done nothing to stop the problem.

Levees also pose a threat to life in the main channel. They cut off the main channel from the backwater areas that many species rely on for food and for reproduction. As we've built levees, we've also narrowed the channel to ensure deep-enough water for barges and to speed away water when the river is high. Channelization is also eliminating many of the shallower backwater areas, which will decrease the abundance and diversity of life in the river over the long haul.

Channelization has also caused more rapid rises and falls along the main channel. During the great flood of 1844, a foot rise in one day was ominous. In contrast, in 2016, the Mississippi River yo-yoed up and down near St. Louis after heavy rains—a twelve-foot rise in two days in November, followed by a sharp drop, then a thirteen-foot rise in three days in late December (December!). On January 1, 2017, the river crested at 42.58 feet at St. Louis, the third highest crest on record, and at an unprecedented height for winter. We have engineered the Mississippi to behave as wildly as a creek.

Record crests are no longer an anomaly. At St. Louis, four of the ten highest flood crests have occurred in the past twenty-five years. It's not because rains are getting heavier. The amount of water in the Mississippi River on New Year's Day 2017 wasn't even among the ten highest observed flows. The river is cresting higher with less water because of the levees that line its banks and the loss of wetlands. Along the Mississippi valley, one hundred- and five hundred-year floods now seem to happen every five or ten years.

Dams on the upper part of the river have cut off the natural north-south migration route for life in the river. This has most severely affected shipjack herring and American eels, but blocking the flow of life in the main channel could have negative long-term consequences for other life in the channel. And just upstream of each dam, higher water levels and waves have conspired to wipe out most of the islands that once dotted the area. The braided channel of the Upper Mississippi—rich with backwater sloughs, islands, and sandbars—is devolving into a single, open channel; the backwaters and islands could soon be just a memory. This isn't a geologic inevitability, but one of our own making.

And we have completely messed up the river's system of moving sediment around. Silt and sand now pile up behind the navigation dams, slowly filling in more of those backwater channels. The effects of sedimentation are hard to see without the perspective of time. From one year to the next, you won't notice much difference, but talk to people who've been on the river for a few decades, and the examples of backwaters filling in come in rapid succession. Ric Zarwell has one of those stories. He grew up near New Albin, Iowa, in the 1950s. He remembers a photograph of his father standing on the running board of a Model A: with a cup in one hand, his father stretched as far as he could to fill that cup with water from an artesian well. Years later, Zarwell had to take a boat to reach that spot, and, once there, reach down to fill a cup from the same well. Ten feet of silt had piled up in the years since his father was photographed. That well today is nearly impossible to find, buried even deeper under sediment trapped by an Upper Mississippi dam.

Meanwhile, dams on the Missouri River are practically starving the Lower Mississippi of sediment. Much of the sediment that the Lower Mississippi still carries rushes out to sea thanks to levees and channelization, falling off the continental shelf into deep water where it can no longer build land along the margins of the sea like it used to. Since the 1930s, the state has lost nearly two thousand square miles of coastal lands, which is like lopping off Delaware and letting it sink into the Atlantic. Louisiana will probably lose another Delaware-size chunk of coastal land in the next forty years.

These are serious challenges to the health of life in the main channel, but they aren't likely to change until more people insist we manage the river in a way that doesn't destroy it.

WETLANDS

SUPREME COURT JUSTICE Potter Stewart wrote that he couldn't define what a wetland is but "I know it when I see it." Okay, maybe he was referencing something else, but the same rule applies. Bureaucrats and scientists have struggled to define exactly what a wetland is. Some places are only wet ephemerally; some never dry out. Trees grow in some; grasses cover others. There's not an ideal choice for a species of plant or animal that lives only in wetlands.

Keeping it simple, where there's water, there will be wetlands, and the Mississippi River has a lot of water. Wetlands form a fluid boundary between the river and the land. At the most basic level, wetlands are places that hold water for at least some portion of the year. For something that is so hard to define, we sure know it by a lot of different names: bayou, bog, estuary, fen, flotant, marsh, muskeg, slough, swamp.

Hiking through prairie landscapes, I can always tell when I'm getting near a wetland: deerflies and mosquitoes come out in force. On a prairie hike in summer 2022, I transformed from a contented hiker into a bug-swatting machine. The bugs were one reason that early Euro-Americans were dismissive, if not outright disdainful, of wetlands. In 1842, Charles Dickens traveled across the United States from January to June. Part of his trip took him by steamboat on the Mississippi River. When they reached Cairo, Illinois, Dickens expressed disgust for the wetlands that spread over the confluence of the Ohio and Mississippi Rivers:

Wetlands at Sherburne National Wildlife Refuge, Minnesota

*At the junction of the two rivers, on ground
so flat and low and marshy, that at certain seasons of the year it is inundated to the house-tops,
lies a breeding-place of fever, ague, and death.
. . . A dismal swamp, on which the half-built
houses rot away: cleared here and there for the
space of a few yards; and teeming, then, with
rank unwholesome vegetation, in whose baleful
shade the wretched wanderers who are tempted
hither, droop, and die, and lay their bones.*

—Charles Dickens, *American Notes and
Pictures from Italy*

The idea of swamps as wasteland—or
wasted land—was enshrined in American
law. When Mississippi, Arkansas, and Louisiana entered the Union, some land went
unclaimed and remained federal property. Much of that land was swamp. In the
mid-nineteenth century, the US Congress
authorized the sale of those swamplands
back to the states so the states could sell the
land to private developers. The states had
to use the money for flood control, though,
which included draining the land. States
built levees and drained swamps to make
the land more attractive for agriculture and
for people (Euro-Americans) to live on. Louisiana sold cypress swamps to big companies
for pennies on the dollar, so they would cut
those trees down to make way for farmers. Many of the initial efforts to drain the
swamps didn't go well, but they picked up
momentum after the Civil War.

What Dickens and other Euro-Americans
saw as dismal and unproductive, though,
teemed with diverse and abundant life, especially amphibians, birds, insects, and reptiles. Native Americans understood this. For
thousands of years, they feasted on fish, harvested plants for medicine, and navigated
the streams.

Wetlands produce oxygen and remove
nitrogen from water (it gets converted to gas).
They store atmospheric carbon dioxide and
capture and filter heavy metals and pesticides.
They provide safe places for many fish to
spawn, and way stations for migrating birds.
Some wetland plants have medicinal benefits.
Wetlands store excess water during floods,
which reduces flood elevations on the main
channel of rivers and recharges aquifers, but
they also store water that is released slowly
back into streams during dry periods. Wetlands reduce periods of extreme highs and
lows. Coastal wetlands absorb energy from
big storms, which reduces their impact on
coastal cities, such as New Orleans. Wetlands
are critical for maintaining the diversity of life
that big rivers support. And maybe best of all,
wetlands require no human management to
do their thing.

WETLAND COMMUNITIES

Wetland communities along the Mississippi
are as diverse as the life they support, and
they change dramatically with the seasons.
Spring snow melts and heavy rains recharge
them, which catalyzes a flurry of activity. Life
slows by summer, and by fall you'd have a
hard time finding some of the places that had
been so active just weeks earlier. Freshwater
communities are most common, of course,
but salinity levels increase near the end of
the river, which supports different varieties
of life than those freshwater communities
away from the sea. Swamps and bogs add
even more variety to the wetlands mix. Let's
take a tour through the variety of wetlands
along the Mississippi and look at the plants
and animals that rely on them.

ALONG THE MAIN CHANNEL

Wetlands develop throughout the river's floodplain and come in many shapes and sizes. Along the main channel of the river, wetland communities vary based on how deep the water is and how often they dry ou completely. Some backwater channels might flow with abundant water in spring, then be completely dry in stretches by fall. Wetland communities form in shallow areas along the riverbank, in front of dams or dikes, in ponds or lakes on islands. Some wetlands appear in the middle of the floodplain after a period of high water, only to dry out completely after the river retreats.

Wetland communities can experience dramatic changes with the seasons, and even from year to year, as water levels vary. Spring almost always means more water, which triggers a burst of growth. Frogs, toads, and salamanders get busy mating. Plants quickly shoot out fresh growth. Migrating waterfowl stop to feast on the new plant growth and amphibians distracted by mating.

From summer to fall, some wetlands dry out. Water recedes into what had been the deeper pools. Dry periods can result in more productive wetlands, though. As the wet bottom dries out, nutrients that had been locked in the mud and under water get released and become food for plants and animals. Some plants—cattails, for example—have deep root systems that keep them supplied with water through dry periods. When moisture returns, wetlands burst back to life with great diversity in plant and animal life.

Wild rice on the northern Mississippi River

Annual Wild Rice

There's an old story that when some Ojibwe People migrated from the St. Lawrence River valley centuries ago, they would know where to build their new homes when they found the place where the food grew on the water. That turned out to be around the western Great Lakes and Upper Mississippi River.

What we call wild rice—what the Ojibwe know as "manomin" and Dakota People call "psin"—is actually an annual grass, what scientists classify as an emergent aquatic vegetation. The plants grow fresh from seed every year once the water temperature rises above 45 degrees Fahrenheit and prefer shallower water with a bit of current. By late August, the kernels ripen and harvest season begins.

(continued)

Traditionally, the harvest requires two people and a canoe. The person in the back of the canoe guides it through the wild rice fields, keeping a slow but steady pace. Meanwhile, the person in front gently taps the stalks with a knocker that releases the kernels into the canoe. It's perfectly fine if some kernels fall back into the water, as that guarantees that wild rice will come back strong next year. The harvested kernels smell a lot like freshly mown grass, and must go through several processing steps before they are ready to eat. Once processed, wild rice will remain good to eat almost indefinitely, as long as it stays dry.

Arrowhead

Wetland communities typically have a gradient of water depth that ranges from mud and muck to deeper pools. Plants that grow near the margins of wetlands have adapted to live with water levels that can vary quite a lot. River bulrush grows in clumps. Annual wild rice waves gently back and forth along the margins of areas with a gentle current. Pickerelweed shoots up clusters of blue flowers that bloom gradually from the bottom up and look like bottle cleaners.

Several varieties of arrowhead (sometimes known as duck potato) thrive in shallow water areas. Broadleaf arrowhead is especially common. It can grow up to three feet tall, but may also completely submerge when the river is high. Its starchy tubers are appealing food for ducks, geese, muskrats, swans, and people, too (they have a starchy texture like potatoes).

As the water gets a little deeper—up to about six feet deep—new species of plants inhabit the wetlands. Some stay almost entirely underwater, whereas others root on the bottom and send up leaves that float on the surface. Several grasses fall in the former category, spending their lives entirely submerged. Coontail—one of the world's most abundant aquatic plants—sticks precariously to the bottom with short stems (coontail does not have a root system). The plant can have a delicate form that resembles baby pine trees. Unlike coontail, wild celery (or eelgrass, probably called such because of the way the plant appears to slither in the water like an eel), puts down deep roots that anchor it on the bottom. Sago pondweed can grow thick in places and annoy recreational boaters while pleasing waterfowl. Grassleaf mud plantain (also known as water star grass) can grow in water as deep as eighteen feet, or on the shorelines of river and lakes.

Coontail

American lotus

As long as the water isn't too deep, the plant produces a tiny yellow flower with long, narrow petals. These underwater grasses provide shelter and food for amphibians, fish, waterbirds, and other inhabitants of the wetlands.

Another group of plants roots on the bottom and sprouts leaves that float on the water's surface, usually in backwaters where the water is warm and shallow. The leaves screen out the sun, so the water doesn't get too hot, and the plants add oxygen to the water. Fish find plenty of places to lie low as they mate and produce children. Water lilies and American lotus are two common (and delightful) varieties of these plants.

The American white water lily prefers still, shallowish water (up to about five feet deep). The plants produce sprawling flowers with white petals with a cluster of dense yellow stamens in the center. The flowers lie flat on the water and smell quite sweet, but are open only in daylight. It's not unusual to see thick patches of water lilies that completely carpet an area.

The American lotus typically grows next to arrowhead in water that is just a little deeper than the water lily prefers. Their blue-green leaves—circular and one to two feet wide—stand above the water and open like shallow saucers. The stems rise from tubers in the mud that look something like a very firm banana. Lotus tubers and seeds were part of the diet for many Native Americans. Lotuses reproduce most efficiently through those tubers, as a fresh shoot can produce flowers in less than a year. Lotus plants that sprout from seeds, in contrast, take two to four years to flower.

Lotuses bloom in August in the Upper Mississippi, and what a sight they are: delicate pale yellow flowers encircle a bright yellow spongy mass (the seedpod) that is surrounded by frilly yellow stamens. The

Duckweed covers a pond

flowers—which also emit a pleasant fragrance—open in the morning, then close in the evening.

Lotus seeds are remarkably durable. As long as the shell stays intact, the seeds inside remain viable for decades. After the petals fall off, the seedpods will, eventually, fall into the water where they float along, carrying potential lotuses to new places. Like lilies, lotuses often spread en masse in shallow areas.

These types of wetlands—with water up to six feet deep—are abundant along the Mississippi north of the Quad Cities, but harder to find from the Quad Cities to St. Louis because of levees and agricultural developments.

Farther out yet into deeper water, there's another group of plants whose entire mass floats freely on the surface, plants such as duckweed. There's nothing inherently problematic when duckweeds are present, as long as they live alongside other vegetation. When duckweeds dominate, though, it often signals serious problems in the ecosystem, and not just because a body of water covered with duckweed interferes with recreational boating. When duckweed takes over, it often means that eutrophication is taking place. When significant amounts of nitrogen and phosphorous accumulate in a body of water—usually because of human activities, such as fertilizer runoff from farms or dumping raw sewage—it triggers an explosion of algae and plants that consume most of the oxygen in the water. Without oxygen, other plant and animal life in the water die. All those nutrients can also start algal blooms, some of which can produce toxins that are deadly to other forms of life, including humans.

ANIMAL LIFE

Some animals live full-time in wetlands; others are tourists. Some spend most of their time in the water, some go in and out, whereas others—red fox, raccoon, black bear—lurk at the edges.

Beavers are probably the best-known mammalian wetland natives. Big rodents—the largest rodent, in fact—they can weigh up to fifty pounds, which is practically tiny compared to their Pleistocene-era ancestors, *Castoroides*, which were as large as today's black bear. Beavers can hold their breath for fifteen minutes, which comes in handy when trying to evade land-based predators. Their diet consists mostly of trees and plants, especially alder, aspen, cottonwood, and willow. They stockpile branches on the bottom of lakes and rivers so they

Beaver

Muskrat

have enough food to get them through winter. We nearly trapped beavers to extinction—their numbers got as low as one hundred thousand in all of North America around 1900. Today, about fifteen million roam North America, which is probably still a fraction of what it was before European colonization.

Beavers live in colonies of four to ten, which typically include Mom, Dad, and their young children. After a year with the parents, the young ones get kicked out to fend for themselves. They build their lodges from branches and mud, in which they live year-round, and that get big enough to look like a small island. Their interior living room sits above the waterline, so they have space to spread out and air to breathe. They also build their iconic dams from mud, twigs, and sticks.

Muskrats are close relatives of beavers but much smaller (weighing less than three pounds on average), and there are more of them. Muskrats prefer to dig a den in a riverbank, but if that's not an option, they will build dome-shaped shelters in shallow water that can stretch nine feet wide and six feet high. Their preferred diet includes clams, fish, and nonnative zebra mussels. They also eat the stems, leaves, and tubers of cattail, bulrush, and arrowhead and will repurpose some of those plant materials

to build their shelters. Muskrats will consume their favorite plants until they are completely gone from an area, which can convert densely covered fields into open water. Eventually, that wetland will dry out when the rains stop for a while, and those plants will come back.

North American river otters are native only to North America. They live in burrows along the riverbank that give them easy access to the water, although they typically move into burrows dug out by other animals such as woodchucks or red foxes, or even abandoned beaver and muskrat lodges. Babies are born blind and toothless but learn to swim within two months and venture out on their own in about a year. River otters are built for aquatic worlds, with long, sleek bodies, webbed toes, and insulating fur that helps them glide through water. They're pretty big. They can stretch three feet from whiskers to tail and weigh twenty to twenty-five pounds. They are most active from dusk to dawn and eat fish mostly, but will sometimes snack on crayfish, frogs, mussels, and even small birds. River otters have been declining in numbers for a while, probably from a combination of habitat loss and pollution.

American minks live solitary lives and don't tolerate other minks invading their territory. They live in burrows, often dug

Mallard

Gadwall

into riverbanks, and are accomplished hunters. Because of their slender bodies, they can enter burrows dug by other animals and hunt them, including muskrats. They swim well and prefer to eat fish, but can catch birds as large as cormorants, drown them, and turn them into dinner.

WATERFOWL AND OTHER BIRDS

Ducks, ducks, ducks! The wetlands of the Mississippi River are rife with ducks. And duck hunters. According to Ducks Unlimited, duck hunters along the Mississippi account for nearly half of all duck hunters in the United States and up to half of the ducks shot in a year.

In stories from Indigenous North American cultures, waterfowl—ducks, especially—are often portrayed as gullible and easily manipulated, which isn't a great characteristic when you spend time around coyotes, foxes, and wolves. Perhaps there's some truth to their gullibility, as hunters today regularly fool some species of ducks with decoys and fake calls. Mallards are especially prone to these tricks. Gadwalls are much harder to fool. And mergansers, well, they won't give

up in the face of hardship, but will, in fact, laugh at it.

Ducks move around wetlands throughout the day to feed and rest, drawn mostly by the availability of food (invertebrates, leaves, seeds, tubers) rather than water. Ducks need a lot of space for nesting, as each pair typically carves out its own territory. After mating, male ducks (drakes) run off together to a big area of water to molt. They drop their fancy attire for a more mundane look that will make them less vulnerable to predators, but during the two weeks when they are waiting for new feathers to grow back, they are extremely vulnerable.

While the drakes molt, Mom is busy raising the chicks. She leads them around to feed on beetles, dragonflies, leeches, mosquitoes, spiders, and other insects. She also protects them from water-based predators, such as alligator snapping turtles, pike, and herons, and from land-based predators such as red foxes, hawks, and owls. The ducklings are ready to fly in about six weeks, at which time Mama goes away for her turn to molt. Ducks typically return to the same nesting areas each spring. Although they are much safer from predators when they are flying, ducks still have to watch out for peregrine falcons, and for human hunters.

We have two basic varieties of ducks along the Mississippi River: dabblers and

Hooded merganser

Cormorant

divers. Dabblers feed on the surface of the water and, occasionally, wander onto land to search for a bite to eat. This group includes wood ducks, pintails, mallards, gadwall, and blue- and green-winged teal. Breeding male shovelers stand out with striking colors: a rusty-brown midsection on a mostly white body, green head feathers, a long flattish black bill, and yellow eyes. We came close to losing wood ducks in the 1920s, but the Migratory Bird Treaty between Canada and the United States triggered active conservation that brought them back. Many wood ducks nest permanently in the wetlands of Mississippi's delta.

Diving ducks do exactly as their name suggests: they dive underwater to feed. They are adept swimmers, which is lucky for them, because they are quite awkward on land. Common diving ducks include redhead, lesser scaup, canvasbacks, bluebill and hooded mergansers, which, as the legends suggest, are adaptable enough to do well in freshwater and saltwater environments. Diving ducks are especially vulnerable to lead poisoning, as they often consume spent lead bullets as they forage on the bottoms of rivers and lakes.

Double-crested cormorants fill the sky in V-shaped flocks but, unlike geese, don't make any noise when flying. Grebes are also divers, but it turns out their closest cousins aren't the coots and loons they resemble but flamingos!

Geese are common in the wetlands of the Mississippi River, including greater snow geese and greater white-fronted (specklebelly) geese. Given how ubiquitous Canada geese are today, it's hard to imagine a time (the 1920s) when naturalists believed they had gone extinct.

Trumpeter swans congregate in shallow lakes and marshes. They are the biggest birds in North America, nearly six feet long on average, with wings that can stretch eight feet when wide open. Their long black bills taper toward black eyes that stand out against white feathers. Mostly, they eat aquatic plants, and once they reach adulthood, face few predators. Their smaller cousins, tundra swans, put on dramatic displays in fall along the Upper Mississippi River. Thousands stop for a few weeks to feed on arrowhead, sago pondweed, and wild celery before continuing their migration to Chesapeake Bay.

American white pelicans are nearly as big as trumpeter swans. They had once been common along the Mississippi but disappeared in the mid-1900s, victimized by habitat loss and the pesticide DDT. In the early 1990s, they returned to the Upper Mississippi and have come back strong. A colony of pelicans now nests on islands near Clinton, Iowa, and

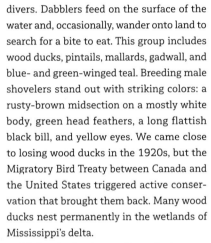

Tundra swans on the Mississippi River

American white pelicans

pelicans are a common sight all along the river today. In winter, look for them along the Lower Mississippi and the Gulf of Mexico.

Brown pelicans, Louisiana's state bird, have had a tortured relationship with humans. Hunting nearly wiped them out, in part because some people considered their feathers a symbol of high fashion. Like bald eagles, DDT made their eggs' shells fragile, so they broke easily, which made it nearly impossible for them to reproduce. From 1962 to 1972, there were no brown pelicans in the Pelican State. They have since come back and are no longer considered endangered.

Herons are one of the many wading birds (or shorebirds) that prowl the shallow waters along the Mississippi for fish and frogs. Great blue herons step gracefully along the shorelines with tall, toothpick-thin legs. They nest in colonies—dozens of great blue herons crammed together at the tops of trees in nests thrown together like shanties. The acidic poop and vomit that falls out of their nests can be toxic to trees, although not to the stinging nettles that thrive under them. They abandon their nests once the young ones can fly, but may return to them the following spring.

Great egrets are abundant along the Mississippi River and nearly as common a sight as deer. They float lazily through the sky,

pulling their heads back for better aerodynamics. Naturalist John J. Audubon thought they looked like royalty, because their "silky train reminded one of the flowing robes of the noble ladies of Europe."

American bitterns are smaller herons but with brown feathers. They make an unusual noise that sounds something like a big drop of water falling out of a faucet, although some have compared it to the sound of a stake being driven into the ground. They are shy creatures and will stand still and try to blend in if approached, though they will eventually take flight if you get too close.

Night herons love the wetlands of the Mississippi and, as the name suggests, are nocturnal. They will eat just about anything: carrion, crayfish, frogs, leeches, small birds, snakes, squid, worms, even trash from the local dump. Yellow-crowned night herons are short and squat with a flowing plume of yellow feathers on top.

Smaller shorebirds include avocets, plovers, ring-billed gulls, and spotted sandpipers that search the shallow waters for insects, invertebrates, and tasty plants. Snipes prefer safety in numbers when migrating (the flocks typically fly at night), but once on the ground, they are pretty solitary.

Red-winged blackbirds are abundant near water and migrate north to wetlands along the Mississippi in early spring. They nest in

Least tern

Eastern snapping turtle

cattails and bulrush and are quite protective of those nests. More than once, I've been strafed by red-winged blackbirds that were angered when I got too close to them.

Belted kingfishers, bank swallows, and least terns nest on the sandbars and sandy banks of the Mississippi. The belted kingfisher nests in tunnels as deep as ten feet. When not nesting, they like to perch high above streams, then dive into water to snatch their prey, although sometimes they will hover. Bank swallows excavate shallow burrows in sandy banks for their nests, digging with their feet and bills until they reach a satisfactory depth. They nest in colonies of a few pairs up to thousands.

Although belted kingfishers and bank swallows remain abundant, least terns—the smallest tern—took a while to bounce back from the days when we hunted them for their feathers. In June, they build nests on sandbars along the Mississippi and Missouri Rivers that rest just above water level. Before humans began engineering the big rivers and changing their natural flows, spring pulses of high water would clear out space on sandbars for least terns (and piping plovers). Now, quick rises are more common because of levees and channelization, and that—plus floodplain development—has erased a lot of the sandy places least terns need for nesting. A sudden rise in late spring can now wipe out many nesting birds. Their numbers have rebounded enough—thanks in part to our efforts to build more sandy islands—so they are no longer classified as endangered, although few would say they are safely back on their feet.

Songbirds migrate along the Mississippi. Spring is the best time to catch finches, thrushes, vireos, and warblers. Birds of prey of various sizes patrol the skies: bald eagles, peregrine falcons, red-tailed hawks, and swallow-tailed kites. And that's just a quick introduction to wetlands' bird life in the Mississippi's world.

REPTILES AND AMPHIBIANS

More than a dozen species of turtles call the Mississippi River's wetlands home. The river's natural backwaters support more species of turtles than the river's impounded sections behind the dams. The middle reaches of the Mississippi have somewhat fewer species, probably because that stretch has lost more backwater habitats to farming and suburbs.

In one study in the mid-1990s, researchers caught more than 4,400 individual

Nonvenomous plain-bellied water snake

turtles from 10 different species. Painted turtles and red-eared sliders preferred the backwater habitats where they loved to bask in the sun on a log or a piece of driftwood (a favorite pastime of river cooters). Spiny softshells were common in the tailwaters around dams.

Eastern snapping turtles are prevalent throughout the Midwest, including the wetlands along the Mississippi River. They will eat just about anything, living or dead, and can make their homes in just about any type of aquatic environment (creeks, lakes, ponds, rivers, swamps).

The eastern musk turtle is one of the smallest species of turtles in the world, with an upper shell that measures about four inches long. They have a gland in the space between their upper and lower shells that can produce a musky scent, which is how they got their name. They also live in a variety of watery habitats, but you won't find many north of Dubuque.

At the other end of the size scale, alligator snapping turtles are the largest freshwater turtle in the world. Their heavily armored upper shells can grow to two feet long. (You could line up six eastern musk turtles on the back of one alligator snapping turtle!) They typically weigh between 100 and 150

pounds but have gotten as big as 300 pounds in captivity. They eat mostly fish and prefer to live in the deep, muddy sloughs next to big rivers. We rarely find them north of St. Louis.

Snakes love the backwaters and sloughs of the Mississippi, too: common water snakes, fox snakes, green water snakes, and northern redbelly snakes, all harmless to humans, except for the pain of a bite. They slink along riverbanks any time of day or night looking for crayfish, a frog, or small fish, birds, or mammals to ingest, while vwatching out for raccoons, opossum, and big birds. Along the middle and lower parts of the river, venomous cottonmouth and copperhead snakes inhabit the Mississippi's wetlands.

The wetlands also offer excellent accommodations for amphibians. Look around for a while and you may find amphibians such as eastern American bullfrogs, American toads, and northern and southern leopard frogs. Central newts begin their lives as small aquatic creatures with gills; they don't leave the body of water where they are born. After three months, the newt matures into a juvenile form called a red eft that leaves its birth home and searches for a new place to live. As juveniles, they shine bright orange (with a hint of red) and tetrodotoxin, the same poison that makes eating puffer fish

Mud puppy

into their burrows to eat them. On the other hand, mud snakes and cottonmouths prey upon amphiuma.

INSECTS

Mosquitoes are among the most abundant (and most irritating) insects, and as far as anyone has discerned, don't matter much in any ecosystem or as a primary food source for any other creatures, even though many animals eat them. Deerflies, horseflies, and blackflies are also abundant and annoying from May to September. Blackflies (also known as buffalo gnats) create their unique brand of havoc for up to six weeks from May into July, whereas deerflies usually peak in June and July. They (just the females) feed on blood by repeatedly stabbing their food source until blood flows. They congregate around water and the edges of wooded areas.

life-threatening, saturates their skin. The bright color warns away potential predators. Newts live as juveniles for up to three years, then transition to adulthood. They settle back into a watery environment, and their skin turns green and slimy. Newts have evolved the very handy ability to regrow limbs they lose to injury or predators.

The common mud puppy lives mostly in the upper half of the Mississippi basin and grows to about a foot long. They spend their lives in the water, breathing via external gills that resemble a feather boa. Those gills grow larger when mud puppies live in water that has little flow to it. They are most active at night and will eat just about anything they can get their teeth into: mollusks, small fish, worms, even spiders. Females don't reach sexual maturity until they are six years old, then lay about sixty eggs in a typical year.

Three-toed amphiuma look like eels but they are salamanders. They prefer thick vegetation in wet areas with a slight current, including swamps and bayous. After a heavy rain, they can slide across land in search of fresh places to hang out. They love snacking on crayfish so much that they will crawl

Whirligig beetles zip across the water's surface with ease. When threatened, they often spin in circles but they can also dive underwater or fly away. The upper half of their body is water-repellent, but the lower half is not. They have remarkable eyes—divided into upper and lower halves so they can see well above and below the waterline.

In contrast, water striders have specially adapted legs that allow them to walk on water without divine intervention. Tiny, water-repellent hairs cover their six legs, each pair a different length, and body. They love spiders and insects, pouncing on them after detecting their presence from vibrations that radiate across the water. Once they've secured their dinner, they pierce the bug's body with a proboscis, inject enzymes that break down tissue, and suck out the juices.

Dragonflies and Damselflies

Dragonfly

A few years ago, I was camping in northern Minnesota just as the deerflies peaked. As I sat in my camp chair swatting away flies in vain, a few dragonflies swooped in and started snatching flies out of the air. A few times, I saw a dragonfly catch a meal, then land on the arm of my chair to eat it. I found the whole thing delightful to watch, and not just because of the spite I feel for deerflies (although that was part of it). Dragonflies and damselflies are among the easiest insects to admire, and not just because they eat mosquitoes and deerflies.

They are beautiful, complex, diverse insects with a deep history. Their ancestors first show up in the fossil record some three hundred million years ago. Worldwide, there are six thousand known species of dragonflies and damselflies, with at least a couple hundred along the Mississippi River. And a dragonfly gets credit for being the largest known insect to have inhabited our planet; a species called *Meganeura monyi*, with a wingspan of thirty inches and a body eighteen inches long, buzzed around 250 million years ago before vanishing into extinction.

Dragonflies and damselflies are relatively easy to tell apart. The bodies of damselflies are more slender than dragonflies. At rest, damselflies hinge their wings above their bodies, but dragonflies keep their wings extended to the sides. Both species utterly depend on wetlands.

Both dragonflies and damselflies spend most of their lives underwater as larvae, where they breathe through gills in their rectum. As air goes in and out,

it also gives them a push so they can maneuver around. They molt as much as fifteen times over a year or two before growing into an adult—but adulthood is brief, just four to six months.

Vision is critical to both insects. They have compound eyes built from twenty-eight thousand pieces called ommatidia. Something like 80 percent of their brain tissue is devoted to processing the visual stimuli that come in through those eyes. They can see everywhere around them except directly behind.

They are masters of flight. They can zip forward at speeds up to thirty-five miles an hour, turn on a dime, fly in reverse (although not nearly as fast as flying forward), and hover for as long as a minute. As they fly, they can snatch prey, and can even mate, although they prefer to do the deed while perched. (When they mate in the air, the process lasts only a few seconds, but they may copulate for three or four minutes when perched.)

They aren't especially picky about what they eat (caddis flies, horseflies, mayflies, mosquitoes, termites), but they prefer flies. A single dragonfly can eat hundreds of mosquitoes in a day, so that's reason enough to adore them. Dragonflies also face a range of predators to watch out for, including birds (purple martins love them), fish, frogs, lizards, and spiders.

Bog in northern Minnesota

PEATLANDS

Pockets of peatlands populate parts of the Mississippi valley. These are areas where the soil is so moist that plants die and pile up faster than they can decompose. This waterlogged blend of partially decayed plants is called peat. The water is usually acidic and cold. Most of the peatlands along the Mississippi are in northern Minnesota. By some estimates, peatlands store twice as much carbon as forests.

Peatlands develop slowly. As shallow lakes fill with dead plant matter, layer after layer of peat accumulates and forms different types of peat. Sphagnum moss in peatlands builds up under shrubs and is a great insulator: in summer, the tops can be hot, whereas the roots are still frozen. Sedge peat grows from the roots and parts of sedges. Woody peat accumulates from the roots and bits of trees.

Two of the most common peatlands along the Mississippi are bogs and fens. Bogs consist of raised peat surfaces near the top of the water table; they may or may not include trees. Bogs are highly acidic but low in nutrients, so the plants in bogs depend on getting nutritional supplements from rain and snow. When trees grow in bogs, the water table is usually lower.

Fens are less acidic than bogs and contain more nutrients, which typically come from water running through them. Rich fens are less acidic than poor fens and, as the name suggests, support more species and contain more nutrients. Water flows more vigorously through rich fens.

Black spruce and tamarack thrive in peatlands. Black spruce can reproduce from their roots. As the water table rises, tamarack send out new shallow roots that replace roots

Tamarack trees in fall at Itasca State Park

deeper down that have become water logged. Tamaracks are the only deciduous conifer in Minnesota, and the needles turn brilliant yellow in the late days of fall.

Some of the most unusual (and interesting) plants thrive in peatlands. Shrubs—mostly in the heath family—developed thick leaves covered with small fibers that help the plants retain water and nutrients. Labrador tea is one of those shrubs. For generations, Native Americans (and other contemporary Minnesotans) have plucked a few of its thick leaves and plopped them into hot water to brew tea. Several varieties of orchids thrive in bogs, including the Minnesota state flower—showy lady's slipper.

Pitcher plants may be the creepiest of the bunch. Leaves grow upward and form an elongated well. The plant generates a sweet-smelling liquid from deep inside that well that seduces insects to come in for a taste. When a bug goes in, fine downward-sloping fibers trap it. Once the victim reaches the bottom of the well, enzymes and bacteria turn the insect into a nutritious soup. Unfortunately, mosquitoes (as well as some aphids, flies, and moths) can live inside the pitcher plant's digestive well without turning into dinner.

Caribou once roamed the peatlands of northern Minnesota, but no longer do so. On the other hand, wolves, mountain lions, and moose—though lower in numbers than before European colonization—still inhabit them. Smaller animals also make their homes in peatlands, including shrews and moles. Bog lemmings also find peatlands agreeable, especially around spruce and tamarack trees. They build their nests in comfortable clumps of moss where they produce several litters a year.

A whole variety of birds enjoys hanging out in the bogs and getting a bite to eat, including a few species for which peatlands provide sanctuary, often for nesting, including yellow rails, sandhill cranes, palm warblers,

Labrador tea

Pitcher plant

and great gray owls. The high acid content of the water—especially in bogs—deters most amphibians and reptiles. Wood frogs find a home in fens, as do garter and redbelly snakes and painted and snapping turtles.

SWAMPS

Swamp. For many of us, the word inspires fear, loathing, maybe even disgust. We have blamed swamps for causing disease. Swamps are full of bugs, and they are dark, dense places where you can't see too far ahead. The water is murky, and God only knows what's living down there.

We have fundamentally misunderstood swamps. They are places of wonder.

Swamps, essentially, are thick forests that are always wet and connect to other water sources, typically a freshwater river. Swamps have trees. Marshes don't. The regular flow of fresh water into a swamp fuels biological diversity and tremendous abundance. When swamp water stagnates, swamps decline; they lose species and abundance. When salt water intrudes, swamps evolve into grassy marshes.

The perpetually wet ground makes it hard for most plants to grow, and those wet soils also make it difficult for trees to stay standing perfectly erect. In the upper reaches of the Mississippi, shrub swamps sometimes appear along the banks of the river. Speckled alder and willow are usually the dominant species.

When left alone and without disruptions such as fire, trees slowly establish and shrub swamps evolve into forest swamps, which are more common along streams with a low flow or old oxbow lakes. They can feature many tree species, from deciduous varieties (American elm, black ash, green ash, paper birch, red maple, trembling aspen) to conifers (black spruce, tamarack, white cedar). Below the trees, ferns and sedges do well.

Heading downriver, cypress swamps become more common around the Ohio River. Cypress and tupelo trees are well adapted to life in a swamp (along with the occasional red maple or black willow), specifically bald cypress and water tupelo. They grow up to two feet a year early in their lives, then, at about fifty years of age, they shift their efforts from growing tall to getting wider. The fat bases offer stability and probably also help move oxygen into their tissues. Bald cypress and tupelo also sprout bumps of tissue around them known as knees that probably help stabilize them. The knees can grow as tall as ten to twelve feet, but bald cypress grow them only when the main trunk is submerged in water. Water tupelo may

Cypress swamp in Mississippi

Horsetail

grow a couple of knees but bald cypress can grow a bunch. Water tupelo, though, are actually better adapted to cope with being and staying wet, so you'll often find them in the deepest waters of a swamp.

Bald cypress and water tupelo may thrive in the wet environment of a swamp, but their seeds will germinate only in dry soil that is rich in oxygen. When the swamp dries out (during periodic droughts, for example), their seeds will finally germinate, so it's common to see clusters of cypress and tupelo trees that are about the same age. Small elevation changes are enough to change the mix of trees in a swamp. Just a foot or so in elevation difference can make the difference between a cypress swamp and a marsh or hospitable ground for live oaks or red maples.

The needles of cypress trees decompose slowly, which is one reason that swamp water is so murky. That murkiness blocks a lot of sunlight, so that limits what can grow below the surface. And what is lurking beneath the surface? The most common fish are those that can make do in low-oxygen environments, or can poke their heads out of the water to suck in some oxygen, such as mosquito fish. Bowfin and gar also enjoy the swamp. Strays may wander in for a bit to raise their young or to feed when the water is high.

Horsetail often grows near cypress trees. This plant traces its roots back to the dinosaur age, so it is among the oldest living plant species on Earth. Most of its mass is belowground (the plants have an extensive root system), but it shoots up hollow stalks in clusters. Other common plants in a cypress-tupelo swamp include buttonbush, palmetto, and swamp privet.

Plenty of reptiles and amphibians are well suited to life in the swamp, including lizards, skinks, and more frogs than you can croak at. Slithery reptiles are well represented, including nonvenomous species such as glossy swampsnake (also called crayfish snake), southern black racer, and red-bellied water snake. Cottonmouth (water moccasin) and copperhead are two species best to observe from a distance, as their bites are venomous. Cottonmouths prefer the swamps, whereas copperheads lurk on the ground in forested areas, blending in nicely with fallen leaves on the ground. In 1970, alligators were teetering on the edge of the endangered species list, and now there is a hunting season. Gulf Coast box turtles are the largest of their species at eight inches long, and they aren't picky eaters (berries, insects, worms).

Swamps accommodate birds large (anhinga) and small (prothonotary warblers). Anhinga are sometimes called snake birds

Marsh hawk

because, when they swim in the water, their head and slender neck rest on the water's surface while the rest of their body is submerged. They don't have oil glands, so they need time to dry off in the sun before they can fly effectively. Prothonotary warblers add splashes of color to the swamp's dark moody palette. Multitudes of wading birds nest in swamps. Other birds you might come across (or hear) include birds of prey such as barred owls, marsh hawks, and red-tailed hawks, along with warblers, woodpeckers, and wrens.

Beaver, muskrat, and otter are swamp natives, whereas nutria are invaders. Nutria are large rodents imported to this country by fur producers who hoped that nutria coats would catch on. They didn't, and instead, nutria escaped into the wilds of Louisiana and have taken over many areas (hundreds of thousands of them inhabit Jean Lafitte National Historical Park and Preserve) and, in the process, have pushed out muskrats from the areas they dominate. Nutria have a taste for tender young cypress shoots, which is short-circuiting the ability of cypress swamps to regenerate.

Swamp-dwelling invertebrates such as clams, shrimp, and snails, and insects thrive, as do the small critters that feast on leaf litter and decaying organic matter (detritivores). Perhaps the best known swamp invertebrate—and one of the most important in terms of its place in the food chain—is the crayfish (or crawfish). Predators with a taste for crayfish include barred owls, bullfrogs, largemouth bass, mink, night herons, some snakes, and, of course, humans.

Coastal marsh near Venice, Louisiana

COASTAL WETLANDS

At the southern end of the Mississippi, the river spreads out into many smaller channels that find their way to the Gulf of Mexico. In the dynamic world near the Gulf of Mexico, even the Mississippi eventually finds a shorter, steeper path to the sea (in relative terms; this is south Louisiana, after all, not West Virginia). Six times in seven thousand years, the Mississippi has altered its route to the Gulf. When its waters are flowing to the sea, the river and the sediments it drops build land. After the Mississippi detours down another path, the sea slowly eats away at land the river built. These areas teem with life—on land, in the sea, in the air—and these forces are the reason that the Louisiana coast claims the largest commercial fishery in the contiguous United States.

The Mississippi is currently building two deltas: the Plaquemines-Balize Delta (the one you're probably thinking of, the one that looks like a bird's foot from the air) and the Atchafalaya-Wax Lake Delta. After a thousand years, the Mississippi is just about done with the Plaquemines-Balize Delta, but the Atchafalaya Delta is relatively new; the river has been building new land there only since the early twentieth century.

The river delta is an area in constant motion. River overflows deposit sediment. Grasses root where they can. As mud and sand pile up, the land gets heavier and sinks. Plants die and enrich the soil. Tides and waves chip away at the edges, forming barrier islands. Hurricanes roar through and rearrange it all.

Marshes and swamps dominate these borderlands in the river delta, and Louisiana is home to more than half of America's remaining coastal marshes. There are many names for the wetlands down here: bald cypress-tupelo swamp, bayhead swamp, brackish marsh, flotant, fresh marsh, gum pond, hillside seeping bog, longleaf pine flatwood savanna, shrub swamp, and more!

Lake Pontchartrain

Lake Pontchartrain

Lake Pontchartrain sprawls over 630 square miles along the northern boundary of New Orleans, its drainage basin a mixture of bayous, forest, marshes, lakes, rivers, and swamps. The lake was probably a saltwater bay until Metairie Ridge formed after the last ice age and cut it off from the Gulf of Mexico.

Technically, Lake Pontchartrain is an estuary, a partially enclosed body of brackish water with freshwater flowing into it, but it also connects to the salt water of the Gulf of Mexico. The lake is pretty shallow, typically twelve to fourteen feet, which allows a lot of sunlight to penetrate to the bottom and feed aquatic grasses. It has historically supported a lot of marine life, including many commercially attractive species, such as blue catfish, blue crabs, brown and white shrimp, red drum, and spotted sea trout, but the estuary also provides space for a variety of animals—not just marine life—to raise their young.

The lake is suffering, though, from the impact of 1.5 million people living around it. Shorelines are eroding from industrial and residential development. Water quality is declining because of stormwater and wastewater discharges, runoff from agricultural fields, and salt-water intrusion caused by industrial canals. Levees have blocked infusions of freshwater needed by cypress swamps. And during periods of very high water on the Mississippi, the Army Corps of Engineers opens the gates of the Bonnet Carré Spillway to divert water away from New Orleans, which sends massive amounts of freshwater from the river into the lake, killing a lot of marine life. The lake is cleaner today than it was thirty years ago and now supports a large population of clams that helps keep the water clean, but we still have a lot of work to do to keep it viable.

MARSHES

Marshes are broad, flat, always-wet areas where only grasses and sedges grow, sometimes around open patches of water (or mud). Marshes grow on highly organic soil (what some folks call swamp muck), the product of layer upon layer of plants that die, fall to the ground, and decay. Sediment washed in by rivers sometimes mixes with the marsh soil.

In Louisiana, marsh habitats vary with the concentration of salt water. As the water gets saltier, plant diversity decreases. Freshwater marshes have no salt mixed in, whereas intermediate marshes may have a salt concentration up to five parts per thousand. Freshwater marshes typically have twelve inches or more of roots and foliage on top of thick beds of clay.

A floating marsh (also called flotant or a floating three-cornered grass marsh) consists of a layer of plants (such as bulltongue) and roots bound together in a squishy zone of loose, organic material (peat) that can be as deep as fifteen feet. Floating marshes can remain in relative balance for hundreds of years; the peat layer may grow thicker over time but stays relatively stable because the soil also sinks as it gets heavier. They rise and fall with water levels and make for unpredictable places to step—some are thick enough to hold the weight of a person, but others are deceptively thin and could give way under a person's weight.

As these areas sink (subside), the freshwater grasses get exposed to more salt water and start dying back, which creates pockets of open water. These brackish marshes have salt concentrations between five and fifteen parts per thousand. Cordgrass (also known as wiregrass, marsh hay, or *paille a chat tigre* [hair of the tiger]) is common. The layer of roots and foliage runs four to eight inches deep and typically rests on top of peat that may be ten feet thick. If you dig below the peat, you'll find dense clay. As the salt concentration gets a little higher, the root/foliage layer gets a little thinner and is likely to rest on top of sturdy blue-gray clay. This is a common type of marsh along the river's border with the Gulf of Mexico.

SALT MARSHES

Saltwater marshes have salt concentrations that exceed fifteen parts per thousand. These are challenging places for plants to thrive because the soil is perpetually water-logged, so it can't hold much oxygen, plus there's all that salt in the water. Salt marshes are biologically productive areas, but not especially diverse because few plants are adapted to this low-oxygen/high-salt water environment.

Marsh grasses such as roseau cane (also called giant reed), like tupelo trees, evolved a handy characteristic to adapt to the low-oxygen context—they create a thin layer of oxygen-rich soil around their roots. Many plants in salt marshes have also developed ways to store oxygen in their tissues. And like desert plants, saltwater plants have narrow leaves and stomates that are buried deep, features that improve moisture retention. But wait—there's more! Many plants in saltwater marshes also developed a mechanism to suck up water while keeping the salt out, although that process uses a lot of energy.

The dominant grass in salt marshes is smooth cordgrass, which grows taller when the layer of organic matter runs deeper. The salt marsh is not a friendly context for seedlings, so smooth cordgrass spreads primarily through rhizomes. Roseau cane, another

Flotant at Jean Lafitte National Historical Park and Preserve

common plant in salt marshes, grows in dense stands in the bird's-foot delta and also manages just fine in salt water. As the canes grow, they trap sediment efficiently, so they stabilize coastal marshes. Invasive mealy bugs , which have so far proven resistant to efforts to control them, have been devastating roseau cane stands in parts of the delta.

Some species of grasshoppers and plant hoppers eat smooth cordgrass, and they are eaten by one of the eighty-one known species of spiders and insects common to southern salt marshes. Most of the salt marsh's biomass, though, gets consumed after the grasses die, by bacteria and fungi, which are eaten by larval invertebrates, protozoa, etc.

Climbing up the food chain a little higher, polychaete worms, snails, shrimp, and crabs enjoy a meal of invertebrates. A single square mile of salt marsh can support hundreds of crabs and snails. The low amount of oxygen in the soil also dramatically slows degradation of dead plants, but daily tides and waves regularly wash detritus out to sea.

Salt marshes support a lot of sea life that we enjoy eating: baby shrimp that grow into adult shrimp, crabs, redfish, sea trout. There aren't many fish that make a permanent home in the salt marshes, but many fish rely on them for reproduction and for raising their young.

Plenty of other animals find life in the salt marsh appealing, too: muskrat and nutria,

Salt marsh in Southeast Pass

plus reptiles and amphibians, including American alligators and Gulf salt marsh snakes. Most birds in the salt marshes are just visitors, but a few make permanent homes, including the long-billed marsh wren and clapper rail. Wandering birds that stay for a while in the salt marshes include common gallinule, coot, great egret, king rail, marsh hawk, roseate spoonbill, sandhill crane, and swamp sparrow.

In tropical areas, mangrove swamps often replace saltwater marshes. Black and honey mangrove trees are common and often root in places where there's a subtle elevation increase in the sea floor, their tangled web of roots rising out of the water. They don't tolerate a freeze, so you have to go out to the scattered islands at the end of the Mississippi to find mangrove swamps, to Timbalier or the Chandeleur Islands, for example, or along the fringes of St. Bernard Marsh. Mangroves stabilize the land around them and provide habitat for a rich tapestry of birds and fish.

CHALLENGES

The single greatest threat to wetlands is, simply, that we have lost so many of them. We have drained and plowed some; others dried up after getting cut off from the main channel by levees. More melted into the Gulf of Mexico.

The most significant ongoing losses are along the Louisiana coast. Although Louisiana is home to 40 percent of the United States's remaining wetlands, coastal marshes are disappearing at an alarming rate. Since the early twentieth century, Louisiana has lost nearly two thousand square miles of coastal marshes, most of which are now open water. The greatest losses have been around the Mississippi's bird's-foot delta, which lost half of its land between 1932 and 1990. There are basically two causes.

Disappearing wetlands near Venice, Louisiana

Historically, the Mississippi River slowed and branched out as it neared the Gulf of Mexico. Periodic overflows spread sediment around, which helped build land. We built levees to prevent those overflows (so we could build houses and businesses in places that used to flood), so all that sediment that used to spread out now stays in the main river channel and, when it reaches the end, falls off the edge of the continental shelf and into deep water. It no longer builds new land.

Industries—oil and gas companies, mainly—accelerated the losses when they dug canals through the coastal marshes to make it easier to get around. The canals allowed salt water to seep farther inland, which killed off the grasses that don't like a lot of salt in their diet. Extracting oil and gas has also caused the ground to sink in some places, which allows more water in. At least the US Army Corps of Engineers no longer dumps the material it dredges from the bottom of the river into wetlands.

We've known about these losses for decades, but only recently has a sense of urgency kicked in, basically since Hurricane Katrina. The US Congress passed the Coastal Wetlands Planning, Protection, and Restoration Act (CWPPRA) in 1990, but the work it authorized is a fraction of what is needed just to stop the net loss of land. Hurricanes Katrina and Rita exposed New Orleans' increasing vulnerability to big storms, a risk that is growing because those lost wetlands slowed big storms and took much of the punch out of them.

Louisiana is now working on an ambitious plan to restore the Mississippi's power to build land. They are planning to cut holes in some levees, which will divert sediment-rich water into areas where it may accumulate again and recreate coastal land. The overall plan will cost tens of billions of dollars, and, of course, there's no guarantee it'll work. And with sea levels projected to rise in the coming century, it's fair to wonder if it's going to be too little too late.

The other major problem relates to sediment. Along the upper half of the Mississippi, navigation dams trap sediment that is piling up in the backwaters. Before we built the dams, some sediment stayed in the Upper Mississippi to form or reinforce islands, but most of it flowed downriver toward the Gulf of Mexico. Not anymore. The pools created by the dams have very little flow, especially away from the navigation channel, so the sediment that enters the river now tends to stay put. Some backwater channels are now inaccessible. Without significant changes in management practices, the Upper Mississippi will lose many of the backwater sloughs and much of the biodiversity that comes with them.

The Lower Mississippi used to carry much more sediment than it does now, much of which came down the Missouri River. After giant dams were built on the Missouri River in the mid-twentieth century, they interrupted the flow of sediment from western mountains and plains to the Gulf Coast. Still, the Lower Mississippi today almost certainly carries enough sediment to build (or stabilize) coastal wetlands.

PRAIRIES AND GRASSLANDS

PRAIRIES ONCE BLANKETED much of North America, from the Great Lakes to the Rocky Mountains, horizon-obscuring open fields of grasses and wildflowers that ranged from the tall gtrasses of Illinois to the short grasses of Montana. On the eastern edge of the prairie belt, the Mississippi River cuts a blue-green path through the landscape.

Early Euro-Americans were not especially fond of the prairies. Many considered them deserts, devoid of life, and poor candidates for farming. After all, if trees couldn't grow there, how fertile could the land be?

Native Americans who had lived in the prairies for thousands of years understood otherwise. The prairie provided well for them. They picked wild strawberries, raspberries, elderberries, and buffaloberries. They dug up prairie turnips, Jerusalem artichokes, and wild licorice, and dried mint. And, of course, they hunted bison, elk, and the other large mammals of the prairies.

Some Euro-Americans recognized the special qualities of the prairie, including Emily Dickinson in her poem "To Make a Prairie":

> To make a prairie it takes a clover and one bee,
> One clover, and a bee,
> And revery.
> The revery alone will do,
> If bees are few.

The beauty of the prairie lies partly in its scale, the vastness of grasslands unbroken from horizon to horizon. "I was born on the

Prairie landscape along the Mississippi River

prairies where the wind blew free and there was nothing to break the light of the sun," Goyathlay (Geronimo) wrote. "I was born where there were no enclosures." There is nowhere to hide from the sun, wind, or rain. Clouds loom like mountaintops in the sky, which feels bigger and bluer. Storm fronts roll onto the prairie with menacing, roiling dark grays and blacks, cloud banks reaching toward the heavens as lightning flashes to the Earth. Roaming through a prairie is to immerse in beauty laced with vulnerability.

Standing in the middle of a prairie, surrounded by grasses that stretch in every direction to the horizon, can feel lonely, but we are hardly alone. The long prairie landscape tempts us to think big, to scan the horizons, but prairie life is all around us, if we're willing to look down. The beauty of the prairie is also in the details.

Blooming pasqueflowers signal the return of spring and the start of a new season, which will be followed with an unbroken succession of wildflowers showing off their colors. Prairie chickens dance and squawk to attract a mate, while sandpipers perch on fence posts and shrubs. Goldfinches and cardinals fly around with flashes of yellow and red. Western chorus frogs wake from their winter slumber and the tiny amphibians fill the air with resonant *cree-eeks* that can travel half a mile. Hundreds of species of beetles, dragonflies, and grasshoppers do their thing in the hidden spaces on leaves or the ground. By the time goldenrod blooms fade, the prairie summer is winding down.

Grasslands spread across North America as glaciers retreated. Hot and dry for much of summer, the landscapes are not favorable places for most trees to grow. With no tree canopy to block the sun, the grasses and wildflowers of the prairie thrive. The prairies we see—the blades of grasses and wildflowers—are dense and productive, but

Pasqueflower

they are just a fraction of the biomass of the prairie. Half or more of the prairie's biomass grows underground, thick networks of roots that have adapted to suck up every available drop of moisture and nutrition to sustain the plant communities. Within and between these root systems, a fungi network moves nutrients and water throughout the ecosystem, while taking a cut for itself.

The Mississippi River passes through some areas where prairies were once the dominant ecosystem. South of Brainerd, Minnesota, the river slices through a transitional area where the forests gradually gave way to tall-grass prairie. South of the Twin Cities, much of the Mississippi valley ran along tall-grass prairies in southern Minnesota, Iowa, Illinois, and Arkansas. Throughout the Mississippi valley, smaller sections of prairie mixed in with wetlands, on sandy soils near the river, and on the tops of bluffs.

We have largely replaced the carpets of grasses that waved with the wind with agricultural fields and suburban developments. Places where prairies once supported multiple species of plants and animals now grow

Big bluestem

monocultures of manicured lawns and rows of commodity crops where one species (us) sprays chemicals to wipe out other species. Across the United States, we have lost 95 percent of our tall-grass prairies.

But the tide has turned—again. We better understand the value of prairies and the dangers of monocultures today. In many places along the Mississippi River, prairie communities are coming back.

GRASSES

Grasses are relatively new in the world, at least in geologic terms. Some species have been around for, maybe, sixty million years. Prairies are even more recent. From what we can tell, the earliest prairies sprouted about thirty-five million years ago; short grasses dominated. Tall-grass prairies didn't emerge until twenty-five million years later.

Grasses grow in relatively dry areas. A waxy substance that reduces the loss of moisture to evaporation covers their leaves. Most of their biomass is underground, though, as much as 90 percent! (In contrast, most of the biomass for plants in a forest is aboveground.) But there's more than one way to grow beneficial roots. Big bluestem, for example, grow roots that sink ten feet deep to tap into groundwater. Little bluestem and switchgrass produce extremely thin roots that quickly and efficiently absorb every drop of rainwater. Just one cubic meter of soil from a tall-grass prairie can contain as much as twenty miles of root systems. Grasses continually regenerate their roots; they replace the whole network about every four years. As grasses die, their roots and leaves melt into the ground and become hummus, one reason that prairie soil is so rich.

The plant communities that thrive in prairies vary with the amount of annual moisture they receive. The tallest grasses grow in prairie regions with more annual moisture, whereas the shorter grasses settle into drier places. Arkansas's Grand Prairie (and the coastal prairies in Louisiana that are west of the Atchafalaya River) are

Switchgrass

exceptions to that rule. The tall-grass prairie in eastern Arkansas spreads over an area that averages fifty inches of rain annually, but the thick clay soil (some dubbed it "hardpan") allows little moisture to penetrate. By summer, the soils in Grand Prairie are quite dry. Trees have a tough time surviving in those conditions (and the fires that rage periodically), but grasses and other prairie plants do just fine.

FIRE

Fire is the other major factor that shapes prairies. Prairies burned regularly before Euro-American settlers began living in them. Prairie fires were dramatic (and frightening)

sights. Flames could burn thirty feet high and a hungry fire could blow across a prairie as fast as a bison could run. George Featherstonhaugh, the first US government geologist, paused during a trip in 1835 to admire one prairie fire, as recorded in his book *A Canoe Voyage Up the Minnay Sotor*:

The appearance of the line of fire on the prairie was very pleasing this night, and detained me a long time from my rest. In every direction the horizon presented brilliant spots, resembling the lamps in an illuminated garden, and would have made a curious and rare picture.

Lightning strikes sparked some fires, but Native Americans regularly set the prairies ablaze to manage them. Burning the prairie yielded many benefits. Fire could drive away rivals or create a more defensible perimeter around their homes. More importantly, though, the fires improved hunting success with open sight lines and by driving herds of game so they were easier targets. After the fires burned, the fresh prairie grasses attracted a lot of bison, which made hunting them less work.

Fire is good for prairie communities, and most prairie plants have evolved so they are not affected adversely by fire (or grazing or being walked on). Since most of the biomass for prairie plants is belowground, losing vegetation aboveground has little impact on the plant's survival. In fact, fires clear off debris from the ground, which allows the sun's light to warm the soil directly. Prairie soils absorb rain more efficiently after a fire, and fires free nutrients that are quickly absorbed. Prairie plants—grasses especially—often grow back stronger and more lush after a fire.

Fires prevent many trees from becoming established in prairie soils (especially aspen and bur oak), so deciduous forests can't spread. Fires also keep nonnative plants under control, as few of them are adapted to survive after being burned to the ground.

PRAIRIE COMMUNITIES

I suppose some people see fields of grasses and assume that one prairie is the same as the next. Not so! Prairies vary by the types of grasses that dominate as well as the life they support. Along the Mississippi, you'll find examples of the most common types of prairies—tall grass and short grass—as well as prairie communities that grow precariously on the edges of Mississippi River bluffs.

TALL GRASS

The Mississippi River passes through tall-grass prairies that range, more or less, from the western Great Lakes to the Missouri River. Vegetation grows tall and thick. In a good year, big bluestem can reach eight feet tall, their stems glowing blue-green by early summer, then turning maroon in fall. Indian grass is shorter, with dense, feathery seed heads; their stalks turn golden in late summer. Prairie cordgrass rises to about the same height as Indian grass, but they differ from other prairie grasses. Their closest cousins are the cordgrasses that grow in coastal marshes along the Atlantic Ocean and the Gulf of Mexico. They grow mats thick enough that homesteaders cut them up and built walls from them, but they also have sharp leaves that can be rough on hands.

Switchgrass can grow nearly nine feet tall, but it is typically shorter than big bluestem; it can be quite happy in an impressive range of settings. Switchgrass grows deep root systems and their leaves form soft naps aboveground, perfect for a quick rest, especially if you're a deer, red fox, or turkey. Many of the same tall grasses grew in Arkansas's Grand Prairie, but because they had been isolated from their Great Plains cousins for thousands of years, they were genetically distinct from the big and little bluestem, switchgrass, and Indian grasses of the Great Plains.

Close to the ground, mints and wild licorice spread out among the grasses. Tall-grass prairies can support a dizzying range of wildflowers, most of which bloom from April to October, depending on the latitude. Pasqueflowers are among the first prairie wildflowers to bloom. Other early spring bloomers include golden Alexanders, prairie trout lilies, prairie violets, and shooting stars.

By June, compass plant (a sunflower, its leaves usually align along a north-south

Grass pink orchid

June grass

axis, coneflowers, leadplant, milkweed, and wild indigo bloom. If you're lucky, you might come across the increasingly rare grass pink orchid. Prairie wildflowers peak in July and August, as some of the earlier bloomers continue to shine, joined by blazing star, Jerusalem artichoke, sunflower, white and purple prairie clover, and ladies' tresses, one of the few orchids that has a scent. Most of the blooms fade away by early fall, but a few plants reach peak bloom then: downy and fringed gentians, heath aster, willow aster.

SHORT GRASS

The Mississippi carries a lot of sand and silt, thanks to its route through the glaciated landscapes of the Upper Midwest. As the river floods, it drops sand onto its floodplains, which really piles up in some places. These heavily sandy soils support ecosystems with flora that are typical of short-grass prairies. In these settings, grasses such as little bluestem, June grass, and poverty oat grass do well.

Wildflowers generally reach their peak with the abundance of water that comes from spring rains. Pasqueflowers, again, signal spring, followed by prairie smoke,

narrow-leaved puccoon, some varieties of sandwort and beardtongue, grass pink orchid, and prickly pear. Early summer bloomers include compass plant, some sunflowers, purple coneflower, blazing star, and golden and silky asters. Clustered poppy mallow blooms from late summer into fall, but you won't find a lot of them.

Some prairies also flourish on the tops of bluffs where a thin layer of soil (typically loess) rests on sandstone or dolomite bedrock, usually on steep south- or west-facing slopes. These hill prairies (also known as goat prairies) are exposed to considerable amounts of sun and wind and don't retain much moisture. They typically cover small patches of land between upland forests and the edges of bluffs. They are especially common in the bluffs along the Upper Mississippi River, in the Driftless Area. Indigenous People managed hill prairies with fire for generations before Euro-American settlement. Without regular fires, red cedar gets a foothold, as does sumac and aspen.

Hill prairies are unique ecological communities. Short grasses, such as little bluestem, and Indian grass tend to do best. The most common flowering plants include silky aster, rough blazing star, purple prairie clover, pasqueflower, leadplant, gray goldenrod, and false boneset. Prairie sagebrush also does well on hill prairies, but it is rare.

Prickly pear

OAK SAVANNA

In the Mississippi valley, oak savannas bridge the space between forests and prairies. As the amount of available moisture declines, trees dot the landscape instead of clustering, and they grow shorter. Grasses cover more space. Savannas thrive in conditions where major disturbances are common, fire especially. The oak trees in these savannas developed thick bark, which insulates their tender inner workings from fires. Grasses come back stronger after a good cleansing fire.

Because they exist between forests and prairies, savannas are home to a diverse collection of plants and animals. Plant life in the oak savannas of the Mississippi valley is like the sun-loving communities in tall-grass prairies with some of the shade-tolerant plants in forests. Bur oak and red oak trees stand as lone sentinels. Turkeys, deer, and other animals feast on the acorns, and turkeys love to nest in the plants that grow under bur oak. American hazelnut spreads out into tall hedges.

Some species are especially fond of the savannas, including purple milkweed, yellow false foxglove, and Culver's root. Red-headed woodpeckers and bobolinks prefer savannas over other ecosystems, which is one reason their numbers are in serious decline now.

Walking around an oak savanna in Minnesota, the experience matched the images in my head of what I expected a savanna to look like (expectations that were, undoubtedly, shaped by *Mutual of Omaha's Wild Kingdom* and similar TV shows). I just didn't get to hang out with lions and zebras. I felt like I was hiking through a prairie—open sun, no escape from the elements—except when one of those scattered trees provided welcome relief with its shade. The ground cover was thick, some of it chest high, sometimes even over my head.

Oak savannas are quite rare now, although some impressive remnants remain. As Euro-American settlers moved into areas where oak savannas were common, they plowed the land for agriculture. They also suppressed fires, so other species of

Oak savanna in Minnesota

trees took over and shut out the sun-loving plants. Where the soils were wetter, for example, savannas grew into forests of red, white, and bur oak, then transitioned to maple-basswood communities.

ANIMAL LIFE

Bison are intimately associated with grasslands for many of us, but most of the animal life found there is not nearly as imposing. Much of it lives on the ground, or just below it. Birds flock to grasslands at certain times of year, even though few species rely exclusively on grasslands for their livelihoods. Reptiles and amphibians find the grasslands quite accommodating, thank you, but of all the creatures that do well in the grasslands, insects may be the most abundant.

MAMMALS

Although bison, elk, and gray wolves no longer roam freely by the millions across the prairies, they still inhabit small pockets here and there, mostly because of reintroduction programs. Still, the prairies support diverse animal life. Pocket gophers—one of the few species that is still abundant in the prairies—burrow through the soil, which creates small mounds on the surface and loosens the soil, making it easier for many plants to grow. Their burrows last a long time and get used over and over, and not always by the original builder.

Black-tailed prairie dogs also burrow underground. Eastern cottontails, black-footed ferrets, western rattlesnakes, and burrowing owls are among the 150 species that use their tunnels. Prairie dogs are also an important part of the diet for badgers, coyotes, ferrets, golden eagles, and great horned owls. Ground squirrels live and

Badger

Greater prairie chicken

feed between the grasses. Badgers feed on gophers and ground squirrels, digging out the gophers' burrows with their long claws and strong front feet. Badgers, which typically roam over four to five square miles, can dig faster than gophers and ground squirrels can get away. The holes excavated by badgers can be big enough to trip up livestock, people, and horses.

If you're roaming around the prairie at night, you may come across coyotes, raccoons, red fox, striped skunks, or weasels. Jackrabbits, deer mice, meadow voles, and short-tailed shrews live close to the ground. Short-tailed weasels invade vole tunnels (they are about the same size), eat them, and take over their nests. Rather rude, if you ask me. When weasels bite prey, they inject a poison that paralyzes them, which means weasels can fight above their weight and eat animals that are bigger than they are.

BIRDS

Forests support more species of birds than prairies, but some prairie birds are quite abundant. There are only a dozen known bird species that nest exclusively in grasslands, though. Wandering around a prairie, we're more likely to see (or hear) birds than

mammals. Some of the most visible birds include the marbled godwit (abundant in spring when they mate) and upland sandpiper, which likes to keep an eye on the prairie from a post or branch perch. Greater prairie chickens have declined as they've lost habitat, but they are quite a sight during mating season. They are flamboyant and loud—their calls can echo over a mile. The males put on a big show to attract a mate in early spring, showing off their best dance moves, which get especially energetic near dawn and dusk. Other common prairie birds include blackbirds (red-winged and yellow-head), bobolinks, meadowlarks, and sparrows (savannah, grasshopper, clay-colored).

Red-tailed hawks and great horned owls typically nest in cottonwoods and other tall trees along streams, but they feed in open areas, including prairies. Other birds of prey that nest and hunt on the prairie include endangered burrowing owls, prairie falcons, northern harriers (sometimes called marsh hawks), short-eared owls, and Swainson's hawks (also called grasshopper hawks). Ferruginous hawks are unique to central North America; they can nest on cliff faces, in trees, or on the ground.

Waterfowl are often abundant in prairie wetlands, including the American white pelican, sandhill crane, and trumpeter swan, plus shorebirds such as piping plover.

Sandhill cranes

During migration season, many varieties of birds, such as black-capped chickadees, eastern kingbirds, horned larks, indigo buntings, and common yellowthroats, rely on the prairies for rest and food. In the evening, listen for the call of the whip-poor-will.

AMPHIBIANS AND REPTILES

More than a hundred species of amphibians and reptiles are native to prairies. Croaks of chorus frogs herald spring. Western chorus frogs may be tiny, but their croaks are audible one-half mile away. Wood frogs don't waste time. They breed in early spring so their tadpoles can mature before winter begins. Wood frogs survive winter by hibernating beneath rocks, leaves, and tree roots. As they settle in, their livers manufacture more glucose, boosting their blood concentration to sixty times greater than in summer. The extra glucose acts as an antifreeze of sorts, which prevents cells from freezing to a point where it would be fatal to the frog.

Tiger salamanders are fairly common but, like most salamanders, they are shy and prefer to hide in moist, dark places. They enjoy the challenge of eating creatures like worms and insects as they move around. Prairie skinks prefer dry prairies and savannas and have a detachable tail that enables them to make a Houdini-style escape. The tail slips right off when a predator grabs it; the skink will grow a replacement tail within a few weeks.

Plenty of snakes inhabit prairie landscapes, but only rattlesnakes are venomous. Gopher snakes can grow as long as six feet on their diet of burrowing mammals. Western hognose snakes put on an impressive show when they are threatened. They roll into a tight coil, then inflate their upper body so they look bigger and more intimidating than they really are. The snake may even hiss and strike, but it's not venomous. In some circumstances, rather than channeling their inner cobra, they will roll onto their belly and play dead. It's good to be flexible.

Endangered Blanding's turtles stand out from the rest of the turtle crowd with their striking yellow lower jaw and throat. They live much longer than your average turtle—eighty or ninety years is common—and show few signs of age-related deterioration. They also take a while to reach sexual maturity, at least twelve years and, sometimes, up to twenty. They'll eat just about anything and are adept enough to catch fish while swimming. When they get spooked, they flee to water for safety, where they'll stay for hours. They need a fair amount of wetlands, sedge, and sandy high ground to breed, which is one reason they are endangered, as there are fewer places that meet all of those requirements.

Antlion

Ornate box turtles are native to the Midwestern prairie. They are rather small, about six inches long at most, with shells marked with decorative strips and blotches of yellow. They burrow in winter, settling several inches underground. All the turtles in the community head to their winter shelters at the same time and emerge in spring within a few days of each other, even though they spend winter in their own individual burrows.

INSECTS

Is there a more common life form on the prairie? Ten thousand species of beetles. Two hundred species of grasshoppers. Five hundred species of dragonflies and butterflies. Insects ensure plants can reproduce by pollinating. They dig in the soil and loosen it, which makes it easier for plants to grow and for burrowing animals to dig. They break down nutrients so other prairie life can eat. And they get eaten by many animals.

Moths and butterflies are among the pollinators. Female monarch butterflies lay as many as four hundred eggs in one breeding cycle, usually on the underside of a milkweed leaf and never more than one egg per leaf. The prairies support many species of bees, but none that produce honey. Most prairie bees live in burrows in the ground. Different species of bees are active at different times of year, but they are always active when the plants they pollinate bloom.

Dung beetles are the prairie's sewage treatment plants. They pick apart pieces of everyone else's dung and roll those pieces until they form a ball. Once they've placed that dungball where they want it, they burrow underneath until it sinks into the dirt, then they feast on it. They remain underground until they have completely consumed that delicious sphere of animal waste, while they also release nutrients back into the soil that feed the prairie grasses. Dung beetles are also an important food source for many prairie animals.

In sand prairies, antlions (some call them doodlebugs) excavate a shallow depression in the soil, then lurk in the middle of it and wait for prey to come to them. Eventually, another insect or ant will get too close to the edge of the circle, and the sand will give way, sending the little creature tumbling into the antlion's trap. The antlion pounces on the little critter and bites it, injecting a paralyzing poison into the prey. The antlion then sticks its fangs into its subdued prey and sucks it dry.

Insect health is a good indicator of the health of prairie ecosystems. If you don't get buzzed by grasshoppers or bees, or if you can't find a single beetle, then the prairie is in deep trouble.

Managing a prairie with fire

CHALLENGES

Once Euro-Americans realized prairies weren't deserts and that their soil was rich and productive, they plowed prairie lands by the millions of acres. We've lost much of our native prairies to agriculture and to suburban development since. In Minnesota alone, just 150,000 acres of the state's pre-settlement twenty million acres survive, a pattern repeated across the Great Plains.

Still, we have probably bottomed out. All across the Midwest, prairies are coming back. New projects are bringing back parcels of prairie all along the Mississippi River, from the tall-grass plains of northern Minnesota to the Grand Prairie in Arkansas. The pace may not be blazingly fast, but at least it's happening. Most of these efforts are converting agricultural lands back to prairie, a worthy endeavor, but one that takes patience. It might take as long as a century to return cultivated land to prairie. Pioneer plants such as ragweed get established pretty quickly, but big bluestem and other grasses may need as long as twenty years to settle in.

Although it took a while for Euro-Americans to recognize the value of fire to prairie ecosystems, we get it now. Conservation groups regularly conduct controlled burns, which is a remarkably cost-effective tool for managing prairie communities.

FORESTS

TREES. WATER MAY define the Mississippi River valley, but trees give it form. In northern Minnesota, the Mississippi emerges from a small lake deep in the forest. After it trickles out of the lake, the river slips through deciduous and conifer forests. Thick forests line the floodplain from the cataract known as Owahmenah/St. Anthony Falls to the Gulf of Mexico. Birch and red and white pine gradually give way to silver maples and green ash, hackberry and pecan, cypress and tupelo. And just about everywhere, willows and cottonwoods steady unstable shores and frame the banks of the Mississippi.

Trees, tall ancient trees, covered thousands of square miles along the river, dense forests that fostered abundance. Trees soared toward the sun and stretched wide to capture every photon of light they could to convert carbon dioxide and water into the fuel that kept them alive: sugars, starches, and oxygen. Hardwood trees reached high in the sky and provided cover for shade-loving and shade-tolerant plants. Wildlife flourished in the dense forest.

Early Euro-Americans saw most of those trees as fuel and an impediment to progress. They occupied land they believed would be better used to grow crops for human consumption. Some Euro-Americans were downright dismissive of trees and forests. In *Domestic Manners of the Americans*, English travel writer and grump Frances Trollope wrote in 1828:

For many a wearisome mile above the Wolf River [at today's Memphis, Tennessee] the only

Forests at Itasca State Park in Minnesota

scenery was still forest—forest—forest; the only variety was produced by the receding of the river at some points, and its encroaching on the opposite shore . . . Where the river has receded, a young growth of cane-brake is soon seen starting up with the rapid vegetation of the climate; these two circumstances in some degree relieve the sameness of the thousand miles of vegetable wall.

The forests are much more than tall trees, of course. Understory trees and shrubs—which get by just fine without a lot of direct sunlight—fill in the gaps between the canopy and the ground. Ivy, grasses, and flowering plants spread across the soil.

Trees that live in communities—forests—have significant advantages over trees that grow alone. Forests reduce the effects of wind and extreme temperatures. Forest communities store water and increase the humidity, which creates better living conditions. Trees in forests live longer than lone trees.

Life in an established forest is intimately connected. Nutrients and water move from trees to ivy to songbirds and insects. As plants and animals die, they fall to the ground and enrich the soil as they decompose. When trees grow, their root systems stabilize the soil. Harvested forests lose much more soil to erosion than old-growth forests, and the soil in harvested forests gradually loses its richness.

Underground, the forest soil grows richer over time as organisms die and melt into the ground. Roots of trees, shrubs, vines—everything growing aboveground—wind together in a thick web. Fungi grow into and around these roots, which extract some nutrients that they can't produce themselves, but they also move nutrients between plants, benefiting the entire forest.

In these underground networks, called mycorrhizal networks among biologists or the "wood-wide web" to punsters, aboveground plants supply sugars generated by photosynthesis, whereas fungi typically provide nitrogen and phosphorus. Fungi can also absorb heavy metals, which pose a greater existential threat to trees than to fungi. As these networks mature, they can also share water through them. Trees use these networks to direct resources to other trees. Dying trees, for example, share their remaining food with other trees in their species to help keep them alive. Trees that are producing abundantly share excess nutrients with neighboring trees. Mycorrhizal networks exist wherever plant communities exist—from the Arctic tundra to tropical rainforests.

Trees can even marshal defenses when they are attacked. Oaks, for example, can produce tannins that make their leaves taste bad to predator insects and can even kill them. When pests attack an oak tree, it can send chemical and electrical signals through the mycorrhizal network to alert other oak trees to the threat. Those trees then produce their own tannins to keep the pests at bay.

Forests benefit the entire planet, including us. They capture carbon and filter and store water. They keep soil from washing away. They support diverse and abundant plant and animal life, which pleases us with its beauty. The complexity of life in forests inspires wonder. Getting lost in a forest may feel scary but losing yourself in a forest can inspire feelings of gratitude, of connection to something greater than ourselves.

FOREST COMMUNITIES

Many forests flourish along the Mississippi. In the headwaters region, the river passes through conifer forests, mostly communities of red and white pine. The Mississippi also passes through deciduous communities, including those dominated by maple and basswood or aspen. Once the Mississippi enters its wide valley around Saint Paul, Minnesota, forests fill the floodplains and provide a long-distance corridor for wildlife, including songbirds. Forests also fill the higher ground along the river, from areas that rarely flood to those that never do. Although many of the forests we see today are second growth, many have already been regenerating for a while and are relatively mature. And in a few special places, we can still find patches of forests that we have never cleared.

NORTHERN CONIFEROUS FORESTS

I first hiked the Bohall Wilderness Trail in Itasca State Park in Minnesota in August 2011, guided by Connie Cox, a long-time park ranger whose broad knowledge of the landscape spilled out in a stream-of-consciousness info dump as we hiked. The trail wound and undulated through a forest dense enough to hide a bear or a wolf just a few yards from where we hiked. Dappled sunlight penetrated to the forest floor that fed hazel brush and a few ferns. Pine needles covered the ground, and every step released a fresh burst of their scent, which I inhaled with deep, revitalizing breaths.

White and red pine dominated the forest, centuries-old trees with tufts at the top that reached upward of two hundred feet. Bogs and shallow lakes broke up the forest's density, opening space for a wider view of the forest and providing breeding grounds for thick clouds of mosquitoes and aggressive deerflies. As we got close to a bog, the firm topsoil gave way to a spongy surface of peat that might tolerate the weight of one average person (average by nineteenth-century standards, anyway) but two people standing in the same spot could sink in the muck two or three feet deep, each step a laborious effort of lifting a foot up and out and into the next spot of thick muck. This is what one portion of the boreal pine forest was like before logging began.

After the last of the glaciers retreated from northern Minnesota some twelve thousand years ago, the massive ice sheets left behind rocks it had pulverized into dust, gravel, and pebbles. Lichen—a symbiotic organism made up of a fungus and alga—carpeted rocks, and a few plants took root in the barren ground. When they died, their organic matter mixed into the ground. Over generations, the ground became richer with organic matter, and more plants took root. Spruce and fir shot up and the first forests emerged. Supersize creatures walked the land: wooly mammoth, buffalo twice as big as the ones we know, and beavers the size of today's black bear. The forests also provided sustenance for people who had moved into the area after the ice had retreated. They lived in sync with the seasons, hunting game like those big bison and collecting nuts and berries along the way.

As temperatures warmed 1,500 years later, the forest trees died away. Oak savannas and tall-grass prairies took their place. After a slight cooling, hardwood forests (oak, mostly) dominated, then, about three thousand years ago, forests of red and white pine took over. (As the planet continues to warm in the coming years, hardwood trees and savannas will again replace the pine forests, which will retreat farther north.)

The trees that thrive in the boreal world don't waste energy by shooting out new leaves every year. Evergreen needles begin photosynthesis with the first drips of water in spring. The trees retain more nutrients throughout the year, so they can survive in soils that aren't especially accommodating and under conditions where the supply of sunlight varies tremendously with the seasons. Spruce trees, for example, have oils in their needles and bark that protect them from freezing in the bitter northern climate.

Fire was essential to the forest life cycle, as important as water and sunlight, a fact understood by Native Americans who lit fires selectively for generations to clear room for hunting and for blueberry bushes to regenerate. Ground fires wiped out shrubs, low-lying plants, and deciduous trees that grew in the understory—aspen, birch, and oak—opening the forest floor to the sunlight needed for red and white pine seeds to germinate and grow (and those blueberries). Mature pines, though, survive ground fires quite well thanks to bark thick enough to withstand intense heat. Fires burned regularly. Researcher Sidney Frissell estimated that fires burned in Itasca State Park every nine years between 1650 and 1922. Red pines did especially well in drier sites that burned regularly.

In the twentieth century, land managers actively suppressed fires, which allowed understory trees to grow taller and interfered with the ability of pines to reproduce. As a result, the surviving pines in today's remaining old-growth stands are taller and older and more susceptible to wind damage. Fire suppression policies have prevented pine seedlings from taking root, so those old-growth stands haven't produced many

Old-growth red pine

seedlings to replace the older generations of pines. Over time, spruce, fir, or deciduous trees such as basswood, birch, or sugar maple will probably replace these old pine stands.

Management policies are shifting, though. Forest managers are using prescribed burns more often and allowing some natural fires to burn themselves out. Allowing this natural process to run its course helps new pine seedlings emerge and replenishes the forests, as long as deer don't eat all the seedlings or climate change doesn't render northern Minnesota too warm for red and white pine.

The northern forests aren't all red and white pine like the stand along the Bohall Trail, though. The Mississippi River also passes through forests dominated by balsam fir; they thrive in areas that are fairly wet and rarely touched by fire. These communities may also include white spruce, paper birch, and, sometimes, black spruce (especially where there are gaps in the forest and the soil is dry). Typical shrubs include beaked hazelnut and mountain maple. On the ground, plants that do well include big-leaved aster, bunchberry, twinflower, wild sarsaparilla, and Canada mayflower.

Communities of red and white pine and balsam fir take a long time to develop, so they aren't the first trees to emerge after disruptions. Logging was a major disruption to northern forest communities, so in areas that we have left to regenerate on their own, jack pines emerge first. The extreme heat from fire opens their cones, so seeds can emerge.

As the soil enriches over time, other trees emerge, often balsam fir, paper birch, and white spruce, assuming another round of fire (or logging) hasn't wiped the slate clean again. Jack pines don't do well with shade, so they'll fade away as these other trees dwarf them.

Snowshoe hare

Plants aren't the only life in the forests, of course. Creatures large and tiny rely on forests for their well-being. Dozens of bird species rely on conifer forests for their summer homes, but most have preferences for particular species of trees or types of vegetation. Kinglets and hermit thrushes prefer older spruce and fir communities, whereas mourning warblers and kestrels flock to areas that have been clear-cut.

Yellow-bellied sapsuckers drill holes into spruce, pine, fir, and aspen and suck out the sap. The holes can loop around the trunk or run up and down in a line; those same holes will sometimes attract hummingbirds or flying squirrels, who also enjoy a little sapsucking. Ruffed grouse make their homes where there are plenty of aspen trees.

Bald eagles often build their immense nests in white pines and tend to use that same nest throughout their lives. Owls are common, too. In some years, large numbers of snowy owls winter in Minnesota's forests. Downy, hairy, pileated, and three-toed woodpeckers are among the few bird species that remain in the coniferous forests year-round.

Snowshoe hares sneak around on the forest floor, their large feet perfect for hopping adeptly across layers of snow. Their white fur helps them hide in plain sight in winter, then in summer that coat turns brown so they don't stand out.

Porcupine

Wolf at the International Wolf Center, Ely, Minnesota

Porcupines lumber to the top of conifers where the bark is softer and easier to chew (maybe even tastier) and twigs are smaller. Raccoons are a common sight. Red foxes are sometimes visible, but not as numerous as raccoons. The forest is also full of creatures that are quite shy around people, so we may catch only a glimpse of them on a trail cam: bobcat, fisher, flying squirrel, lynx, marten, even an occasional mountain lion.

Northern forests also provide a home for plenty of amphibians and reptiles. If you look closely, you may see a blue-spotted or tiger salamander or any of a variety of toads. Snapping and painted turtles inhabit forested wetlands, and harmless redbelly and garter snakes patrol the ground.

Deer are abundant (probably too abundant) and beavers have made a spectacular comeback. Both animals are especially easy to see in forests that are rebounding from fire or logging. Most of the larger mammals are a rare sight, though, especially on a short hike.

Black bear (which can be brown or black) roam the northern forests, where they forage for blueberries, cherries, hazelnuts, insects, raspberries, and the occasional small mammal. They retreat to dens in winter but aren't true hibernators. Sure, they rarely eat or poop, but they will sometimes get up and move around and may even leave their den briefly. Cubs are born in January and February and nurse while Mom is still dormant. By the time warmer weather arrives in spring, the cubs are active and agile.

Moose are rebounding in northern forests. They are big animals with big appetites: they consume about thirty pounds of food every day. Summer delicacies include water lilies, wild rice, and other aquatic plants as well as willow, mountain maple, hazelnut, balsam fir, and aspen. Moose are also roaming tick colonies. As many as forty thousand ticks can cover a moose's hide, which is as annoying as it sounds. They rub their bodies against trees to remove them, which sometimes also scrapes off layers of fur.

Coyotes used to roam prairies almost exclusively but now they're more likely to be found in forests. They will eat just about anything but feast primarily on small animals such as hares, mice, and porcupines. Occasionally, a pack will go after a deer. We're more likely to hear than see coyotes, especially in the evening. If you hear a cry that sounds like whiny dogs or little children howling, that's a pack of coyotes.

Consider yourself lucky if you spy gray wolves (also known as timber wolves) in the wild. They are reclusive and usually live in remote areas in small family groups of five to eight (usually siblings with their parents) and typically range over fifty to a hundred miles. They eat primarily whitetailed deer

Luna moth

have molted a few times—they spin a web that shields them during winter. In spring, they emerge—hungry again!—and feed on fir needles and buds for a few weeks. They eventually morph into pupae, then ten days later become a moth and begin the cycle all over again. Spruce budworms can do a lot of damage to fir stands. Birds eat them and usually keep them in check, but sometimes their numbers far exceed the appetites of their predators, so they munch on and kill a lot of trees. As the damage spreads, they lose their primary food source, and their numbers drop again.

If you're lucky, you may catch sight of the stunning luna moth, with its delicate green wings dotted with prominent eye-spots, a white body, and tail feathers that twist around and flutter in the night. They're big for a moth, with wingspans that typically stretch four and one-half inches but can reach seven inches. They reproduce only once a year in the northern forests, in late May or early June, and when the adult moths emerge, they live only about a week.

Cecropia moths are in the same family as luna moths. They are the largest moths in North America (five- to seven-inch wing-spans) and dazzle with colors and patterns that the painter Claude Monet would have loved. As caterpillars, spiky ridges line their bodies, so expect to feel a sting if you try to touch one.

but will occasionally snack on beavers, snow-shoe hares, and other small animals, and sometimes even berries. One wolf eats about twenty deer every year, but they almost always take the oldest and weakest ones. They are about twice as big as coyotes and don't share territory with them. If you see a wolf or coyote running in the woods, one way to tell them apart is by watching their tails: coyotes run with their tails between their legs, whereas wolves' tails stay outstretched.

And let's not forget the smallest creatures in the forest: insects. Pine sawflies—which are actually nonstinging wasps—come equipped with an appendage that resembles a saw that they employ to slice a gap in pine needles where they can deposit their eggs. When the larvae emerge, they feed on the needles for a while, then fall to the ground, where they build cocoons among the fallen leaves and decaying organic matter. Some remain comfortably sheltered in their cocoon for two years before emerging as adults.

In forests dominated by balsam fir, spruce budworm sometimes thrives. The female moths lay their eggs on the needles in July, then two weeks later they hatch as hungry larvae. Some of them spin a thread that allows them to drop to the ground to search for food, but sometimes a breeze blows them into unfavorable places, such as lakes or oak or maple trees. By late summer—after they

NORTHERN DECIDUOUS FORESTS

In its five-hundred-mile course from Lake Itasca to the Twin Cities, the Mississippi River also passes through a few deciduous forest communities. The trees you'll see in a deciduous forest vary depending on the richness of the soil, how much moisture the area receives, and how often fires burn. Deciduous forests often intermingle with brushland, savannas, and wetlands. Some of the deciduous forest types in Minnesota today probably emerged as a consequence of the fire suppression policies adopted by Euro-Americans.

Deciduous trees shed their leaves as the weather cools. As fall approaches, trees suck the nutrients out of the leaves and into the trunk and roots. Many will then generate a hormone that stimulates the growth of a new cell layer that forms at the point where the leaves attach to the limbs. The extra layer protects the limbs from bitter cold, but it also severs the flow of water and nutrients to leaves, so they will gradually dry up and fall off. As photosynthesis slows, the green pigments of chlorophyll—the magical chemical that allows plants to convert light to fuel— fade away. As a result, the yellows, golds, and reds that had always been present in the leaves shine brightly before the leaves fall to the ground and turn into humus. In spring, flowering plants on the forest floor bask in the open canopy before the trees' leaves fill out and block the sun again.

Before logging companies leveled the trees, sugar maples dominated many northern forests, with a lot of hemlock mixed in. Other prominent species included aspen, basswood, beech, yellow birch, and white ash. Logging changed the mix of trees quite a bit, so today's second-growth forests have a different character. Communities of aspen, which root quickly, and birch are common now, with American hazelnut, shining clubmoss, and wild sarsaparilla growing on the surrounding ground.

Trembling (Quaking) Aspen

Trembling (or quaking) aspen typically grows in thick clusters that brighten the fall landscape with splashes of bright golden yellow. The tree's flat leaves stick out on long, thin stalks, so when a breeze blows through, the leaves flap, hence the name. Those easily fluttered leaves expose both their upper and lower parts to the sun, which is handy, because trembling aspens are one of the few trees that can photosynthesize from both sides of a leaf. Trembling aspens have another unusual feature: the white bark photosynthesizes, something that is done only by the leaves of other trees. In winter, when other trees can feed only on stored nutrients, trembling aspens continue to produce new food.

Trembling aspen

Gray tree frog

The Mississippi also passes through communities dominated by maple and basswood trees, which are typically forest communities that have been intact for a while. They rarely burn, so basswood and sugar maple trees are common, but you may also see ash, bitternut hickory, butternut, elm, and red oak. Sugar maples can live up to four hundred years and are generous neighbors. The nutrients that feed their leaves stay in the leaves rather than being redirected into the trunk as the weather gets colder, so when their leaves hit the ground, those nutrients get recycled into the soil, which becomes richer and richer over time.

The canopy in a maple-basswood forest is dense. It can screen out up to 95 percent of sunlight. Violet, trillium, Dutchman's breeches, bloodroot, and bellwort get most of their growth in early spring before the trees fill out and the canopy closes. Shade-tolerant herbs then dominate the forest floor, including zigzag goldenrod, enchanter's nightshade, and ostrich and lady ferns, with the occasional wild ginseng mixed in. If the soil is quite damp, wood nettles may stake out some territory.

Deciduous forests teem with life. Black bears roam the northern deciduous forests along the Mississippi River. Whitetail deer are abundant in forests today, although historically they preferred more open spaces around the edges of prairie and forest where they could easily spot predators. Where deer are abundant, you won't find much sumac, red osier dogwood, or mountain maple.

Closer to the ground, small mammals like cottontail rabbits keep busy grazing and reproducing. They replenish their ranks with up to four litters a year, each with up to eight bunnies. Woodchucks (also known as groundhogs) graze primarily on grasses and berries but will sometimes snack on insects, and even baby birds. They live in underground burrows, which is where they hibernate in winter, but they are also adept swimmers and can even climb trees.

If you're lucky, you might catch sight of a southern flying squirrel. They don't technically "fly," but glide thanks to a membrane called a patagium that stretches between their limbs. After a running start or a fall (and an assist from gravity), they float from tree to tree or limb to limb and can make quick adjustments in flight to maneuver around obstacles. If you want to see one, you'll need to prowl the forest at night. They're nocturnal.

Creatures with wings abound in deciduous forests, too, including birds of prey, such as the broad-winged hawk and barred owl, and songbirds such as the tufted titmouse, red-eyed vireo, and ovenbird. Insect-feasting birds include the Acadian flycatcher, the least flycatcher, and pileated woodpecker. Wild turkey and ruffed grouse prowl the ground.

Amphibians and reptiles are abundant in deciduous forests. Gray tree frogs are virtuoso climbers, and they can change their skin color to camouflage their presence. Turtles and some species of frogs survive the northern winters by burying themselves in the muddy bottoms of lakes and rivers. Salamanders and snakes burrow into the ground just below the frost line. Those gray tree frogs will slip under leaves for winter, which doesn't provide much insulation. The outer layers of their bodies freeze, but their body cells below the surface contain enough glycerol to prevent water in their body from freezing, so the cells aren't

Wood tick

damaged. When the weather warms, those frogs thaw and get busy climbing trees and hiding from predators again.

Webworms, sawflies, cankerworms, and other insects live off the bounty of plants but rarely kill them. Aphids and spittlebugs get their nourishment by sucking juices from plants. Tent caterpillars emerge in ten- to twenty-year cycles and, when they come out, they can cover an entire deciduous forest. Affected trees typically bounce back, but it can take a while to recover.

Ticks are probably the insects most of us associate with forests. They are cousins of mites and spiders. In northern decidu-ous forests, the most common varieties are deer ticks and wood ticks. The life cycle of a tick spans two years and three blood donors. Larval ticks start the cycle by hooking up with their first host, typically a white-footed mouse. After gorging for two days, they drop to the ground, where they will stay for the next year. They emerge as a nymph and climb onto a tree limb or blade of grass, where they wait to ambush their next blood donor. After feeding for a few days, they drop off again and slumber through another winter. They come out in spring as an adult and are ready for their last meal, which is often blood from a deer (or us). The adults mate while feeding off their host. After binging on blood and sex, the male drops off and dies, while the female falls onto the ground and lays her eggs, which will hatch the following spring and start the cycle all over again.

FLOODPLAIN FORESTS

Floodplain, or riparian, forests share many of the characteristics of other forests, with an important difference—disruption is a feature, not a bug. Water levels rise and fall. The river occasionally cuts a new channel through the middle of a floodplain forest. The soil is some-times sandy, sometimes heavy with gravel, sometimes thick with gooey sediment. High water can sweep the forest floor clean and also wash out vulnerable trees, which opens holes in the canopy. Plants in riparian communi-ties also get their rewards, though. When the water recedes, the river leaves behind a fresh blanket of nutritious sediments. Trees and plants near the river have, therefore, had to adapt to living with disruption.

Willow and cottonwood saplings are among the first to bounce back after high water. Both have seeds primed to sprout quickly and each will shoot up fast, which stabilizes the ground. Cottonwoods can grow ten to fifteen feet a year and top out over one hundred feet, which is one reason red-tailed hawks and great horned owls nest in them. They can live well over a hundred years but need repeated flooding to reproduce.

Silver maple

Silver Maples

Silver maples are well adapted to life in the floodplain and are increasingly dominating them as species diversity declines. They tolerate a wide range of temperatures—they range from northern Minnesota to the Gulf of Mexico—and can survive long periods of being flooded or drying out. They are remarkably resilient. Cut one down and fresh shoots emerge from the decapitated trunk. When sediment covers it, it grows new primary roots on top of the new soil. Seedlings can survive for years in shaded areas until a hole opens in the canopy and sunlight reaches them, then they grow quickly.

They are the first tree to bloom in the floodplain of the Upper Mississippi (typically late February to early March), but they need to get started early so they can transfer nutrients from their roots to the trunk and stems before the ground surrounding them floods. Once their roots go underwater, they won't be able to move nutrients around. By the time floodwaters recede, their fertilized seeds in the familiar helicopter pods are ready to float free. Many seeds land on the water, then settle on the ground as the river recedes.

Without regular overflows, cottonwood forests would age and die out. A single cottonwood tree, by the way, can produce an astonishing forty-eight million seeds that are often released gradually over a few weeks in white balls of fluff. Cottonwoods were of a handful of tree species that Native Americans carved into dugout canoes.

As floodplain forests mature, other flood-tolerant species join cottonwoods and willows, such as silver maple, green

TOP: *Flooded forest* / **ABOVE**: *Upland forest at Stemler Cave, Illinois*

ash, American elm (which grows until it can produce seeds, then succumbs to Dutch elm disease), and swamp white oak (which produces tasty acorns in fall). Occasionally, hackberry and box elder also find room to grow, especially in the spaces vacated by elm trees. At slightly higher elevations, in places that only rarely get wet, oaks and hickories dominate. The species along the river don't vary just by elevation. The mix also changes somewhat from north to south along the river.

Along the Upper Mississippi, species including swamp white oak, silver maple, river birch, hackberry, green ash, cottonwood, and black willow dominate the floodplain forests. Below the canopy, you'll find buttonbush, plus plants like ostrich fern, nettle, gray-headed coneflower, and cardinal flower.

As you get farther south, more pecan, box elder, and American elm trees grow in the floodplain forest. Still farther south, the rich floodplain forests of the Mississippi Delta are mostly oak-gum-cypress, elm-ash-cottonwood, and oak-hickory, with live oaks mixed in.

Below the canopy, shade-tolerant plants fill in but don't cover the forest floor: cardinal flower, frost grape, poison ivy, woodbine (Virginia creeper), and wood nettle. Crayfish feast on plants on the floodplain floor; raccoons (and us) eat crayfish. Migratory birds depend on the continuous forest communities to complete their journeys. Ephemeral pools of water provide safe breeding places for amphibians such as toads, salamanders, and frogs.

Floodplain forests provide critical habitats for migrating birds. Some species of migratory birds spend close to a third of their lives flying back and forth. Riparian forests come to life earlier in spring than nearby upland forests, which makes their flowers and leaves important food for quite

a range of migrating birds, including American redstart, Baltimore oriole, common yellowthroat, great crested flycatcher, warbling vireo, and yellow warbler.

UPLAND FORESTS

Upland forests don't get wet. That's basically what distinguishes them from the other forests in this chapter. They might grow just a few feet above the floodplain, which is just enough to keep their feet dry. Others grow on top of ridges, such as Crowley's Ridge in northeast Arkansas and southeast Missouri. In the Upper Mississippi, they grow on the sides or tops of rocky bluffs, whereas along the Lower Mississippi, they spread across loess hills.

In the bluffs of the upper river, trees vary by how steep the terrain is, how much sun they get, and the type of soil beneath them. The south- and southwest-facing slopes are usually dry. In these areas, black oak, northern red oak, and white oak are common. North- and northeast-facing areas usually get more moisture, so basswood, beech, slippery elm, and sugar maple take root.

Along the Lower Mississippi, westerly winds picked up dust that, sometimes, found a place to stick, which grew into a series of isolated bluffs over millennia. The first of these bluffs, known as the Chickasaw Bluffs, rises north of Memphis. Atop each bluff, forest communities developed that were not affected by occasional floods but had to root in the loose, fine dirt known as loess. These upland forests are utterly unlike their neighbors down in the floodplain. Common trees include white oak, tulip poplar, sweet gum, sugar maple, and bitternut hickory. Underneath, dwarf red buckeye, flowering dogwood, hop hornbeam, pawpaw, and spicebush spread out. Look even lower, and you'll spot catbrier, crossvine, grape, poison ivy, trumpet vine, and Virginia creeper.

These forests also tend to attract different birds. Common species include barred owls, black-billed cuckoos, broad-winged hawks, eastern wood-pewees, hairy and pileated woodpeckers, least flycatchers, red-eyed vireos, white-breasted nuthatches, and yellow-billed sapsuckers.

CHALLENGES

We lost most of the trees in floodplain forests during the steamboat era to fuel the boats. In some places, we've also cleared them for agriculture, dams, and for logging. Some forests have come back, especially along the Upper Mississippi Refuge and in the batture lands, between the levees, of the Lower Mississippi.

Forests along the Mississippi River, though, remain heavily altered by human use. The processes that drive their growth and renewal are increasingly artificial and determined by our actions. Structural changes to forested areas are driving declines in productivity and viability, from land lost to suburban developments to changes in flood pulses to higher water levels and islands washing away. Some of these challenges directly result from our efforts to manage the Mississippi River for barges.

In floodplain forests, a monoculture of silver maples is replacing what had been diverse forest communities. Fewer plants are surviving in the understory and young trees and plants are having a harder time getting established. Trees in floodplain forests are getting older and there's not much coming along to replace them. Some biologists are concerned that we've completely altered the forest's ability to take care of itself.

The ideal floodplain forest maintains species diversity, variations in size and age of trees and plants, a range of plant types, and complex layers from top to bottom. We're losing much of that now. Losing taller trees will probably mean fewer bald eagles, cerulean warblers, great blue herons, and great egrets. Fewer sections of connected forest will mean fewer songbirds and a decline in red-shouldered hawks. Remaining stands of forests are getting cut off and isolated, which will create more edge habitats that are less diverse and more vulnerable to nonnative species, such as the reed canary grass that is crowding out native plants and turning forested areas into grasslands. We have some challenges ahead to restore the vibrancy and self-sufficiency of our forests.

NONNATIVE SPECIES

NONNATIVE, OR INVASIVE, species are a fact of life, not just along the Mississippi River, but around the world, although not all of them stoke concern. Honeybees, for example, aren't native to North America, but no one would suggest that we wipe them out. Along the Mississippi, some nonnative species are more problematic than others.

Our approaches to dealing with nonnative species are still a work in progress. Some methods are time-consuming and expensive to execute, and it's not entirely clear whether they will even work. We've also learned, though, that nonnative species generally have an easier time getting a foothold in ecologically impaired areas. Nonnative species can become established in prairies that no longer burn, in forests where tree harvests have left isolated stands, in rivers degraded by pollution and channelization. Once in place, the changes these nonnative species bring can be hard to reverse. By one estimate, the Mississippi basin is now home to more than 160 nonnative species, about half of them fish.

It's our fault. Most nonnative species get a foothold in new habitats because of human actions, especially the ease with which we get around the world today. Zebra mussels hitched a ride in the ballasts of ocean freighters. Well-intentioned but poorly conceptualized management practices have sometimes been to blame. In 1871, the US Congress created the Commission of Fish and Fisheries. One of their priorities was to introduce more game fish to the Upper Mississippi River, so a few years later, biologists introduced salmon, but they didn't do well. Grass carp, though, did just fine. Some nonnative species also enter North American habitats accidentally. Bighead carp, silver carp, and nutria, for example, escaped domestic farms and have dramatically affected habitats along the Mississippi River.

In the river itself, carp cause the most trouble, although their impact is not equally distributed along the Mississippi. River managers introduced common carp at the end of the nineteenth century, primarily because they were a desirable species to eat. Carp had been a staple of European diets for centuries (after Europeans imported them from Asia); Germans were especially fond of them. Common carp have been in the Mississippi basin for so long now that many people don't realize they aren't native. Biologists have also had a tough time figuring out just how much of an impact they have had on river habitats, as the areas where common carp have settled in have also been degraded by agricultural expansion, pollution, and urbanization. Common carp are quite tolerant of poor water quality, so in some places they have replaced native species that weren't so tolerant. They are now one of the most common species in the Mississippi River and won't be going away soon.

Grass carp are native to the big rivers in Russia and China. Wildlife managers in Arkansas introduced them to North American waters in the 1960s, mainly to control

Common carp

Bighead carp

vegetation and for sport fishing. They now inhabit much of the Mississippi and Missouri Rivers. They typically top out at about two and one-half feet long but can grow to nearly twice that size. Ecologists are concerned that the grass carp's need to consume loads of aquatic vegetation could permanently alter river communities (fewer waterfowl, more turbid water) and could push out some native species, but so far, those effects have been minimal.

Silver and bighead carp, on the other hand, are headline-grabbing nonnative species, thanks to their tendency to jump out of the water when disturbed. Both are native to Asia, and both found their way into the Mississippi basin when they escaped confinement. Both species of carp were imported to the United States in the early 1970s to improve fish production in ponds and to control phytoplankton in sewage ponds. They escaped within a few years, at least some of them, after floodwaters overran one of those ponds.

Both species have been quite happy in the Mississippi River's waters (and other rivers in the basin) and their numbers are expanding quickly. They are filter feeders and could squeeze out native filter feeders such as paddlefish, gizzard shad, and buffalo fish. They reproduce and grow rapidly, which makes them much harder to control. They are especially abundant in the Illinois River and along

parts of the Middle Mississippi above and below the Illinois River.

Silver and bighead carp have not yet settled in the upper reaches of the Mississippi, but concerns about them taking over the Great Lakes and the lakes of northern Minnesota and Wisconsin are so great that wildlife managers have spent a lot of time and money looking for ways to stop their spread. The US Army Corps of Engineers has installed an electric "fence" around a dam on the Illinois River, hoping the shocks will keep the invasive carp from spreading to the Great Lakes. In Minneapolis, the decommissioned Upper St. Anthony Lock and Dam is being maintained to provide a physical barrier that may prevent the carp from spreading to northern Minnesota's waters. On the other hand, we have evidence now that silver and bighead carp do best in parts of the river where pollution and overengineering have degraded the environment. Although it's not clear whether affected parts of the river can ever return to pre-carp days, restoring or maintaining a healthy river ecosystem might be the best long-term solution to limit their spread and protect native species.

Several nonnative plants are changing the landscape of the Mississippi's islands and shorelines. Fungi that aren't native to North America cause Dutch elm disease; native and nonnative beetles spread the fungus. Oak

Reed canary grass

Japanese hops

wilt fungus, which probably came up from Central or South America, is devastating oak trees in the Mississippi basin. Gypsy moths have taken a toll on hardwood trees, black willow in particular.

As the canopy opens up in floodplain forests, invasive reed canary grass multiplies. It grows quickly and crowds out native vegetation. Perpetually high waters caused by construction of navigation dams have also taken out floodplain trees such as swamp white oak, silver maple, and cottonwood, which also opens up space for reed canary grass. If these trends continue, some floodplain forests will convert to open grasslands.

Common (European) buckthorn and garlic mustard can take over fields and forests and crowd out native plants. The vines of Japanese hops are increasingly spreading across places in the Mississippi valley. They spread fast—they can grow as much as thirty-five feet in a year—mostly in sunny areas, and often on islands. As they spread out, they form thick mats that choke out native plants. Unfortunately, they are not used to make beer, and the prickly hairs on the stems can irritate skin enough to cause small blisters.

Water hyacinth forms free-floating mats in wetlands that can spread quickly and choke out native plants (and pose a barrier

Water hyacinth blocks a Louisiana bayou

Eurasian water milfoil

Nutria

to boat traffic). Louisiana spends a couple million dollars a year to control its population, mostly with chemical sprays. Eurasian water milfoil root in shallower parts of wetlands and send up frilly stalks that grow in thick clumps. They're probably spread by recreational boaters who unknowingly pick up fragments on their boat; when they take their boat to a different lake or river, those fragments get established in a new place. They form thick concentrations that can block boat traffic and crowd out native plants; few native animals find them tasty.

Purple loosestrife puts out tall, pretty purple flowers, but the plant is native to Asia and Europe. It was introduced to the United States more than a century ago for ornamental uses, but you can't buy it in most of the country now because of its impact on habitats. Purple loosestrife crowds out native aquatic plants and few native animals eat it.

Regular burns control most nonnative plants in prairies. Native prairie plants have evolved to thrive with fire, whereas nonnatives (sweet clover, spotted knapweed, leafy spurge) haven't.

Although most of the trouble-making nonnatives are fish and plants, one invasive rodent has created a heck of a lot of trouble: nutria. The McIlhenny family of south Louisiana (the makers of Tabasco sauce) imported nutria from South America to Avery Island in the 1930s. The McIlhennys had hoped that nutria furs would become the next big fashion trend. They didn't, and some got away and found Louisiana's wetlands much to their liking. They are fairly prolific. A female can mate again just a couple days after giving birth, and will, on average, give birth to two dozen babies during her lifetime. Nutria are rough on wetlands, though. They eat the stems of plants, which kills them and clears out large swaths of grasses, which leads to erosion and wetlands converting to open water. Even with incentives for trapping them, the nutria population remains robust.

HUMAN IMPACTS ON THE RIVER

MARK TWAIN underestimated the tenacity of the US Army Corps of Engineers. In *Life on the Mississippi*, he wrote:

The military engineers of the Commission have taken upon their shoulders the job of making the Mississippi over again—a job transcended in size by only the original job of creating it . . . . One who knows the Mississippi will promptly aver—not aloud but to himself—that ten thousand River Commissions, with the mines of the world at their back, cannot tame that lawless stream, cannot curb it or confine it, cannot say to it "Go here," or "Go there," and make it obey; cannot save a shore which it has sentenced; cannot bar its path with an obstruction which it will not tear down, dance over, and laugh at.

We have tamed the Mississippi River, not as well as a domesticated dog but more like a wolf cub raised by humans. We have straightened the river, confined its channel, and covered its banks and riverbed with rocks and concrete. We have modified its essential nature, taken away much of the wild river that supported many, and replaced it with a superhighway for bulk transport for the profit of a few. The scale of the work is unprecedented. There is really no part of the 2,350-mile-long river that we have not engineered.

THE RIVER'S MAKEOVER

At Itasca State Park in northern Minnesota, summer visitors line up to step carefully across the stones that mark the spot where the Mississippi River emerges from Lake Itasca, to wade into the mythology of a deeply fabled river. If the placement of the stones looks just a bit too perfect, it is.

The stones sit on top of a dam. Before the dam was built, the Mississippi River oozed out of Lake Itasca into a marsh, then pulled itself together into a stream about one-half mile downriver. Park officials of the day believed that the officially designated start of the Mississippi didn't do justice to the river's superstar status. Park Superintendent Earl Lang wrote in 1933: "At this time I am sorry to say that the established source of our great river is a swampy, muddy, and dirty sight . . . . This is, indeed, a sight that is not becoming to such a great river."

In the 1930s, the Civilian Conservation Corps (CCC) built a concrete dam at the edge of Lake Itasca and excavated a two-thousand-foot channel below it. The CCC gave visitors a prime photo op and the mythical river a more visually appealing start. In 2020, park officials renovated the

The dam at Lake Winnibigoshish

area to correct bank erosion and to make it look a little more natural.

The shallow river, however, encounters its first obstruction just eight miles from Lake Itasca—Vekin's Dam, a wooden structure that was built in the late 1800s at the height of the logging era. In the five hundred river miles from Lake Itasca to St. Anthony Falls in Minneapolis, the river is a small stream that occasionally passes through broad marshes with little current and vast lakes where a gentle breeze can feel like a gale force wind. This part of the Mississippi River feels wild and isolated, yet, in those five hundred miles, there are twelve dams, including the dam that flooded the Pokegama Rapids.

Four more dams block the river through the Twin Cities, including one at what was once the only waterfall on the Mississippi: the place Dakota People called *Owahmenah* and Ojibwe People called *Kakabikah*; today, we know it as St. Anthony Falls. The falls attracted Europeans who saw them as an easy way to generate power for their burgeoning frontier town.

South of the Twin Cities, the Mississippi River splits into a braided channel. Instead of a single strong current, the river's flow once split into smaller channels that snaked their way between and around islands. By late summer, the river was sometimes shallow enough in places that a person could walk from one side to the other without getting their hair wet. This made navigation difficult for boats with a deep draft. After decades of lobbying by agricultural and business interests in the Midwest, the federal government, in the 1930s, built a series of locks and dams from Minneapolis to St. Louis to maintain a more predictable channel depth for bulk transportation.

By the time the river reaches the Missouri border, most of the floodplain has been drained and plowed and protected by tall levees. From the Twin Cities to the Quad Cities, only 3 percent of the floodplain is

*Pokegama Dam near Grand Rapids,
Minnesota*

behind a levee; from the Quad Cities south to St. Louis, more than half of the floodplain is behind levees; south of St. Louis to the Ohio River, more than 80 percent of the floodplain is cut off by levees. Those levees exist almost exclusively to protect agricultural land from flooding; few people live in those areas.

South of the Ohio River, the Mississippi River enters a broad, flat alluvial valley known as the delta or Mississippi Embayment. When the Mississippi River ran free, it had a habit of cutting new channels as it meandered through the soft soil. The river constantly reshaped the land. A dynamic river isn't too good for boats trying to navigate it, though, so we built wing dams, piled rocks to stabilize riverbanks, (no one stacks rocks better than the Corps of Engineers!), cut new, shorter channels between meanders to speed the flow of water to the Gulf of Mexico, and sank concrete mats on its bed to ensure more stability and predictability in the river's channel.

Navigation dam at Alma, Wisconsin

Rocks placed to stabilize shoreline

In Louisiana, the Mississippi River fans out into several channels. The ones that branch away to carry water from the Mississippi to the sea are called distributaries. The largest distributary is the Atchafalaya River, which feeds the largest freshwater swamp in North America and will, one day, be the main channel of the Mississippi. Most of the other distributaries (a series of bayous, some of which are old river channels) were closed off with dams and levees to allow the land on the other side to dry out for farming (mostly sugarcane) or to build homes and businesses on.

As the Mississippi River nears the Gulf of Mexico, it forms a wide delta where the main channel spiderwebs, creating a lush network of wetlands and a maze of shifting sandbars that can make navigation tricky. When Europeans first explored the Gulf Coast in the sixteenth century, the mouth of the river was nearly impossible to find because thick clumps of driftwood and wide sandbars hid it.

Jetties at the Mississippi River's end

Levee along the Lower Mississippi River

In 1876, James Eads devised a series of jetties that cut through the sandbar at South Pass, and, within three years, deepened the channel from nine to thirty feet, allowing bigger boats to pass through. Within a few years, the Port of New Orleans boomed from the ninth busiest in the United States to the second busiest. The Army Corps of Engineers used a similar process to create a thirty-five-foot channel in Southwest Pass.

Twain also underestimated the drive of American capitalists to make a buck. In 1883, St. Louis businessman Richard Smith Elliott neatly summarized the dominant view of the day toward the Mississippi:

The United States will have a population of about sixty-three million in 1890, and eighty million in 1900. The majority will be west of the Alleghenies. To say that we shall allow the great river to remain in its present imperfect and destructive condition, is to say that we do not understand the interests of the nation, or our own power.

Because of these engineering projects, homes flood less often, shipping bulk goods is more reliable, and big farmers have cheap transportation to export their commodity crops (because public money pays for navigation infrastructure). Some people have profited from the changes to the river.

These projects have also fundamentally altered the river's world. Silt is accumulating behind navigation dams, filling backwater habitats. Islands have washed away upriver of the dams, which has created open expanses of water and less habitat. The Mississippi increasingly acts like a smaller river, with rapid rises and falls after heavy rains or dry periods. Louisiana is losing coastal wetlands at an alarming pace. Plant and animal life is less abundant. This is a system out of balance.

ENGINEERING A SOLUTION

We engineered the river to make water levels more reliable for barges and to hold back floodwaters from low-lying areas. At first, engineers made calculations and drew up plans focused solely on maintaining a channel that was reliably deeper. Over time, they gradually expanded their priorities to manage flood heights. In 1986, the US Congress added environmental restoration to the Corps' responsibilities with a program called the Upper Mississippi River Restoration Program, a recognition of the damage done to the river by past engineering efforts.

We still prioritize navigation and flood control projects over everything else, though. When shipping interests wanted a deeper channel at the Gulf of Mexico, the Corps and the state of Louisiana spent nearly $240 million to dredge five additional feet deeper. Meanwhile, a proposal to create a new environmental restoration program has a $300 budget. For the entire river. Congress has never come close to allocating enough money to mitigate the damage caused by engineering the river for shipping. There's little reason to believe that is going to change.

We are trying to manage a complex natural system to meet a handful of contemporary priorities, but we don't even fully understand how to manage such a system, and probably never will. Rivers are dynamic. They rise and fall throughout the year; the difference from high to low water levels varies from twenty-three feet at Saint Paul to sixty-three feet at Helena, Arkansas. Low-lying areas near the river can, therefore,

be inundated with deep water, covered with mud, or parched. Animal and plant life in the river's world evolved to thrive in that dynamic environment. We've chosen altering the river over adapting to it.

The river managers and their allies try to quantify (some) costs and (some) benefits of the engineering projects, but the process is as much art as science, and requires assumptions about the future that the Corps has often gotten wrong. And it's much harder to attach a dollar value to some things than to others.

How do we value habitat for migrating birds and spawning fish? Can we quantify the economic value to the mental health benefits of spending time in the natural world? Maybe we can quantify the cost of removing pollutants that threaten the quality of our drinking water, but it's not as easy to place a value on a diverse ecosystem that relies on that same water. Some policy makers today better understand the value of a Mississippi River with productive wetlands, especially for reducing flood risks, but we have to restore a lot of wetlands to realize those benefits, and deciding where wetlands will be restored will be contentious.

We have had a rich but complicated relationship with the Mississippi River. We have relied on it for our lives and livelihoods, even as we felt deeply afraid of the river's power. In modern times, though, most of us gave up on the Mississippi. We turned it over to engineers and lobbyists who have tried to engineer the river into a barge canal that we can wall off and forget about. Still, through it all, the Mississippi River—like many rivers—has kept a powerful grip on our imaginations, on our spiritual aspirations, and on our well-being. If we want a different future for the river, we'll need to take it back.

EXPERIENCE THE RIVER

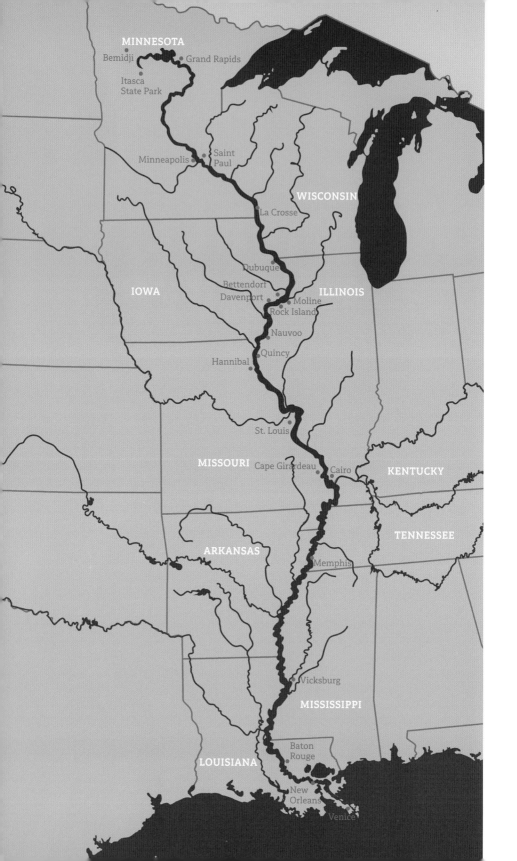

EXPLORE THE RIVER STATE BY STATE

WE ARE BLESSED with a lot of public land along the Mississippi River. We're lucky. These lands open up much of the river's world for us to experience, and they conserve everything from upland forests and hill prairies to backwater sloughs and remote islands. Multiple organizations tend to these places.

The federal government manages large swaths of the river, much of it through national wildlife refuges within the US Fish and Wildlife Service. The US Army Corps of Engineers also manages a lot of space along the river, often in cooperation with state and local agencies but prioritizes navigation and flood control over everything else. The federally managed areas—the refuges, in particular—typically prioritize conservation first and public access second, so they may or may not have facilities such as a visitor center and maintained trails. Some of them also close public access part of the year to protect migrating birds.

State parks, on the other hand, usually prioritize recreation and public use, with conservation a close second. Many offer full-service campgrounds and a network of trails they tend regularly.

Many states also own properties that may be called "wilderness" or "natural" areas. States typically manage these areas for conservation, but many also prioritize access for hunting and fishing. Although anyone can visit, these areas may or may not have groomed trails, and most offer just bare-bones services, such as a gravel parking lot and a pit toilet. Although state parks often get a lot of visitors, wilderness areas don't. If you desire an experience where you aren't likely to encounter many other people, check out a wilderness or natural area. Just be prepared to hike your way through brambles, between trees, and across muddy fields. It's a good idea to avoid hiking around these areas during hunting season, though, especially during deer season.

Some private organizations also own and manage property along the Mississippi River. Conservation and restoration are almost always the main (or only) goals, so these areas may or may not be open to the public. When they are, most organizations will, at least, maintain a trail or two through the property but probably won't offer any other visitors' services.

As much as I'd like to write about every place along the Mississippi that is open for public use, it's just not practical. I had to make choices about which ones to include or face the wrath of my editors. For the most

OPPOSITE: *The Mississippi River*

part, I used the following criteria to guide my choices about which places to include in this guide:

- Reasonably easy access
- Four-wheel drive not required to get around
- Possible to hike without needing back-country gear
- Offer a variety of experiences and exposure to different aspects of the river's world

Some places in this book might satisfy your curiosity in an hour, whereas you could spend several days at others and still not see all there is to see. Most places in the book maintain hiking trails for recreational use, but a few are accessible only in a boat (such as a canoe or kayak).

When you visit also matters. Spring and fall are always rewarding times of year to travel anywhere along the Mississippi River. Summers are spectacular along the Upper Mississippi, but along the Lower Mississippi, summer heat and humidity will drain your energy like a refrigerator with the door left open. Southern summers are best managed with lots of shade, avoiding hikes in peak heat, and ice-cold water (or beer, after the hike). And remember, hurricanes and tropical storms pose a threat to places along the Lower Mississippi from June through November. Winter in the Lower Mississippi is typically mild, with an occasional cold spell that might leave behind some snow or ice. Birds fill the wetlands. Winter in the Upper Mississippi brings prolonged periods of cold, some of it extreme. Blizzards can blow through and shut down roads for a few hours. Still, it's an underappreciated time of year to visit, just one that requires layers of insulation (including a heavy winter coat), good boots, and hot chocolate (or a brandy old-fashioned).

Follow the pilot wheel sign to drive the Great River Road.

Whenever you go, consider following the Great River Road, a signed route that runs from where the river begins at Lake Itasca, Minnesota, to where the pavement ends at Venice, Louisiana. For most of the route, it runs on both sides of the river, so you have choices!

MAKING THE MOST OF BEING OUTSIDE

Spending time outside is good for us. If you're reading this book, you already know that. It improves mental health and helps us feel more connected to the rest of the life on our planet. Spending time outside also helps us understand, viscerally, the value of conserving places where other life can thrive.

Spending time outside also comes with a few easily managed risks. Bugs are abundant, including flies, mosquitoes, and ticks. They are more annoying than a genuine threat to your health, but ticks transmit Lyme and other diseases, which aren't much fun to deal with. Cover bare skin when hiking through forested areas and tall grasslands. You may also wish to spray on bug repellent. After your hike, search your body for ticks (or ask someone else to do it, if you prefer).

Poison ivy thrives along the length of the Mississippi. It's nearly impossible to avoid. Many people are allergic to the oil in the leaves and stems of the plant and will develop a rash if they come in contact with it. To avoid exposure, wear long pants. If you think you walked through a patch of poison ivy, change clothes right away and throw them in the wash. Wear gloves when handling exposed clothing. If your bare skin gets exposed to poison ivy, wash it as soon as possible to remove the oil. A handful of moist sand often does the trick, but you need to clean off the oils within an hour or so of exposure to avoid a rash.

A few species of venomous snakes find the Mississippi valley quite accommodating. Watch for rattlesnakes if you're hiking around the bluffs of the Upper Mississippi. Farther south, cottonmouths and copperheads

TOP: *Poison ivy* / ABOVE: *Cottonmouth*

inhabit the wetlands and adjacent areas. If you see a snake, just back away slowly. They aren't aggressive unless provoked.

Check the weather before you set out for a hike or paddle, and dress appropriately. Storms can blow in quickly and, during spring and fall, the weather can change dramatically in just an hour or two. Keep in mind that cell service can be spotty, especially in remote areas, so, again, check the weather before you leave.

The Mississippi River sometimes floods. Expect high water from January through May along the Lower Mississippi. Farther north, high water may linger from March into June. Many of the places in this book will be closed when the river is high. Call in advance if you're concerned about that. And never, ever, ever drive across a flooded road.

If you're interested in paddling a canoe or kayak on the Mississippi, go for it. Paddling on the Mississippi is much safer than most people believe, but it's not a good place for

Storm rolling in over the river at Alma, Wisconsin

beginning paddlers. If you have little experience paddling a canoe or kayak, partner with a more experienced paddler and stick to a backwater channel; you won't have much current or other boat traffic to worry about.

Check the weather before you hit the water. Even a small amount of wind can make paddling difficult. Wear a personal flotation device (life jacket) the entire time you're on the water. No exceptions. Wear a hat and sunscreen to avoid a serious sunburn; sunlight reflects off the water, so you get exposed from above and around. Bring drinking water. Big rivers require bigger boats—fourteen feet long for a kayak, sixteen feet long for a canoe. Get more tips here: mississippiriverwatertrail.org/safety.

MINNESOTA

Bemidji • Grand Rapids

Itasca
State Park

Brainerd •

St. Cloud •

Saint
Paul
Minneapolis •

Winona •

MINNESOTA

THERE ARE MANY Mississippi Rivers in Minnesota, and I'm going to take you to all of them! There's the small forest stream that snakes through the Northwoods, the prairie river that flows from Brainerd to the Twin Cities, the river of the falls and gorge through Minneapolis, and finally, the river of our imaginations that begins around Saint Paul. Continental glaciers shaped much of the river's world in Minnesota.

All of Minnesota's rivers, except for the Mississippi, are postglacial. They have followed their current courses for only twenty thousand years, which is a blink of the eye in geologic time. About fifteen thousand years ago, alternating pushes and retreats of ice shaped and reshaped the land north of the Twin Cities. The St. Croix Moraine formed about that time in the area between today's Minneapolis and Little Falls. The Mississippi flowed along the western edge of it, getting some of its flow from water that emerged from tunnel valleys under the retreating glaciers.

Near the end of the Wisconsin glaciation, a lobe of ice lingered in the western part of the state. As it migrated to the northeast, it passed over the St. Croix Moraine and pushed the flow of the Mississippi River around its northern tip, while blocking its flow to the south. This blockage created Glacial Lake Grantsburg. Water from the lake drained down the St. Croix River and, eventually, into the Mississippi. As the ice melted, the Mississippi flowed around the northeast edge of the ice and gradually reconnected with its previous channel, which is why the Mississippi in northern Minnesota follows a fishhook-shaped course today.

Below Minneapolis, glacial meltwaters carved the deep valley we know today. Goat prairies and observation decks perch hundreds of feet above the Mississippi and satisfy visitors with stunning views. If you're in the area, stop by Barn Bluff in Red Wing, or Latsch State Park, and take the steep hike up to the overlooks, or swing by Winona's Garvin Heights Park where a much easier walk will get you to the edge.

You'll find plenty of places to stop and stay along the Great River Road in Minnesota. In the headwaters region, Bemidji, Grand Rapids, Brainerd, Little Falls, and St. Cloud have much to offer. Below the Twin Cities, Red Wing is a good place to base, as are Lake City, Wabasha, and Winona.

You'll find most of the highlighted places in this guide on or very near the Mississippi River. I've included a few, though, that are farther away, because they offer a good way to experience ecosystems that are part of the Mississippi's world.

ITASCA STATE PARK

DeSoto Lake, far from the crowds at Itasca State Park

ITASCA STATE PARK is one of Minnesota's most visited public lands (and on my short list of personal favorites), and it won't take long to understand why. People flock to the park to stand in the shallow waters where the Mississippi River slips out of Lake Itasca to begin its 2,350-mile journey to the Gulf of Mexico. The park offers quiet isolation—the nearest city, Bemidji, is thirty miles away. Pockets of old-growth trees and renewing stands of second-growth forest offer plenty of wildernesses and wildlife to seek out, including gray wolf and black bear. And the park offers a full range of services for visitors to enjoy, especially in summer.

The Ojibwe People have lived in the region for hundreds of years. Although we adopted many of their place-names into English (including the words that gave us

Mississippi), the name of the lake we identify as the source of the Mississippi—Itasca—is not one of them. William Boutwell, part of Henry Schoolcraft's 1832 expedition that searched for the source of the Mississippi, teamed with Schoolcraft to coin the name. They took the middle letters from the Latin words *veritas caput*, which translate as "true head." The Ojibwe knew the lake as *Omashkoozo-zaaga'igan* (Elk Lake).

As loggers clear-cut forests across northern Minnesota, a few concerned folks convinced the Minnesota legislature to save a few acres from destruction. The legislation passed in 1891—by one vote in the Senate—and Jacob Brower was appointed the first commissioner of the park created from those protected acres: Itasca State Park.

Logging continued in the park boundaries anyway, despite courageous efforts in

1903 by Superintendent Mary Gibbs to stop them. A logging company had been operating illegally in the park, and Gibbs, backed by the local sheriff, confronted them. Her victory proved temporary. The governor replaced her and logging resumed. Although loggers took many of the park's trees, a few stands of old-growth pine remain today.

It's hard to get a full Itasca experience without staying at least one night in the park. Itasca State Park maintains more than two hundred campsites in two full-service campgrounds as well as eleven backcountry sites for those who want to get away from the crowds. It's a good idea to reserve a site in advance, especially on weekends and during peak season. (You must register for the backcountry sites in advance.) The park also offers a range of lodging options, from motel rooms at Douglas Lodge to large cabins away from the crowds. Most of the lodging options are open from Memorial Day weekend until early October, but the four-season suites and Headwaters Inn are available year-round. The Douglas Lodge Restaurant and Mary Gibbs Café are open from Memorial Day until early October, but may shorten operating hours early and late in the season.

The park is open year-round but peak season is July through mid-August. By the third week of August, the park is much quieter. Weekends are always busier than weekdays. Come in January, and you'll have much of the park to yourself. The park offers fewer services in winter, but you can still stay in a cabin, rent a pair of snowshoes, and talk with a ranger. A few people cross-country ski on the thirteen miles of groomed trails in the park. Others explore the thirty-one miles of snowmobile trails. Spring brings mud with the melting snow and ice, and highly variable weather. Temperatures can still dip below freezing into May. Pleasant daytime temperatures and cool nights characterize June. By July, some lakes are warm enough for a swim, and the campgrounds fill up. The crowds thin by mid-August, and by mid-September, deciduous trees show off their colors. In early October, tamarack trees—deciduous conifers—turn a striking yellow before the needles fall off, one of the last trees to go bare for winter.

Note: You must purchase a vehicle permit to enter a state park in Minnesota. You can purchase a day pass, but if you're going to stay multiple days or visit other Minnesota state parks, you're better off buying an annual permit.

Orchids

Orchids dazzle with bold colors and shapes that look like something designed by a fantasy writer, especially the petal shaped like a lip. I used to assume that orchids were strictly tropical, but they aren't. Minnesota, which will never be mistaken for Bora Bora, has forty-six native varieties.

The tubers of some orchid species have an oblong shape that resembles a certain part of the male anatomy, which is where we get the name "orchid." The word comes to us from Ancient Greek and means "testicle." There are more than twenty-eight thousand known species of orchids worldwide, one of the most abundant types of life on the planet. They grow in just about every habitat around the world. Many are epiphytes, meaning they grow on other plants and get their food directly from air and rain instead of soil. More than half of Minnesota's orchids live only in wetlands, places such as the bogs at

Showy lady's slipper

Itasca and Lake Bemidji State Parks or Pennington Bog near Bemidji. Most bloom from mid-May to the end of June. One of those orchids is the Minnesota state flower: the showy lady's slipper.

HIGHLIGHTS

Although the park draws a lot of visitors, most don't go far beyond the Mississippi headwaters and the road between the east and north entrances. Even in peak season, you can escape the crowds with a hike into the backcountry or a bike ride along Wilderness Road.

Still, everyone wants to visit the spot where the Mississippi begins, the headwaters. A short, paved trail leads from the Mary Gibbs Mississippi Headwaters Center to the star attraction. Park managers have substantially altered the site from its natural state. Still, it's a fun experience to flip off your shoes and walk through the shallow water from bank to bank. ("I walked across the Mississippi!") In peak season, you'll be sharing the experience with a lot of people. If you prefer a smaller crowd, go early in the morning or try to visit another time of year (such as June or late August, if you're traveling in summer).

The park offers far more than a photo op at the beginning of the Mississippi, though. The exhibits in the Jacob V. Brower Visitor Center and around the Mary Gibbs Mississippi Headwaters Center give a nice overview of the river and the history of the area, as do the exhibits in the museum near the beach and amphitheater. If you have time for a leisurely visit, you'll find plenty of places to hike, bike, fish, visit historic sites (such as the Old Timer's Cabin), browse exhibits, or just relax. You can rent a canoe or kayak to take on Lake Itasca or a bicycle to ride around the park, and a boat takes folks on Lake Itasca for narrated tours.

The park also features several places where you can view the legacy of the continental glaciers that once loomed more than a mile high. The glaciers left behind several small hills known as knobs that were built from debris that accumulated on the margins of a sheet of ice or by streams of meltwater that flowed under a glacier. Sometimes, a block of ice got stuck in the ground, which formed depressions known as kettles that often filled with water. Many of the park's lakes formed this way.

Between the park road and the east arm of Lake Itasca, a small esker rises sixty feet. Eskers form when a glacier stops moving and streams under the ice deposit drift (sand and gravel). Because the glacier is stationary, the stream melts the ice above it. As gravel and rocks fall out of the melted ice, the pile of drift grows taller and taller. After all the ice above the stream is melted, a narrow ridge remains.

HIKING AND BIKING

The park offers forty-nine miles of hiking trails, many of which are relatively flat. Along Wilderness Road, there are several places to stop for a hike:

- The Aiton Heights Trail (one mile round-trip) passes through a stellar maple-basswood community and ends at a fire tower you can climb; the views of the forest from the top are fantastic.
- The Bohall Wilderness Trail (one mile round-trip) highlights a stand of old-growth red and white pine.
- For a longer hike, the DeSoto Trail (2.9 miles one way) winds through aspen communities and along some wetlands.

Other hikes in the park worth some time include:

- The Dr. Roberts Trail, a two-mile loop that begins at Douglas Lodge. It's an easy place to spot native orchids, such as showy lady's slipper, when they bloom, as well as other wildflowers.
- The Schoolcraft Trail just west of the headwaters winds along Lake Itasca and through a tamarack swamp (two miles round-trip).

If you'd like to bike around the park, there's a six-mile paved biking trail between the headwaters and Douglas Lodge. Cars and bicyclists share the park road, but biking on the eleven miles of Wilderness Road would probably be a more rewarding experience.

CONTACT

Itasca State Park
36750 Main Park Drive
Park Rapids, MN 56470
(218) 699-7251

DIRECTIONS

From Bemidji: Itasca State Park is about forty minutes from Bemidji. Go south on US Highway 71, continuing south after it merges with Minnesota Highway 200. Enter the park at the east entrance, or continue on Highway 200 to the north entrance.

LAKE BEMIDJI STATE PARK

LOCATED ON THE northern shore of Lake Bemidji, the state park spreads out over 1,726 acres and offers camping in a thick forest and multiple ways to pass the time. The name *Bemidji* comes from the Ojibwe *bemiji-gau-maug*, which translates as "the place where the current cuts across," a reference to the way the Mississippi River slices diagonally through the lake's waters. The Mississippi enters the lake from the south and exits on its northeast side. Summer is the most popular time of year to visit, but the park also has much to offer in winter.

Note: You must purchase a vehicle permit to enter a state park in Minnesota. You can purchase a day pass, but if you're going to stay multiple days or visit other Minnesota state parks, you're better off buying an annual permit.

HIGHLIGHTS

The beautiful beach on the north shore of Lake Bemidji is a great place to spend a summer day and listen to the call of the loons. Among the many hiking trails, the Bog Walk is, arguably, the most interesting. The boardwalk winds through a small bog, where you can spot some unique plants, including carnivorous pitcher plants and round-leaved sundew. If you are visiting from mid-May to

Common loons

the end of June, you are likely to see several species of orchids, including the state flower, the showy lady's slipper.

CONTACT

Lake Bemidji State Park
3401 State Park Road Northeast
Bemidji, MN 56601
(218) 308-2300

DIRECTIONS

From Bemidji, head north on Bemidji Avenue out of town, then turn right on Birchmont Beach Road and follow it to the park entrance. The park is about ten minutes from downtown Bemidji.

Loons

The star attraction for many people who visit the northern forests, the common loon, is striking. For me, a visit to the Northwoods isn't complete until I hear the loon's somber call. Loons are swift in the air and skilled divers but hilariously clumsy on land. They can get airborne only from water and need a long, clear stretch to succeed. In the air, they've been clocked as fast as seventy miles an hour. They can also stay underwater for long periods of time (up to five minutes), something you quickly figure out when you try to take their photograph. Their preferred habitat is forested lakes, and they often nest on isolated islands. Both parents stay involved in raising chicks, and often teach their young to dive by tossing them small fish for which the chicks must submerge themselves to retrieve. Within ten weeks, the young ones will grow to be as big as their parents. Loons typically leave the north in late October for the Gulf or Atlantic coasts and return to the Northwoods around the end of April. Fun fact: Loons are more closely related to penguins than they are to ducks.

CHIPPEWA NATIONAL FOREST

Old-growth forest at the Lost Forty

SPRAWLING ACROSS 660,000

square miles of northern Minnesota, Chippewa National Forest encompasses boreal forest, northern deciduous forest—most of it second growth—and prairie. Much of the land that forms the national forest was taken from the Ojibwe People without their consent. The Dawes Act of 1887 forced most Native American communities to give up collective ownership in favor of individual ownership. The federal government assigned parcels to individual tribe members, then sold off plots of land that weren't assigned. By the 1930s, the Dawes Act and other policies had reduced Native American land ownership in the United States from 138 million acres to 48 million acres.

In Minnesota, the availability of so much land triggered debate. Many people wanted to clear the forests and develop the land to attract new residents, but the Minnesota Federation of Women's Clubs wanted some of the land preserved, especially since developers were rapidly clearing most of Minnesota's native forests. Their initial idea for a national park

got little support, so they proposed a managed forest instead. In 1902, the US Congress created the Minnesota Forest Reserve; it was renamed Chippewa National Forest in 1928.

Logging continued in the forest, though, so about 90 percent of the forest's trees have been cut down and the land replanted. Over time, the Ojibwe People have also regained some access to traditional hunting and fishing areas within the forest, access that is guaranteed by treaties with the federal government. Today, they also directly manage large tracts of the forest.

Chippewa National Forest is divided into several units; each manages multiple campgrounds, hiking trails, and other recreational access. Overall, there are twenty-one campgrounds, three hundred miles of hiking trails, dozens of lakes and rivers to paddle, bike trails, and space to hunt and fish. There are remote areas and backcountry camping opportunities as well as nice resorts that offer all the creature comforts we expect. The forest is rich with plant and animal life, including black bear and bald eagles.

HIGHLIGHTS

The Norway Beach Interpretive Trail is an easy one-and-one-half-mile walk through the woods that comes with interpretive signs about the forest. It's in Norway Beach Recreation Area near Cass Lake.

Star Island sits in the middle of Cass Lake and offers six miles of hiking trails through thick forests to Lake Windigo, a lake on an island in a lake. You'll need a boat to get there.

The Lost Forty is a rare stand of old-growth forest, 144 acres with old red and

Joyce Estate, Chippewa National Forest

Black bear at the North American Bear Center, Ely, Minnesota

white pine trees. A short hiking trail winds through the forest. It's about fifty minutes from Deer River. From Deer River, take State Highway 46 to County Road 34, keep heading north as the road becomes County Highway 4, then continue north on County Highway 126. Turn right on County Highway 29, then left on County Highway 26. It's not as difficult as it sounds.

The Edge of the Wilderness Scenic Byway follows State Highway 38 for forty-seven miles from Grand Rapids to Effie. The road passes through Chippewa National Forest, so you'll find many places to stop and hike, such as in the Suomi Hills, a rugged area of rolling terrain, thick forest, and clear glacial lakes. Nineteen miles of hiking trails crisscross the area, some of which are open to mountain biking and provide access to primitive campsites. You'll also cross the Laurentian Divide. Water on one side flows to the Mississippi River, while on the other side, water ends up in Hudson Bay. Begin the drive from US Highway 2 at the west end of Grand Rapids.

David Joyce made a fortune from logging and built a summer retreat in the Northwoods between 1917 and 1935, complete with its own airplane hangar and forty buildings. The Joyce Estate on Trout Lake served as an escape from the bustle of their Chicago home until the 1970s. From Grand Rapids, follow State Highway 38 to County Road 60. After 1 mile, go north on County Road 335 until you reach the trailhead for Trout Lake Tract. It's an easy (one-way) three mile hike to reach the compound and remaining buildings.

Black Bear

Several thousand black bear call the woods of northern Minnesota home. They can, in fact, be brown or black and they are voracious berry eaters (blueberries, cherries, raspberries). They'll also snack on hazelnuts, insects, and small mammals. Cubs are born in January or February and will feed off Mom while she's still hibernating. By the time spring arrives, they are pretty adept at getting around. They aren't aggressive, and you aren't likely to see any; they are quite shy. If you pay close attention, though, you may spot signs of their presence, such as scat on the trail.

CONTACT

Chippewa National Forest
Supervisor's Office
200 Ash Avenue NW
Cass Lake, MN 56633
(218) 335-8600

CRANE MEADOWS NATIONAL WILDLIFE REFUGE

CRANE MEADOWS NATIONAL

Wildlife Refuge is a relative newcomer to the world of public lands. Established in 1992, the refuge conserves what was one of the largest remaining tracts of wetland complexes in central Minnesota. Crane Meadows covers more than two thousand acres across fourteen tracts of land that preserve sedge meadow, prairie, oak savanna, and forest habitats. The Platte River runs along portions of the refuge. The refuge provides critical habitat for migrating birds as well as native wild turkey, deer, and other animals.

Along the Platte River at Crane Meadows

HIGHLIGHTS

The Platte River Trail is a peaceful walk across flat terrain that passes through prairies full of native flowers, striking oak savanna, and wetlands. The shortest loop goes through prairie and oak savanna, but if you go the full 3.7 miles (round-trip), you'll also walk through forest and by wetlands.

Farther afield, the Sedge Meadow Overlook offers expansive views of a wetlands complex. It's best visited during migration season, and a pair of binoculars comes in handy.

CONTACT

Crane Meadows National Wildlife Refuge
19502 Iris Road
Little Falls, MN 56345
(320) 632-1575

DIRECTIONS

To reach the Platte River Trail from Little Falls, go south on US Highway 10, then left (east) on County Highway 35. Travel four-and-one-half miles to the Platte River Bridge. After crossing the bridge, take the first left to the trailhead.

Continuing on from the Platte River Trail to Sedge Meadow Overlook, go east on County Highway 35 for three miles to County Road 36 (Lake Road); turn left. After one mile, turn left on 230th Avenue and follow it for three miles. When it dead-ends at 133rd Street, turn left. The parking lot for the Sedge Meadow Overlook will be one-half mile on the left.

SAND PRAIRIE WILDLIFE MANAGEMENT AREA

HIGHLIGHTS

Several trails wind their way through the open prairie and into the woods, which offer an easy way to observe the succession of prairie plants that bloom from late spring into fall. The wetlands are in the eastern and northern parts of the WMA. There's a good bit of noise from the highway and nearby industries, but it lessens the deeper you get into the WMA.

THE GLACIERS LEFT their mark on Minnesota in many ways. As they retreated, the meltwaters carried tons of sediment dredged by the ice, much of which dropped out as the flow of water slowed. Around St. Cloud, one of those areas where glacial drift accumulated is part of Sand Prairie Wildlife Management, 650 acres of prairie, wetlands, and aspen stands. The prairie communities support 150 plant species and a few animals that are rare elsewhere in Minnesota, such as the yellow rail, nonvenomous plains hognose snake, and the endangered Blanding's turtle. The frog population is also doing well.

CONTACT

Sand Prairie Wildlife Management Area
(320) 223-7869

DIRECTIONS

Sand Prairie WMA is two miles southeast of St. Cloud along US Highway 10. It's slightly confusing to reach, so don't worry when you see the gate for Minnesota Highway Safety and Research Center. Just turn right and follow the gravel road to the parking lot.

SHERBURNE NATIONAL WILDLIFE REFUGE

Mahnomen Trail at Sherburne NWR

SHERBURNE NATIONAL WILDLIFE

Refuge covers thirty thousand acres in the borderland where northern forests gradually give way to prairies. The government acquired some of the refuge land through eminent domain beginning in 1965, and although some resentments still linger, the refuge enjoys widespread appreciation today. As it should. It's easy to pass a half day here and feel you've just scratched the surface. It's one of the best places in northern Minnesota to experience oak savanna habitats, but there are also sublime wetlands and patches of prairie and forest to visit.

HIGHLIGHTS

The Mahnomen Trail is a flat, three-mile hike through prairie, woodlands, and wetlands. The prairie lights up with flowers, whereas the wetlands are popular with waterfowl. Look closely at the plants along the lake border and you may spot orchids. It can get buggy, so be prepared to deal with mosquitoes and deerflies.

Another easy trail leads around restored prairie and oak savanna habitats behind the Oak Savanna Learning Center. It's a good place to observe a variety of wildflowers.

The Blue Hill Trail is a bit more work as it winds its way to the top of a hill through oak savanna. The trail can get a little bushy as

A view from Wilderness Drive at Sherburne NWR

you ascend, but the views at the top are good. If you finish the longest loop, the distance is five miles, or you can take the shorter loop that goes to the top of the hill and back to the parking lot.

Save time for a leisurely circuit around seven-mile-long Wilderness Drive. The gravel road passes small bits of prairie plus oak savanna and sedate wetlands, and there are a couple of places to get out of the car and walk around. The prairie trail is a pleasant diversion and passes a stand of trembling aspens. During one summer visit, I spotted a beaver working on a limb on land, sandhill cranes and trumpeter swans, and lots of other waterfowl. Near the end of the loop, there's a massive eagle's nest. To get to the start of Wilderness Drive from the visitor center, continue west on County Road 9 until you reach a stop sign at County Road 5. Turn left. The entrance to Wilderness Drive is two miles down on the left.

CONTACT

Sherburne National Wildlife Refuge
17076 293rd Avenue NW
Zimmerman, MN 55398
(763) 389-3323

DIRECTIONS

The refuge visitor center is just north of the town of Zimmerman on County Road 9 (289th Avenue NW) about four miles west of US Highway 169.

SCHOOLCRAFT STATE PARK

The Mississippi River at Schoolcraft State Park

ONE OF THE least visited state parks, Schoolcraft State Park occupies a quiet slice of the Mississippi in northern Minnesota. The park manages a small campground.

HIGHLIGHTS

The park features short hiking trails through pine forests and along wetlands, plus it borders the main channel of the Mississippi. Waterfowl are easy to spot in summer. It can be a rewarding place to sit and watch the river flow, especially toward sunset.

Note: You must purchase a vehicle permit to enter a state park in Minnesota. You can purchase a day pass, but if you're going to stay multiple days or visit other Minnesota state parks, you're better off buying an annual permit.

CONTACT

Schoolcraft State Park
9042 Schoolcraft Lane NE
Deer River, MN 56636
(218) 328-8982

DIRECTIONS

The park is twenty-five minutes west of Grand Rapids. Take US Highway 2 west to State Highway 63. Turn left (west) and drive about nine miles to Highway 6. Turn left (south), then take the first right onto the Great River Road north and drive two miles, then turn right to enter the park.

BASS BROOK WILDLIFE MANAGEMENT AREA

Bedrock outcropping along the Mississippi River at Bass Brook WMA

BASS BROOK WILDLIFE Management Area occupies a quiet, wooded corner of Cohasset that runs along the Mississippi River.

HIGHLIGHTS

Several trails wind through the thick woods (aspen, some red pine and other conifers) and swamps of the WMA. One trail parallels the Mississippi River for about a mile. On a good day, you might see beaver, mink, and muskrat. The trail also leads to an outcropping of Pokegama quartzite, which is a rare glimpse at bedrock in this part of Minnesota.

CONTACT

Bass Brook Wildlife Management Area
(218) 328-8865

DIRECTIONS

The easiest way to access Bass Brook is by parking at Pokegama Recreation Area (34385 US Highway 2) and walking across the dam into the WMA.

CUYUNA COUNTRY STATE RECREATION AREA

A fall morning at Cuyuna Country State Recreation Area

CUYUNA COUNTRY STATE Recreation Area is an interesting case study in how an old industrial site (iron ore mining) can be converted into a more natural state and repurposed for recreation. The former iron ore pit mines are now deep blue lakes. Piles of debris form challenging hills for world-class mountain biking trails. Although mountain biking is the principal attraction, there are multiple campgrounds, lakes to swim in or paddle, and hiking trails, too.

HIGHLIGHTS

You are welcome to hike the biking trails unless you see a sign that indicates the trail is restricted to bikes only (few are). The paved Cuyuna Lakes State Trail runs an easy eight miles from Crosby to Riverton. The hills between Alstead Mine Lake and Huntington Mine Lake (Mucker Mountain and Miner's Mountain) are dense with trails that range from relatively easy to steep inclines. If you don't mind an uphill hike, you'll find good views from the overlooks on these trails.

CONTACT

Cuyuna Country State Recreation Area
307 3rd Street
Ironton, MN 56455
(218) 772-3690

DIRECTIONS

Most of the recreation area is just north of Minnesota Highway 210 near the towns of Crosby and Ironton.

CROW WING STATE PARK

Mississippi River at Crow Wing State Park

ONCE THE SITE of a frontier outpost, Crow Wing State Park today sits at the scenic intersection of the Mississippi and Crow Wing Rivers.

HIGHLIGHTS

The park preserves a building from the old settlement and part of the historic oxcart trail that ran from Saint Paul to the Red River in North Dakota. The park is a convenient place to put in a canoe or kayak for a paddle, plus there's a hiking trail that winds through prairie and deciduous forest.

Note: You must purchase a vehicle permit to enter a state park in Minnesota. You can purchase a day pass, but if you're going to stay multiple days or visit other Minnesota state parks, you're better off buying an annual permit.

CONTACT

Crow Wing State Park
3124 State Park Road
Brainerd, MN 56401
(218) 825-3075

DIRECTIONS

The park is about ten minutes south of Brainerd, just west of Minnesota Highway 371.

RIPLEY ESKER SCIENTIFIC AND NATURAL AREA

Prairie at Ripley Esker

ANOTHER REMNANT OF Minnesota's glacial past, Ripley Esker rises sixty feet above the plains and snakes across the land for nearly seven miles just east of Camp Ripley. Built by a stream of meltwater that ran underneath a glacier, the ridge is easily visible as you drive along State Highway 371 near Camp Ripley.

HIGHLIGHTS

You'll find prairies and oak-aspen woodlands on the esker, with oak savanna between them. The primary goal of this SNA is conservation, so you won't find much in the way of well-trod trails, but two separate spots (each just big enough for one parked car) offer access to the site.

CONTACT

Ripley Esker Scientific and Natural Area
(651) 259-5800

DIRECTIONS

From Little Falls, go seven miles north on State Highway 371, then 0.7 mile east on County Highway 48 (233rd Street), then 1.4 miles north on County Road 282 (165th Avenue). As you drive along 165th Avenue, you'll see pull-ins at the north and south ends with an entrance by each.

MISSISSIPPI NATIONAL RIVER AND RECREATION AREA

THE MISSISSIPPI NATIONAL

River and Recreation Area (MNRRA) runs seventy-two miles through the heart of a major metropolitan area, the Twin Cities of Minneapolis and Saint Paul. It's a remarkable stretch of river. The modest prairie river at the northern end passes over the only waterfall on the Mississippi, through a gorge, then at Saint Paul enters the valley so many of us are familiar with. Along the way, homes and industry have altered much of the river's natural landscape, but remarkably, many areas near the river are protected from further development.

The park's role is mostly to promote access to the river and interpret river history, so it doesn't own much land in the corridor. Instead, the park offers a wealth of resources about places to visit that are owned and managed by federal, state, and local units of government. If you can find a copy of the park service's *Mississippi River Companion*, grab one. It is a comprehensive guide to the sites along the MNRRA's seventy-two miles.

HIGHLIGHTS

Stop in to one of the visitor centers for exhibits about the river and tips on exploring the Mississippi River in the Twin Cities. In Minneapolis, head to the St. Anthony Falls

Visitor Center. In Saint Paul, check out the visitor center in the lobby of the Science Museum of Minnesota.

South of downtown Minneapolis, the area around Coldwater Spring features oak savanna and prairie in various stages of restoration. The area has a long history as a meeting place, and the removal of a large office complex in 2012 created an opportunity to restore native habitats. A few trails pass through the area. Follow State Highway 55 (Hiawatha Avenue) south from downtown to reach the site.

The park service also maintains Paddle Share stations at a few locations in the Twin Cities. These are kiosks where anyone can rent a kayak, paddle a few miles on the Mississippi, and return the kayak to a downriver kiosk. Nice Ride bike stations are located near the Paddle Share kiosks, so you can rent a bicycle to pedal back to where you started.

CONTACT

Mississippi National River and Recreation Area
(651) 293-0200

St. Anthony Falls Visitor Center
1 Portland Avenue
Minneapolis, MN 55401

Mississippi River Visitor Center
120 West Kellogg Boulevard (Science Museum of Minnesota lobby)
Saint Paul, MN 55102

Coldwater Spring
5601 Minnehaha Park Drive South
Minneapolis, MN 55417

MINNEAPOLIS RIVERFRONT

MINNEAPOLIS HAS ONE of the best Mississippi riverfronts, and it promises to get even better in the future. Much of the land directly next to the river is public, so green spaces and trails run along much of it. Flour mills once lined the river, but most have closed. A few of the buildings still stand, and one was converted to the Mill City Museum (704 S. 2nd Street), which is worth a visit; don't miss the balcony near the top that offers fantastic views of the river.

HIGHLIGHTS

Downtown, walk the Stone Arch Bridge for views of St. Anthony Falls. On the east bank of the river, the lower trail in Water Power Park descends to the river through grasses and vegetation and among industrial ruins. You'll find the entrance to the trail just downriver of the intersection of SE Main Street and 3rd Avenue SE.

Bike trails run along both sides of the river, and many bridges are bicycle-friendly, so it's easy to loop back to where you started your ride. For example, one easy loop would be along West River Parkway, across the Stone Arch Bridge, up the path along SE Main Street, then back across the Mississippi River on the Central Avenue Bridge (or the Hennepin Avenue Bridge for a slightly longer ride), then back down West River Parkway. If you didn't bring a bike with you, look for a Nice Ride station where you can rent one.

CONTACT

Meet Minneapolis
(888) 676-6757

DIRECTIONS

Downtown Minneapolis is easy to walk around. Park at one of the metered spots or parking lots near the river and walk from there. On the east bank, you can walk to the Stone Arch Bridge from SE Main Street at 6th Avenue SE. On the west bank, you'll find pedestrian access to the Stone Arch Bridge from West River Parkway at Portland Avenue.

FORT SNELLING STATE PARK

Confluence of Minnesota and Mississippi Rivers

FORT SNELLING STATE Park is an oasis in the middle of the city. Not to be confused with the historic fort on top of the bluff, the state park sits at river level at the confluence of the Mississippi and Minnesota Rivers. The Dakota People know the place as bdote, the place where life began, according to some creation stories. Bottomland hardwood forests cover much of the area, with assorted ponds and wetlands mixed in.

HIGHLIGHTS

The visitor center includes exhibits on the human and natural history of the area. Outside, you'll find a memorial to the Dakota People who died while interned after the US-Dakota War of 1862.

The park includes eighteen miles of hiking trails, some of which are also open to bicycles. In winter, many of the trails are groomed for cross-country skiing and snowshoeing. The trail on Pike Island (Wita Tanka to the Dakota People) passes through a forest with cottonwood, silver maple, willow, and other flood-tolerant trees to the tip of the island, where the Minnesota and Mississippi Rivers meet.

Note: You must purchase a vehicle permit to enter a state park in Minnesota. You can purchase a day pass, but if you're going to stay multiple days or visit other Minnesota state parks, you're better off buying an annual permit.

CONTACT

Fort Snelling State Park
101 Snelling Lake Road
Saint Paul, MN 55111
(612) 279-3559

DIRECTIONS

Fort Snelling State Park is about fifteen miles south of downtown. Follow State Highway 55 (Hiawatha Boulevard) to State Highway 62 east, take the exit at State Highway 5 west, then exit at Post Road. Follow Post Road into the park.

SAINT PAUL RIVERFRONT

LIKE ITS NEIGHBOR (and rival) Minneapolis, Saint Paul is remaking its Mississippi River corridor. Bicycle and pedestrian paths run along the river, and more changes are coming to the downtown riverfront to connect the city to the Mississippi. Away from downtown, three parks in and near Saint Paul offer a chance to enter the river's world.

HIGHLIGHTS

On the west bank of the river, Lilydale Regional Park offers a pleasant escape from the city. At one time, a few hundred people lived near the river in this area, but repeated flooding, especially the record flood in 1965,

convinced folks to move to higher ground. The park still floods occasionally, but when it is dry, you can hike through the floodplain forest, enjoy the dog park with your pet, bike through on the Lilydale Trail, or put in your canoe or kayak at the boat ramp for a paddle on the river. To reach the park from south of downtown Saint Paul, take I-35E to the Minnesota Highway 13. Exit and go north, then right on Lilydale Road to the park.

Just down the river (or road) from Lilydale Park, Harriet Island Regional Park is one of the most frequently visited parks in the area. The park sits along the main channel of the river and has a lot of room to picnic and hang out or walk. The park hosts some of the city's major festivals as well as a company that offers riverboat tours. From Lilydale Park, continue north on Lilydale Road (it will become West Water Street). Go left on Dr. Justus Ohage Boulevard and follow it to Harriet Island.

On the other side of the river (and upriver from downtown), Hidden Falls Regional Park has seven miles of trails and room to spread out near the river below the bluffs. You'll also find a boat ramp and one of the Paddle Share stations. From downtown Saint Paul, take Shepard Road south. At Minnesota Highway 5, continue on Mississippi River Boulevard. The park entrance will be about a mile on the left.

CONTACT

Visit Saint Paul
  (651) 265-4900
Lilydale Regional Park
  400 Water Street
  Saint Paul, MN 55108
Harriet Island Regional Park
  200 Dr. Justus Ohage Boulevard
  Saint Paul, MN 55107
Hidden Falls Regional Park
  1313 Hidden Falls Drive
  Saint Paul, MN 55116

WAKAN TIPI/BRUCE VENTO NATURE SANCTUARY

WHAT WAS ONCE a busy (and dirty) industrial area is undergoing a transformation back into a more natural state while also paying tribute to the Indigenous history in the area. A cave in the bluffs here known as Wakan Tipi (spirit house) holds deep spiritual meaning for the Dakota People.

HIGHLIGHTS

The cave is closed off today, but the surrounding area is a joy to walk around. Prairie plants bloom in succession as the weather warms, and small ponds and wetlands attract a variety of wildlife.

CONTACT

Wakan Tipi / Bruce Vento Nature Sanctuary
  265 Commercial Street
  Saint Paul, MN 55106
  (651) 266-6260

DIRECTIONS

The sanctuary is tucked into a corner of downtown between highways and railroad tracks. One way to get there from downtown Saint Paul is to follow 5th Street northeast. Turn right at the stadium, then left on Prince Street. Follow it around a curve where it becomes Walnut Street, then turn right on 4th Street. The entrance to the sanctuary is on the right.

GREY CLOUD DUNES SCIENTIFIC AND NATURAL AREA

Grey Cloud Dunes

THEY ARE AN unexpected sight far from oceans and big water, but just south of Saint Paul, fifty-to-one-hundred-foot-tall sand dunes roll across the land next to the Mississippi River. The dunes formed at the end of the last ice age. Glacial River Warren dropped sediment that formed a wide, sandy terrace, then a few thousand years later, winds reshuffled some of that sand into the tall dunes we see today. Plants that prefer dry, well-drained soils thrive in the site's two hundred acres, including little bluestem, silky prairie clover, and gramma grass. You'll also find patches of oak savanna and floodplain forest as you descend to the bottom of the dunes.

HIGHLIGHTS

There are no maintained trails, but you can follow the informal footpaths that wind through the area.

CONTACT

Grey Cloud Dunes Scientific and Natural Area

7501 110th Street South
Cottage Grove, MN 55016
(651) 259-5800

DIRECTIONS

From Hastings, go north to Grey Cloud Dunes on US Highway 61, then west on US Highway 10. Exit at Jamaica Avenue and go south. Turn right on 100th Street, then left on Ideal Avenue. After a mile, turn right on 110th Street and follow it to the parking lot at the end of the road.

HASTINGS SAND COULEE SCIENTIFIC AND NATURAL AREA

Hastings Sand Coulee

TUCKED INTO A narrow, sandy valley behind a subdivision, Hastings Sand Coulee Scientific and Natural Area preserves small patches of old Minnesota landscapes. Most of the valley consists of dry prairie on a base of sand and gravel left behind by glaciers, but the SNA also has small stands of oak trees and prairies where the ground is slightly wetter.

HIGHLIGHTS

The SNA is divided into south and north units. The north unit offers a better visitor experience, with a groomed trail that passes through much of the tract.

CONTACT

Hastings Sand Coulee Scientific and Natural Area
(651) 259-5800

DIRECTIONS

From Hastings, follow US Highway 61 south to State Highway 316. After two miles, turn left on Tuttle Drive. Follow the road for about one-half mile and look for the trailhead on the left.

FRONTENAC STATE PARK

Hiking at Frontenac State Park

FRONTENAC STATE PARK offers a lot of variety in a compact area. Most of the 2,200-acre park sits atop a bluff along Lake Pepin (a natural widening in the main channel of the Mississippi).

HIGHLIGHTS

Hiking trails wind through upland forests and prairies. Overlooks offer panoramic views of Lake Pepin. The Lower Bluff Side Trail descends to the river and through a bottomland hardwood forest. The park also manages a campground with serene sites between the trees of an upland forest as well as a few cart-in sites in the middle of a prairie.

Note: You must purchase a vehicle permit to enter a state park in Minnesota. You can purchase a day pass, but if you're going to stay multiple days or visit other Minnesota state parks, you're better off buying an annual permit.

CONTACT

Frontenac State Park
29223 County 28 Boulevard
Frontenac, MN 55026
(651) 299-3000

DIRECTIONS

From US Highway 61 in Red Wing, go south for ten miles to County Road 2 in Frontenac. Turn left and follow the road to the park entrance.

WEAVER DUNES PRESERVE

Weaver Dunes

SAND DUNES ROLL across the Mississippi's floodplain south of Wabasha, more relics of the state's glaciated past. Glaciers left behind sand and gravel, and winds blew them around to form the dunes. The sandy soil supports prairie plants that flower from spring through fall and grow amidst little bluestem and June grass as well as a few plants that don't grow in many other places or are considered endangered, such as sand milkweed, wild indigo, and seabeach needlegrass. The dunes also provide critical habitat for endangered Blanding's turtles; females need the sandy dunes to lay their eggs. If you encounter the turtles during a visit, please keep your distance.

HIGHLIGHTS

The site doesn't have any groomed trails, but the dunes are easy to walk around. Wander slowly and watch your step.

CONTACT

Weaver Dunes Preserve
(612) 331-0700

DIRECTIONS

From Wabasha, drive south on US Highway 61. At Kellogg, turn left at the water tower (County Highway 18), then turn right on Dodge Street, then veer left onto County Highway 84. After about six miles, look for the address 60042 (on a blue marker) and turn left to park.

UPPER MISSISSIPPI RIVER NATIONAL WILDLIFE AND FISH REFUGE/WINONA DISTRICT

Reno Bottoms, Upper Mississippi Refuge

IN 1924, CONGRESS created the Upper Mississippi River National Wildlife and Fish Refuge after pressure from groups such as the Izaak Walton League to save remaining wetlands and forests from development. The refuge today spans 261 river miles and includes 240,000 acres of protected areas from Wabasha, Minnesota, to Rock Island, Illinois. Three million people visit the refuge every year, which includes all those who enjoy fishing its waters. Four district offices share responsibility for managing it all.

HIGHLIGHTS

In the Winona District, the best recreational options are on the water. The refuge maintains several signed water trails. The Halfmoon Water Trail loops five miles around the backwaters near Kellogg from Halfmoon Landing (12067 622nd Street); thick vegetation in late summer can slow progress along the trail. The Reno Bottoms Water Trail has three access points along State Highway 26, so it's possible to paddle from three to fourteen miles through a dense backwater area where bald eagles are abundant. The refuge website offers complete descriptions of all the water trails (with maps): fws.gov/library/collections/water-trails-upper-mississippi-river-national-wildlife-and-fish-refuge.

CONTACT

Winona District Office
102 Walnut Street, Suite 205
Winona, MN 55987
(507) 454-7351

GREAT RIVER BLUFFS STATE PARK

THE UPPER MISSISSIPPI has many splendid parks and preserves, and Great River Bluffs State Park is among the best. The park sits atop some of the highest bluffs along the river and, as one would expect, offers terrific views of the valley. Thick upland forests of oak, maple, hickory, and basswood end at hill prairies with wildflowers that bloom from spring into fall. Hawks and other raptors circle above the bluffs searching for their next meal or just to enjoy a cozy thermal.

HIGHLIGHTS

Six miles of hiking trails lead through forests to goat prairies and overlooks. The trails are mostly flat, with just a gentle incline here and there. Great River Bluffs is a pretty reliable place to enjoy bright colors in fall. The park also manages a campground and a few remote camping sites.

Note: You must purchase a vehicle permit to enter a state park in Minnesota. You can purchase a day pass, but if you're going to stay multiple days or visit other Minnesota state parks, you're better off buying an annual permit.

Foggy upland forest at Great River Bluffs State Park

CONTACT

Great River Bluffs State Park

43605 Kipp Drive

Winona, MN 55987

(507) 312-2650

DIRECTIONS

The park is between Winona and La Crosse. Follow Interstate 90 west away from the river. Exit at Nodine and turn right, then follow County Road 3 to the entrance.

WISCONSIN

UNLIKE IN OTHER states, the river's world doesn't change that much along Wisconsin's border, which is just fine. Folks somehow make do with 230 miles of imposing bluffs, thick forests, wetlands alive with birds and fish, and thousands of secret spots to enjoy it all. Wisconsin is blessed with some of the best scenery along the Mississippi River and the people who live up here know it (but won't brag about it).

The Great River Road follows right along the river in some places, but it never strays far from the water or woods. Small towns line the river from Prescott down to Potosi. The biggest river town is La Crosse, which will never be mistaken for Chicago but is a terrific place to spend a few days. Regardless of where you are, you're never far from a place to sleep or get a good meal. Any of the communities along Lake Pepin would be a satisfying place to base, as would Prescott to the north or Alma and Fountain City to the south. Other river towns that have options

for accommodations and food include Trempealeau, Prairie du Chien, Cassville, and Potosi.

Along the way, you'll find no shortage of places to pull over and enjoy views of the river. Stop as often as you can. Drive up to the overlooks that look down on the river's world from a few hundred feet high. Don't miss the views from Buena Vista Park in Alma and Grandad Bluff in La Crosse, for example. But along the Great River Road, you'll also find pullouts at river level in front of shallow wetlands where it's easy to stay for a bit and watch birds and other wildlife do their thing. As always, take your time. The longer you linger, the greater the rewards.

Wisconsin offers breathtaking views and inviting public lands along the river, and just a couple of those are popular state parks. Many of the best places to hike are state natural areas that get relatively few visitors, and even the federal refuge lands can be quiet places.

MAIDEN ROCK BLUFF STATE NATURAL AREA

View from the hill prairie at Maiden Rock Bluff

WHEN THE CHIPPEWA River meets the Mississippi, it carries more sediment than the Mississippi can sweep away. Over time, that extra sediment has accumulated into a spit of land that acts as a natural dam and backs up the Mississippi into an area we call Lake Pepin. It's one of the most scenic parts of the river, and you can get an unbeatable view from Maiden Rock Bluff State Natural Area. The bluff has been a landmark for travelers for generations and continues to inspire wonderment today. The state natural area preserves nearly six hundred acres on the top of the bluff, and the views of Lake Pepin from four hundred feet above it are spectacular.

HIGHLIGHTS

Hill prairies layer the blufftop, and they come with magnificent views of the river. Little bluestem, pasqueflowers, and wild bergamot grow in the dry soil next to red cedar. Raptors rest on the rocky bluff face when they aren't catching thermals and coasting in circles above the bluff. After a short walk from the parking lot through upland forest (about ten minutes), the trail opens onto the first hill prairie and the best view. Follow the trail around the top of the bluff for other great views of the surrounding hills.

CONTACT

Maiden Rock Bluff State Natural Area
(608) 685-3252

DIRECTIONS

Maiden Rock Bluff is north of Stockholm. From State Highway 35 and County J, drive north on J for three-quarters of a mile. Turn left on County E and drive a mile to Long Lane. Turn left and follow Long Lane to the parking lot.

TIFFANY WILDLIFE AREA/ NELSON-TREVINO BOTTOMS STATE NATURAL AREA

Chippewa River Delta

THE CONFLUENCE OF the Chippewa and Mississippi Rivers forms a thick maze of narrow channels, forests, and pockets of wetlands. Tiffany Wildlife Area protects 14,000 acres in this delta, and Nelson-Trevino Bottoms preserves another 3,600 acres. Between them, they cover a large, contiguous tract of bottomland hardwood forests, and a dynamic one, at that. High water often reshuffles the placement of water and sediment. Small channels sometimes shift course, and new islands pop up. Birds are abundant, and the rivers provide habitat for beaver, mink, and many other animals. Silver maples fill the floodplain next to American elm, cottonwood, and river birch.

HIGHLIGHTS

You'll need a boat to get around the area. If you just want to hang out and watch, try one of the boat ramps along State Highways 35 and 25. If you want to stay a night or two, the state allows primitive camping, but you need to get a permit in advance. Call the number below to get a permit.

CONTACT

Tiffany Wildlife Area/Nelson-Trevino Bottoms State Natural Area
(608) 685-6222

DIRECTIONS

You'll find several boat ramps along State Highways 35 and 25 between the towns of Nelson and Pepin.

WHITMAN DAM WILDLIFE AREA

Looking toward Whitman Bottoms from Minnesota

THE THICKET OF river bottoms around Buffalo City is the former stomping grounds of famed riverman Kenny Salwey. His book, *The Last River Rat*, is a must-read for anyone interested in a detailed description of the flow of life in the lowlands along the Mississippi. Whitman Bottoms, today, remains a popular place to hunt and fish and is replete with life. Most of the area consists of bottomland hardwood forests with silver maples and cottonwoods, but there are some marshes, too.

HIGHLIGHTS

You won't find a hiking trail, but you're welcome to walk around and make your path. From the parking lot near Buffalo City, you can walk pretty far along the dike. The Whitman Bottoms are a good place to paddle around, too. There's another boat ramp between Buffalo City and Merrick State Park that offers access to the southern end of Whitman Bottoms.

CONTACT

Whitman Dam Wildlife Area

(608) 685-6222

DIRECTIONS

To reach the dike, follow Highway OO south in Buffalo City. When the highway takes a sharp turn left, continue forward on South River Road. When you reach the parking lot for Upper Spring Lake Landing, park and walk toward the river; you'll see a footpath on the dike heading downriver. To reach the other boat ramp from State Highway 35 at Cochrane, turn west into Cochrane on 5th Street, then turn left (south) on Highway O. Continue forward when it turns into County Highway OO and continue forward on Prairie Moon Road. When Prairie Moon Road veers left, continue forward on Kamrowski Road. After one and one-half miles, turn right and follow the road until it ends at a boat ramp.

TREMPEALEAU NATIONAL WILDLIFE REFUGE

GOSH, I LOVE this place. Maybe I shouldn't tell you that. Trempealeau National Wildlife Refuge is one of the few public lands along the Upper Mississippi that doesn't have railroad tracks right next to it. It's a ways away from a highway, too, so it can be pleasantly quiet—quiet enough to distinguish the calls of many species of waterfowl. And there are often a lot, especially during migration seasons. Within the refuge, you'll find a shallow bay and other wetlands, sand prairie, sand dunes, forest, and small areas of oak savanna.

HIGHLIGHTS

The four-and-one-half-mile Prairie's Edge Loop is an easy way to get to know the refuge; you can drive, bike, or walk it.

Near the visitor center, you'll find an observation deck overlooking the wide, shallow bay that abuts the refuge. The deck is just far enough away from the water so visitors standing there don't scare away the birds. Just north of the observation deck, you can access the trail along Pine Creek Dike. The (one-way) one-half mile walk across a narrow path passes wetlands rich with life and ends at a point where you have water almost all around you. The refuge often floods in spring.

CONTACT

Trempealeau National Wildlife Refuge
W28488 Refuge Road
Trempealeau, WI 54661
(608) 539-2311

DIRECTIONS

From Centerville, head north on State Highway 35 for three miles to West Prairie Road. Turn left. The refuge entrance is one mile on the right.

PERROT STATE PARK

PERROT STATE PARK has enough to keep someone busy for a couple of days, so it's a good thing they have a campground. It sits along one of the narrowest sections of the Upper Mississippi's channel, although the valley is nearly six miles wide nearby. The Mississippi used to flow on the other side of the park's bluffs. The park has a mix of wetlands, bottomland forest, upland forests, and hill prairies.

Perrot State Park from Brady's Bluff

HIGHLIGHTS

Twelve miles of trails cut through the park. Brady's Bluff East Trail (0.7 mile one way) follows a series of switchbacks to reach the top of the bluff, so it's a relatively easy hike up. Brady's Bluff West Trail (0.5 mile one way) is a steeper climb and a little more work. Both end at a hill prairie at the top of the bluff (520 feet above sea level) with fantastic views. The Riverview Trail is much flatter and runs along the Trempealeau and Mississippi Rivers (two and one-half miles one way). There's also a canoe trail along the Trempealeau River and through the wetlands around its confluence with the Mississippi.

The pyramid-shaped land just north of the Trempealeau River is called Trempealeau Mountain. The only way to get there is by boat, and, if you do, walk carefully. There are no trails, and the mountain has deep spiritual significance for many Native Americans.

Note: Wisconsin charges a fee (per vehicle) to enter state parks. You can purchase a daily permit, but if you're going to visit a few state parks, you're better off buying an annual permit.

CONTACT

Perrot State Park
W26247 Sullivan Road
Trempealeau, WI 54661
(608) 534-6409

DIRECTIONS

Heading north on State Highway 35 in Trempealeau, turn left (south) on Main Street. At the river, turn right and follow the road for about two miles to the park entrance.

VAN LOON WILDLIFE AREA

HIGHLIGHTS

In the first half of the twentieth century, a narrow road ran through the area, which was connected by six rather rare bowstring arch steel truss bridges. Those bridges, all built between 1905 and 1908, are now part of the hiking trail through the area. Fall is a terrific time for a hike at Van Loon. From the parking lot, it's a 3.7-mile hike to the sixth bridge and back, all of it across flat terrain.

VAN LOON WILDLIFE Area runs through the floodplain of the Black River near its confluence with the Mississippi. The Black River splits into a few smaller channels through the area, which is a rich mosaic of floodplain forest, oak savanna, and sand prairies. Sand and gravel deposits from the Black River form much of the soil base. Silver maple and swamp white oak are common forest trees. Birds are, as you might guess, quite happy here. Songbirds regularly rest here in spring. Nesting birds include cerulean and prothonotary warblers and yellow-crowned night herons.

CONTACT

Van Loon Wildlife Area
N8327 Amsterdam Prairie Road
Holmen, WI 54636

DIRECTIONS

From State Highway 35 in Holmen, drive about a mile west of US Highway 53 to Amsterdam Prairie Road. Turn right. The parking lot is 1.6 miles on the left.

HOLLAND SAND PRAIRIE

HOLLAND SAND PRAIRIE protects sixty-one acres of remaining sand prairie on an old river terrace that the Mississippi River built at the end of the last ice age. In those twelve thousand years, winds have sculpted sand into gentle hills that break up an otherwise flat terrain. About 150 species of native prairie plants, including wild bergamot, wild rose, and black-eyed Susan, do just fine in the dry, well-drained soil and bloom in a steady succession from spring through fall.

HIGHLIGHTS

If you take your time walking around, you may spot some plants that you won't see in many other places, such as silky prairie clover and prairie smoke. The grasses in Holland Sand Prairie include June grass, side-oats grama, and little bluestem. The flat, mowed paths through the prairie offer good access throughout.

CONTACT

Holland Sand Prairie
W7781 County Road MH
Holmen, WI 54636
(608) 784-3606

DIRECTIONS

From the intersection of County DH (Main Street) and East McHugh Court (County MH) on the north side of Holmen, go west on County MH for one and one-half miles to a parking area on the south side of the road.

UPPER MISSISSIPPI RIVER NATIONAL WILDLIFE AND FISH REFUGE/LA CROSSE DISTRICT

Prairie at Upper Mississippi Refuge office

IN 1924, CONGRESS created the Upper Mississippi River National Wildlife and Fish Refuge after pressure from groups such as the Izaak Walton League to save remaining wetlands and forests from development. The refuge today spans 261 river miles and includes 240,000 acres of protected areas from Wabasha, Minnesota, to Rock Island, Illinois. Three million people visit the refuge every year, which includes all those who enjoy fishing in its waters. Four district offices share responsibility for managing it all.

HIGHLIGHTS

The La Crosse District operates a visitor center in Brice Prairie that is a good place to start. Once you're done with the exhibits, you can walk around the native prairie near the visitor center, which pops with wildflowers from spring through fall. You can also walk the dikes at Upper Halfway Creek Marsh area. The hikes along the dikes are pretty short, but they give a good look at marshes, wet meadows, and other restored wetlands that attract a lot of birds. To reach the dikes, exit the visitor center parking lot and turn right on County Z, then turn left on County Road ZN. After about one-half mile, you'll see a small gravel parking lot.

The refuge offers better opportunities by boat than on foot and maintains several signed water trails, such as the Long Lake Trail that zigzags for five miles through the backwaters south of Trempealeau. To reach the Long Lake Canoe Trail, turn south on Fremont Street from State Highway 35 in Trempealeau. Follow it south for nearly two miles (it will become Lake Road) to the boat ramp.

The refuge website offers complete descriptions of all the water trails (with maps): fws.gov/library/collections/water-trails-upper-mississippi-river-national-wildlife-and-fish-refuge.

CONTACT

Upper Mississippi River National Wildlife and Fish Refuge/La Crosse District
N5727 County Road Z
Onalaska, WI 54650
(608) 779-2399

DIRECTIONS

The La Crosse District office and native prairie trail are located in Brice Prairie. From Onalaska (at Main Street), follow State Highway 35 north for two miles to County Highway Z. Turn left. The office is about two and one-half miles down the road and on the left.

GREAT RIVER STATE TRAIL

Biking the Great River State Trail

THE GREAT RIVER State Trail offers a chance to tour a part of the river's world from the seat of a bicycle (or on foot). In winter, people snowmobile and cross-country ski on the trail. The crushed limestone path runs twenty-four miles from Onalaska to Trempealeau National Wildlife Refuge. You'll find a visitor center at the Onalaska trailhead with plenty of parking and bathrooms, and self-service machines to purchase a trail pass (you'll need one for each biker sixteen years old or older). Food and water are available in a few places along the way, but bring your own if you're going to be riding for a while.

HIGHLIGHTS

The trail passes prairies and wetlands and through some forested areas in two wildlife refuges and a state park. The trail offers good birding opportunities, and you may spot other riparian wildlife as well. You'll also see a couple of Native American mounds.

CONTACT

Great River State Trail

101 Irvin Street (Trailhead/Great River Landing)

Onalaska, WI 54650

(608) 534-6409

DIRECTIONS

If you're driving north on Highway 35, Great River Landing in Onalaska is on the left at Irvin Street, just a block south of Main Street.

HIXON FOREST

Hiking at Hixon Forest

YOU'LL FIND A lot of places to enjoy the outdoors in and around La Crosse, but few offer the range and variety of hiking as eight-hundred-acre Hixon Forest, which is divided into upper and lower units. The Hixon Forest Trails connect to other trails in the La Crosse area (including to Grandad Bluff), so you can get around much of the city on a bicycle (or walking) without crossing many city streets.

HIGHLIGHTS

Thirteen miles of trails wind up, down, and around the bluffs and through deciduous forests on the eastern edge of the city, many of which are open to bicycles, as well as hikers (and can get busy on summer weekends). Some trails lead to overlooks with expansive views of the city and river valley (and so require an uphill climb). The best views of the river are from the trails in lower Hixon, such as the Vista and Miller Bluff Trails. In winter, some trails are open for cross-country skiing and snowshoeing.

CONTACT

Hixon Forest
(608) 789-7533

DIRECTIONS

To reach the trailheads for lower Hixon Forest, take US Highway 16 north from La Crosse Street for 0.3 mile. Turn right on Bluff Pass, then turn right onto Milson Court and follow it into the parking lot.

GOOSE ISLAND COUNTY PARK

Sunset from Goose Island County Park

ON THE SOUTHERN edge of La Crosse, Goose Island County Park offers a nice variety of river-themed experiences. The park also manages a large campground (nearly four hundred sites).

HIGHLIGHTS

Trails wind through bottomland forests and next to wetlands that attract a lot of birds (many of which you may also see while driving into the park). A boat ramp offers access to a signed, seven-mile canoe route around the island and through backwaters. Part of the trail goes upstream, which might be a little work when the river is high and the current strong. Assume it'll take at least three hours to complete the route. You can rent a canoe in the park during summer.

CONTACT (CAMPGROUND)

Goose Island County Park
 W6488 County Road GI
 Stoddard, WI 54658
 (608) 788-7018

DIRECTIONS

From State Highway 35, drive one-and-one-half miles south from the intersection of US Highway 14. Turn right on County Road GI and follow it into the park.

GENOA NATIONAL FISH HATCHERY

IT'S NOT A place you're going to spend hours hiking around, but Genoa National Fish Hatchery offers an insider's look at some of the behind-the-scenes work that keeps our public lands and waters vibrant. When Congress created the hatchery in 1924 (at the same time it created the Upper Mississippi River National Wildlife and Fish Refuge), its work focused on supplying populations of sport fish, such as bass and panfish. Today, it focuses more on conservation, so endangered species are its primary focus. The hatchery now raises fifteen species of mussels as well as lake sturgeon and the Hine's emerald dragonfly.

HIGHLIGHTS

Start with a tour of the visitor center, then you can follow a self-guided tour around the hatchery site's ponds and buildings.

CONTACT

Genoa National Fish Hatchery
S5631 State Highway 35
Genoa, WI 54632
(608) 689-2605

DIRECTIONS

The fish hatchery is two miles south of Genoa along State Highway 35.

RUSH CREEK STATE NATURAL AREA

Hill prairies at Rush Creek

RUSH CREEK STATE Natural Areas conserves 2,400 gorgeous acres in the blufflands of southeast Wisconsin. At river level, you'll pass through bottomland hardwood forests and prairie. At the top, two hill (goat) prairies offer unobstructed views of the river and provide habitat for rare plants such as prairie sagebrush, but you're more likely to see little silky aster, bluestem, and leadplant.

HIGHLIGHTS

From the parking lot, a trail passes through prairie, then it follows an old dirt road to the top. Follow side trails to get to the hill prairies. Assume two hours to hike to the top and back. Rattlesnakes inhabit Rush Creek SNA,

so watch your step. The SNA is a good place to view fall colors, but you'll want to avoid hiking its woods during deer hunting season.

CONTACT

Rush Creek State Natural Area
(888) 936-7463

DIRECTIONS

Take Wisconsin Highway 35 north from Ferryville for three miles to Rush Creek Road. Turn right. You'll see a parking lot on the left. Cross the road to hike into the SNA.

WYALUSING STATE PARK

Wisconsin River from Wyalusing State Park

WYALUSING STATE PARK is another splendid public park along the Mississippi River and full of enough diversions to occupy a weekend. The Wisconsin River runs along the park's northern boundary, whereas the Mississippi passes to the west. The area has attracted human settlers for a long time, and you can still find a few Native American mounds within the park today. You'll also find bottomland hardwood forests, prairies, cliff faces, dramatic views, and quiet backwater sloughs.

Wyalusing State Park also manages a campground. Some sites in the Wisconsin Ridge Campground are along the edge of thet bluff, so you can enjoy million-dollar views from your tent or RV.

HIGHLIGHTS

Fourteen miles of trails wind through the park, some of them with steep inclines (or declines). The Mississippi Ridge Trail, which you can bike or hike, runs 1.8 miles through the southwest corner of the park and along the Mississippi, with some good views from the top. The Sentinel Ridge Trail runs 1.6 miles along the Wisconsin River, then turns along the Mississippi and heads down to river level. You can loop back before the descent for a shorter hike.

The park also maintains a six-mile signed canoe route through the backwaters. Put in from the boat ramp at the end of Long Valley Road and follow the signs. Logs or trees sometimes appear to block the route, but the park cuts small openings through them that are big enough for a canoe or kayak to pass through. The park rents canoes in summer.

Note: Wisconsin charges a fee (per vehicle) to enter state parks. You can purchase a daily permit, but if you're going to visit a few state parks, you're better off buying an annual permit.

CONTACT

Wyalusing State Park
13081 State Park Lane
Bagley, WI 53801
(608) 996-2261

DIRECTIONS

From Prairie du Chien, go south on State Highway 35 for about five miles. After crossing the Wisconsin River, turn right on County Highway C. After three miles, turn right on County Highway X. The park entrance is about a mile on the right.

NELSON DEWEY STATE PARK

Camping at Nelson Dewey State Park

NAMED FOR WISCONSIN'S first governor, Nelson Dewey State Park occupies about eight hundred acres of blufflands in the southwest corner of the state. The scenic park offers several short hikes that are worth a visit.

HIGHLIGHTS

The Mound Point Trail runs about one-half mile (one way), some of it through hill prairie with good views of the Mississippi. The Prairie Trail (0.2 mile one way) features native prairie habitat and another view of the river. The park also manages a campground in an upland forest.

Note: Wisconsin charges a fee (per vehicle) to enter state parks. You can purchase a daily permit, but if you're going to visit a few state parks, you're better off buying an annual permit.

CONTACT

Nelson Dewey State Park
12190 County Highway VV
Cassville, WI 53806
(608) 725-5374

DIRECTIONS

From central Cassville, follow State Highway 133 for one-half mile to County Road VV. Turn left. The park entrance is on the right.

IOWA

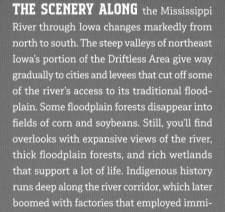

THE SCENERY ALONG the Mississippi River through Iowa changes markedly from north to south. The steep valleys of northeast Iowa's portion of the Driftless Area give way gradually to cities and levees that cut off some of the river's access to its traditional floodplain. Some floodplain forests disappear into fields of corn and soybeans. Still, you'll find overlooks with expansive views of the river, thick floodplain forests, and rich wetlands that support a lot of life. Indigenous history runs deep along the river corridor, which later boomed with factories that employed immigrants from around the world.

Iowans spend a lot of time along the Mississippi. It's a popular place for hunting and fishing. You'll find clusters of pleasure boaters (especially on weekends), drawn to isolated islands with sandy beaches. Paddlers enjoy the same islands, and many of the remaining backwaters are ideal places to explore in a canoe or kayak.

Driving along the Mississippi River through Iowa, you're never far from places to stay or eat. The bigger cities along the river (Dubuque, Clinton, Bettendorf, Davenport, Muscatine, Burlington, Fort Madison, Keokuk) all offer the full range of visitor services. You'll also find plenty of satisfying options in smaller communities such as Lansing, Marquette, McGregor, Guttenberg, Bellevue, and LeClaire.

You'll find the most spectacular public lands—the tallest bluffs and the thickest backwaters—and the highest concentration of places to visit in northeast Iowa. Don't miss the sites in the southeast, though, particularly the sublime Port Louisa Refuge, which is probably best explored in a canoe or kayak but does offer hiking trails, too.

YELLOW RIVER STATE FOREST

Fog hangs over the hills of Yellow River State Forest.

WHATEVER YOUR IMAGE of Iowa is, it's probably wrong and nothing will make that more obvious than visiting lush Yellow River State Forest. Just a few miles west of the Mississippi, the Yellow River flows through part of the Driftless Area. Deciduous forests cover the hills and bedrock outcroppings, and trout streams run through the valleys. Maple-basswood and oak-hickory forest communities dominate the uplands, whereas ash, cottonwood, and other hardwood trees thrive in the river bottoms. It's a great place to hike, mountain bike, fish for trout, canoe or kayak, and camp. The area is rich with wildflowers in spring, birds in summer, and bright colors in fall.

HIGHLIGHTS

The state forest consists of several units, but most of the recreation opportunities are in the Paint Creek unit, which has much to offer. Forty miles of trails wander through the unit, some of them designated for multiple uses (hiking, mountain biking, and horseback riding). The Paint Creek Trail loops through the forest for thirteen and one-half miles, some of it along the Yellow River, and some segments head up into the hills. You can hike the entire trail or easily divide the walk into shorter segments. The Paint Creek unit also is the proud home of the only fire tower in Iowa, which you can reach via Firetower Trail (or Firetower Road, if you prefer to drive). You can walk around it but not up into it.

Three of the Yellow River Water Trail's thirty-five miles pass through the forest. If you're paddling over a couple of days, the water trail has a primitive campsite that's accessible only from the river.

DIRECTIONS

The Paint Creek unit is fifteen miles north of Marquette. Take State Highway 76 north from town to State Forest Road B25, which runs into the Paint Creek unit.

CONTACT

Yellow River State Forest
729 State Forest Road
Harpers Ferry, IA 52146
(563) 586-2254

EFFIGY MOUNDS NATIONAL MONUMENT

The Mississippi River from Effigy Mounds

FOR HUNDREDS OF years, Native Americans crafted mounds from dirt to honor their ancestors and to bury their dead. They built many of those mounds on the tops of bluffs along rivers, including along the Upper Mississippi. Effigy Mounds National Monument preserves the site of dozens of mounds that were built between 1,400 and 800 years ago. Although that would be reason enough to visit, the landscape is absolutely captivating, and worth a half day or more to hike around. The North Unit includes the visitor center, but most of the rest of it is on top of a bluff that runs along the Mississippi River. The South Unit consists of upland forests, whereas the Sny Magill Unit (south of McGregor) occupies atmospheric bottomland forest along a backwater channel of the Mississippi.

HIGHLIGHTS

Start with a tour of the visitor center. The hiking trail in the North Unit begins with a hike uphill where most of the mounds are located. You'll also pass several places where you can take a quick detour to a spectacular overlook of the Mississippi. The hike to the end at Hanging Rock and back is seven miles.

The hike to the Marching Bear Group in the South Unit is four miles round-trip with several elevation changes, but the scenery is beautiful and the mounds are among the most interesting in the national monument. To reach the Marching Bear Trail, go south one-half mile on Highway 76 from the visitor center; turn left, and follow the gravel road over the railroad tracks to the parking area, then walk back to the trailhead, which is on the other side of the highway.

The Sny Magill Unit is farther afield, but it preserves over a hundred conical and linear mounds in floodplain forest along a quiet backwater slough; it's an area that feels like it was meant to encourage silent reflection. The Sny Magill Unit is subject to seasonal flooding.

CONTACT

Effigy Mounds National Monument
151 Highway 76
Harpers Ferry, IA 52146
(563) 873-3491

DIRECTIONS

The park entrance is three miles north of Marquette along State Highway 76. The Sny Magill Unit is four miles south of Pikes Peak State Park along County Highway X52 and adjacent to a boat ramp. The entrance is unmarked but is just north of Sny Magill Creek and Keystone Road.

PIKES PEAK STATE PARK

PIKES PEAK STATE Park has a commanding presence atop a bluff in one of the most scenic parts of the Upper Mississippi River. Just across from the park, the Wisconsin River emerges from a gap in the tall bluffs, then disappears into a maze of islands and sloughs and the flow of the Mississippi. Visitors stop at the park to walk to an observation deck that offers splendid views of the confluence of these two rivers. The park also manages a campground, if you'd like to stick around for a while.

The Wisconsin and Mississippi Rivers from Pikes Peak State Park

HIGHLIGHTS

The views are unbeatable, absolutely. But most visitors to the state park go no farther than the overlook. If you stay longer, you'll discover that the park also has several miles of trails that are every bit as interesting as that overlook as well as fossils to be discovered and an ancient Native American mound. From the overlook, walk down to Bridal Veil Falls (one mile round-trip). For a longer hike, follow the Point Ann Trail, which passes through the upland forests to another good overlook. The walk from the Homestead parking lot to the overlook is about two and one-half miles (one way).

CONTACT

Pikes Peak State Park
32264 Pikes Peak Road
McGregor, IA 52157
(563) 873-2341

DIRECTIONS

In McGregor, follow Main Street southwest (away from the river). Turn left when it ends at 7th Street, then right onto County Highway X56. At the top of the hill, turn left into the state park.

TURKEY RIVER MOUNDS STATE PRESERVE

Atop Turkey River Mounds

IT'S NOT THE biggest preserve around, but it offers a lot in its sixty-two acres. Turkey River Mounds State Preserve is, basically, a narrow ridge at the confluence of the Turkey and Mississippi Rivers. Forty-three mounds dot the top of the ridge, all built between 2,500 and 1,100 years ago. Most are conical or linear, but one mound resembles a panther. Because of varying microclimates around the ridge, you can find several plant communities in this compact area. The top of the ridge is a mix of aspen, eastern red cedar, and red and white oak, but patches of prairie grow along some edges. Down below, the south-facing forests are mostly white oak, shagbark hickory, and eastern red cedar, whereas the north-facing forests have a mix of basswood and sugar maple.

HIGHLIGHTS

The ridge itself is a delight to hike from end to end. The preserve does not have a groomed trail, but it's okay to walk around, just stay off the mounds. Getting up and down requires some care (and effort), as the side of the ridge is steep in places. You can walk up to the top from the northwest corner of the ridge, then walk to the other end, although there are places where you will need to climb up or down a few feet to keep going. When you reach the southeast corner (about a mile's hike), you'll find an American flag and good views of the Mississippi and Turkey Rivers.

CONTACT

Turkey River Mounds State Preserve
 (563) 873-2341

DIRECTIONS

From Guttenberg, follow US Highway 52 south for five and one-half miles. Turn left (east) on Estes Park Road and drive two miles to the parking lot.

NATIONAL MISSISSIPPI RIVER MUSEUM AND AQUARIUM

THE NATIONAL MISSISSIPPI

River Museum and Aquarium is one of the best museums along the river, which is part of the reason it earned an affiliation with the Smithsonian Institution. The exhibits fill room after room, and although many of them highlight river-themed history, the aquarium offers an intimate look at the animals that live in the river, many of which we rarely get to see. (Beavers are notoriously shy, after all.)

Mississippi-themed aquarium, National Mississippi River Museum

HIGHLIGHTS

The river-themed aquarium tanks show off native fish, mammals, turtles, snakes, and much more. The main channel display offers a close-up peek at river giants such as sturgeon, paddlefish, and blue catfish. Outside, the museum also maintains a small section of wetlands. When you're done with the river exhibits, wander to the Gulf of Mexico aquarium for a look at life in areas where the river meets the sea.

CONTACT

National Mississippi River Museum and Aquarium

350 East 3rd Street
Dubuque, IA 52001
(563) 557-9545

DIRECTIONS

The aquarium is in the Port of Dubuque, just east of downtown. From Main Street, follow 3rd Street east to get there.

MINES OF SPAIN STATE RECREATION AREA

Horseshoe Bluff, Mines of Spain

IN 1788, JULIEN DUBUQUE negotiated a deal with the Sauk and Meskwaki Peoples to mine the abundant lead deposits in the area around Catfish Creek. He then filed a land claim with the authorities who governed the area at that time, who were representatives of the Spanish crown. That, in a nutshell, is why the magnificent park south of Dubuque is called the Mines of Spain. Mines of Spain covers nearly 1,400 acres of bluffs and lowlands along Catfish Creek where it meets the Mississippi. Upland deciduous forests run up and around the high ground, bottomland hardwood forests and wetlands fill the floodplain, and fields of tall-grass prairie occupy many of the places in between.

HIGHLIGHTS

The E.B. Lyons Nature Center serves as the visitor center for the park and features wildlife exhibits and a one-half-mile walk around a butterfly garden, a flower garden, and prairie. For a nice view of the river and Dubuque, head to the Julien Dubuque Monument.

Twenty-one miles of trails wind through the park. The 1.6-mile Horseshoe Bluff Trail loops up and into an old quarry, with a couple of scenic views along the way. The trail passes through oak-hickory forest and rocky areas with sedges and flowering plants such as cinquefoil.

Catfish Creek runs through the northern part of the park, and six hundred acres around it make up Catfish Creek State Preserve, which has patches of hill prairie and wetlands between limestone bluffs. You can wander the area on the Catfish Trail (two miles), which passes through stands of birch trees and a small savanna with Native American mounds and a few old-growth oak trees. Expect some elevation changes.

CONTACT

Mines of Spain State Recreation Area
8991 Bellevue Heights (E.B. Lyons Nature Center)
Dubuque, IA 52003
(563) 556-0620

DIRECTIONS

Mines of Spain adjoins southern Dubuque. To reach the nature center, follow US Highway 61/52 south. Turn left onto US Highway 52 where it splits from Highway 61, then make an immediate left onto Bellevue Heights Road. To reach the trails in the southern half of the park, head south on US 52 to Olde Massey Road and turn left. The quickest route to Catfish Creek and the Julien Dubuque Monument is to head back to Highway 52 and turn right onto US Highway 61/52, then exit at Grandview. Turn right, then right again onto Julien Dubuque Drive. Take the first right to reach the parking lot for the Catfish Trail as well as the monument and overlook.

BELLEVUE STATE PARK

Butterfly garden at Bellevue State Park

ANOTHER STATE PARK, another overlook! The observation deck at Bellevue State Park offers more stellar views of the river, showcasing the village of Bellevue and the lock and dam next door, but like the other state parks, there's more to do than take in a single view. The park is divided into the Nelson Unit and the Dyas Unit. The campground is in the Dyas Unit.

HIGHLIGHTS

The park maintains a lovely one-acre butterfly garden in the Nelson Unit that is a delight to wander around. Two miles of hiking trails are also available in the Nelson Unit; they wander mostly through upland forests. In the Dyas Unit, the park maintains four miles of hiking trails that range through the hills.

CONTACT

Bellevue State Park
24668 Highway 52
Bellevue, IA 52301
(563) 872-4019

DIRECTIONS

From Bellevue, take US Highway 52 south. After crossing the bridge at the south end of town, turn right and follow the road to the Nelson Unit. To reach the Dyas Unit, return to US Highway 52 and drive south about two miles to the park road.

GREEN ISLAND WILDLIFE MANAGEMENT AREA

THE LABYRINTH OF backwaters along the Mississippi River supports a lot of animals, but we've lost many of those wetlands to development and siltation. Green Island Wildlife Management Area conserves a couple thousand acres of those critical backwater habitats. Green Island occupies a quiet area just north of the town of Sabula and is a popular site for birders. Waterfowl fill the lakes, ponds, and sloughs during migration season, but several species of birds find the area just perfect for nesting (least bittern and prothonotary warblers, for example).

Green Island

HIGHLIGHTS

There aren't really any trails to hike, but you can walk along the levees and a couple of roads that run right next to wetlands. Otherwise, drive slowly and pull over often. The wetlands are east of US Highway 52. On the west side of the highway, you can walk around an area where state wildlife officials are restoring native prairie.

DIRECTIONS

To enter Green Island WMA, follow US Highway 52 for about eight miles south from Bellevue. The prairie restoration area is just past the Maquoketa River, as are a couple of parking lots. To reach the wetlands, continue south on US Highway 52 to Green Island Road and turn left. Follow it into the WMA.

CONTACT

Green Island Wildlife Management Area
Iowa Department of Natural Resources
(563) 927-3276

QUAD CITIES RIVERFRONT

Davenport riverfront

THE MISSISSIPPI RIVER flows to the west through the Quad Cities. Some thirty thousand years ago, a southern push of ice forced the river's channel to divert to its current course. Davenport and Bettendorf are the big cities on the Iowa side of the Quad Cities, with LeClaire, Pleasant Valley, and Riverdale just north of them. Before the federal government built the navigation dam at Rock Island, a series of rapids flowed between LeClaire and Rock Island. Boats traveling through had to unload most of their cargo at one end, ship it by land to the other end, then reload. Local pilots who knew the river well guided the boats through the rapids. Eventually, large factories were built along the river and churned out farm equipment. When those factories closed, the cities converted the old industrial areas into public parks.

HIGHLIGHTS

From Credit Island upriver to the Interstate 74 bridge, much of the riverfront is now green space. Credit Island covers 450 acres, with baseball fields, a disc golf course, and lots of room to picnic, but the western end preserves a nice stand of bottomland hardwood forest, which you can wander through on a trail. Birds are often abundant in the sloughs and ponds around the park. The park is subject to seasonal flooding.

A string of city parks east of Credit Island are pleasant public spaces that are fine places to fish or watch the river flow. The Mississippi River Trail connects them all, and is a great way to see the cities and the river. The trail runs nearly nineteen miles along the river in Iowa from Credit Island to Bettendorf.

CONTACT

Visit Quad Cities
1601 River Drive
Moline, IL 61265
(800) 747-7800

DIRECTIONS

To reach Credit Island from downtown Davenport, follow West River Drive for about two miles. The entrance will be on the left. You'll find multiple places to access the Mississippi River Trail. If you're driving to it, you'll find plenty of parking at Credit Island Park, any of the parks at downtown Davenport, Lindsay Park in East Davenport, and Leach Park in Bettendorf.

NAHANT PRESERVE, EDUCATION, AND RECREATION AREA

Bottomland forest trail at Nahant Marsh

NAHANT PRESERVE IS a feel-good success story. For decades, members of a sporting club hunted in the marsh, but their shot pellets fell into the water and created dangerous levels of lead pollution. The federal Environmental Protection Agency eventually classified the marsh as a Superfund Site, and federal officials worked with state biologists and local citizens to clean it up. The marsh today is a thriving 305 acres of wetlands that attracts a variety of birds.

HIGHLIGHTS

The Education Center features exhibits on wildlife and hosts public programs. Three trails wind around the marsh; if you walk them all, you'll cover just under two miles. The trails pass through bottomland forest and patches of wet meadow and prairie. Lotuses cover the shallow areas of the marsh near shore by summer. You'll also find a blind just off the trail where you can observe the marsh. The trails are flat, an easy stroll. The grounds are open daily, so if the gate is locked, enter the trails from the parking lot.

CONTACT

Nahant Preserve, Education, and Recreation Area
 4220 Wapello Avenue
 Davenport, IA 52802
 (563) 336-3370

DIRECTIONS

From downtown Davenport, follow West River Drive west for about three miles to Iowa Highway 22. Turn south on Highway 22, then turn left on Wapello Avenue and follow it Nahant Marsh. The entrance is on the left just before the railroad tracks.

Along the Sycamore Trail at Port Louisa NWR

PORT LOUISA NATIONAL WILDLIFE REFUGE

PORT LOUISA NATIONAL Wildlife Refuge preserves twenty-four thousand acres of the river's world in its four divisions. The refuge protects critical habitat for waterfowl and fills with birds during migration season. Several species of birds, including bald eagles, also nest in the refuge, and herons, egrets, and American white pelicans stick around until fall.

HIGHLIGHTS

The Louisa division's 2,600 acres offer the best public access. The refuge office sits atop a bluff above the river. If the office is open, stop in for the scoop on the latest wildlife sightings and tips about where to hike. The park staff are restoring native prairie plants to the grounds around the office. The overlook next door offers a good view of the floodplain forest, and you may see some birds from it. A better option, though, is to hike down into the floodplain forest from the trailhead at the observation deck. You can follow a couple of short loops around the bluffs and down to the floodplain forest, or you can take the longer route (one and one-half miles one way) along lush Muscatine Slough. Even in late summer, you're likely to find large flocks of birds, including American white pelicans and Canada geese. Wildflowers bloom into fall.

You'll also find four designated paddling trails in the area (the Odessa Water Trails). The North Trail is three miles long (one way) and goes into the heart of the Port Louisa Refuge and through narrow backwater channels. This trail runs between the boat ramps at Schafer Access and a parking lot at 120th Street, so you can either shuttle between those two points or paddle up and back. To reach the boat ramp at Schafer Access, go south on County Highway X61 for a mile to 97th Street. Turn left and follow the road down to the ramp. To reach the parking lot on 120th Street, go north on County X61 for two miles to 120th Street and turn right. The parking lot is one and one-half miles down the road.

Most of the Louisa division closes to public access from September 15 to January 1 to provide sanctuary for migrating birds.

CONTACT

Port Louisa National Wildlife Refuge
10728 County Road X61
Wapello, IA 52653
(319) 523-6982

DIRECTIONS

The refuge office is about eighteen miles south of Muscatine. From central Muscatine, follow US Highway 61 Business (it is West Mississippi Drive downtown) for one and one-half miles to County Highway X61 (Oregon Street). Turn left, and stay on Highway X61 for about fifteen miles to the entrance.

STARR'S CAVE STATE PRESERVE

JUST A FEW miles west of the Mississippi River, Flint Creek cuts a narrow path through limestone and dolomite bedrock. The fossil-rich cliffs rise one hundred feet above the river. Starr's Cave State Preserve conserves 184 acres along this scenic area, and it is a special place. Originally a farm and winery operated by William Starr and family, the property today consists of bottomland forests, prairie, and cliffs.

Starr's Cave education center

HIGHLIGHTS

Trails follow along Flint Creek, with multiple places to stop and dip in a toe. They are mostly flat and well maintained, perfect for a lazy stroll.

Starr's Cave is closed to the public to protect the resident bats from white-nose syndrome, which is caused by a fungus that visitors can carry unknowingly into the cave on their shoes. (Big and little brown bats are the most common residents, but endangered Indiana bats also live in the cave.)

William Starr's barn now serves as the nature center and houses displays about the area's natural history and hosts public programs.

CONTACT

Starr's Cave State Preserve
11627 Starr's Cave Road
Burlington, IA 52601
(319) 753-8260

DIRECTIONS

From US Highway 61 in Burlington, turn right on Sunnyside Avenue, then left on Irish Ridge Road for about a mile to the entrance.

ILLINOIS

IF YOU VISIT the Mississippi River in northwest Illinois, you may not recognize it when you visit it again in the southwest part of the state. The steep hills and deep valleys of the Driftless Area give way to a broad, flat floodplain and a much bigger river. In between, the limestone bluffs fade away, but shine gloriously one last time around Grafton and Alton. Scenic small towns spread farther apart, and pleasure boats give way to barges. A river confined to a valley five miles wide now commands a floodplain that stretches dozens of miles.

In Illinois, the Mississippi runs for 581 miles and defines the state's western border. The river also runs deep in the state's history. Abraham Lincoln guided two flatboats down the Mississippi to sell goods in New Orleans, trips that almost certainly shaped his views on slavery. Agriculture is a big deal along the river, with miles of levees that guard corn and soybean fields from the river's whims.

You'll find no shortage of places to base. In the northwest corner, Galena is a popular tourist destination and is well stocked with accommodations and restaurants. Just a little way down the road from Galena, Savanna is also a good place to base. The Quad Cities region, which includes Moline, East Moline, and Rock Island on the Illinois side, offers a full range of diversions and places to stay. Farther south, Quincy offers all the creature comforts and grand architecture, too.

The stretch from Grafton to Alton is one of the most beautiful parts of the river anywhere and is a popular place to spend a weekend or a couple of nights. In metropolitan St. Louis, you'll find the greatest range of lodging on the Missouri side, but Collinsville and Fairview Heights in Illinois also have options. As you head farther south, Chester would be a good place to base for a night or two. You won't find many places to stay along the most southern reaches of the Mississippi in Illinois, but Cape Girardeau is nearby, as are parts of Shawnee National Forest.

Even though much of the river's world in Illinois is cut off from the main channel by levees, you'll still find a striking mix of ecosystems, from upland forests atop tall bluffs to sand prairies to expansive wetlands. A hike in these places may, therefore, require climbing steep inclines or slogging through Mississippi mud (and shaking it off your boots when you're done).

WITKOWSKY STATE WILDLIFE AREA

Hiking through upland forest at Witkowsky

WITKOWSKY STATE WILDLIFE Area offers visitors a chance to hike through a thousand acres of varied ecosystems at the southern end of the Driftless Area. Upland forests of red and white oak and hickory occupy patches along the ridges next to prairies. As you descend the creek valleys, bottomland forests, wetlands, and prairies intermingle.

HIGHLIGHTS

Ten miles of well-maintained trails criss-cross through the wildlife area. You'll find six parking areas next to trailheads that offer access to the interior of the property. Expect gentle rolling hills, thick stands of trees, limestone outcroppings, and patches of prairie grasses and flowers. If you have time, the 5.7-mile Walnut Trail loop passes through these areas, but there are options for shorter hikes, too.

Blackjack Road gets a little busy at certain times of day (for a country road), but you won't hear any car noise once you're in the woods. Witkowsky is popular with hunters, too, so it is closed to hiking during firearms seasons. The best time to hike is, essentially, from mid-May to mid-October.

CONTACT

Witkowsky State Wildlife Area

    Jo Daviess Conservation Foundation

    (815) 858-9100

DIRECTIONS

It takes about fifteen minutes to reach Witkowsky from Galena. Follow US Highway 20 east from the Galena River and turn right on 4th Street, then veer left onto Blackjack Road. The first parking lots for Witkowsky are about eight miles down the road, but the miles will pass quickly as you enjoy the scenic drive.

HANLEY SAVANNA

TUCKED INTO A narrow valley between rising hills and cultivated land, Hanley Savanna is a work in progress, and the work is progressing quite nicely. What had been 160 acres dedicated to row crops and a tree plantation is now a mix of tall-grass prairie, oak savanna, and stands of black oak trees in a rural area filled with quiet. In spring and summer, a nice variety of wildflowers blooms among the grasses and sedges, from hoary puccoon in early spring to button blazing star in late summer.

HIGHLIGHTS

Several mowed trails wind through the area. At a relaxed pace, you could walk to West Savanna and The Pines and back to the parking lot in about an hour. The shelter next to the parking lot has displays on the restoration efforts and trail maps. Hanley Savanna is closed to the public from November 15 to May 15.

CONTACT

Hanley Savanna
9417 Whitton Road
Hanover, IL 61041
(608) 638-1873

DIRECTIONS

Hanley Savanna is about fourteen miles northwest of Savanna. From Savanna, take Illinois Highway 84 north for about nine miles. Turn left (west) on Whitton Road and drive 4.3 miles to the parking lot (next to a shed).

UPPER MISSISSIPPI RIVER NATIONAL FISH AND WILDLIFE REFUGE/LOST MOUND UNIT

Mississippi River overlook at Lost Mound

THE LOST MOUND Unit of the Upper Mississippi River National Fish and Wildlife Refuge represents an even more ambitious (and longer-term) restoration project than Hanley Savanna. From 1917 to 2000, the US Army operated a munitions factory on this site. A short time after the base closed, the US Fish and Wildlife Service assumed management for nearly ten thousand acres of the property and has been busy cleaning up what it can and helping it all return to a more natural state. The work takes time and

money (the $200 million spent so far is just part of what's needed), and they may never entirely clear some areas of the pollution from the munitions days. About one-third of the refuge has been cleaned up so far. Some companies have moved into other portions of the old base (a railroad car storage operation, for example), but parts of the refuge and most of the nonrefuge property around it are strictly off-limits to the public.

Still, plants and animals are returning and breathing life back into the land, the largest remaining sand prairie in Illinois. The refuge provides a home for forty-seven rare and endangered species, including fragile prickly pear, James' clammyweed, and ornate box turtles. You'll also find sections of bottomland hardwood forest, but the sand prairies are the most accessible areas.

HIGHLIGHTS

The refuge has few hiking trails. Your best bet is the Prickly Pear Trail, which passes through sand prairie (and a lot of prickly pear!) and ends at an overlook of a backwater slough that birds love.

The refuge road continues past the office and through a section of the old base that could be a suitable location for a movie set in a postapocalyptic world. The road gets little traffic, so it's not unusual to encounter wildlife while driving it; I've seen wild turkeys several times. When you see a gate across the road, you've reached the end. You'll find a parking lot that's a short walk to an overlook of the river, from which you get a good perspective on how high the sand prairie sits above the river.

The extensive sand prairies and wetlands are the primary reason that the Audubon Society named the Lost Mound Unit an Important Bird Area. The grasslands offer secure breeding habitat for birds such as upland sandpiper and grasshopper sparrow, whereas the shrubs support loggerhead shrikes and cuckoos (yellow-billed and black-billed). The Lost Mound Unit also provides critical habitat for common nighthawks, and a couple dozen species of waterfowl.

CONTACT

Upper Mississippi River National Fish and Wildlife Refuge/Lost Mound Unit
3159 Crim Drive
Savanna, IL 61074
(815) 273-2732

DIRECTIONS

From Savanna, go north on State Highway 84 for about seven miles. Turn left (west) on Army Depot Road and follow it around for one and one-half miles to the refuge office. The trailhead is just past the office.

MISSISSIPPI PALISADES STATE PARK

Hiking at Mississippi Palisades State Park

JUST NORTH OF Savanna, towering limestone-faced bluffs hug the river's banks. People have lived in this area for a long time, and it's easy to understand the attraction. The river corridor offers all of life's essentials and is beautiful, too.

Illinois created Mississippi Palisades State Park in 1973, and it's become one of the most popular in the state, for good reason. The bluffs—the palisades in the park's name—entice a detour to explore them. Once you've parked your car, it's easy to linger longer than you thought you might. The park's trails pass through bottomland hardwood forests and prairies and a few end at overlooks with wide views of the river. If you wish to extend your stay overnight, the park manages a large campground, so there's no need to rush.

HIGHLIGHTS

With fifteen miles of trails, the park offers plenty of options for hikes that vary in length and difficulty. The trails in the northern part of the park are a little more work, as they rise from river level to the tops of the hills. The High Point Trail, for example, follows an old service road for one and one-half miles (one way) through an upland forest of elm, oak, and walnut trees. The trail ascends steadily under a dense canopy (and through small but noticeable temperature variations) until it ends at a shelter overlooking the river. In summer, trees—some of them red cedars—partially obstruct the views.

The trails in the southern half of the park are typically flatter and lead to overlooks with clear views, but footing is trickier when the trails are wet (especially when walking across limestone instead of dirt). Whether wet or dry, keep your distance from the edge of the bluffs, as the rocks sometimes give way. The Sentinel Trail runs about a mile through the upland forest and occasionally passes near the edge of the bluffs. Along the park road, you'll also find three places where you can take a short walk to an overlook. The Prairie View Trail loops about one-half mile around a section of grasslands.

CONTACT

Mississippi Palisades State Park
16327A State Highway 84
Savanna IL 61074
(815) 273-2731

DIRECTIONS

The state park is just north of Savanna. Follow State Highway 84 about two miles to the first entrance. The second entrance—which provides direct access to the campground—is another mile up the road.

QUAD CITIES RIVERFRONT

Biking along the Mississippi River in East Moline, Illinois

JUST NORTH OF the Quad Cities, at Rapids City, the Mississippi River takes a sharp turn to the west, a course it follows for the next forty-three miles. About thirty thousand years ago, large sheets of ice crept south and blocked the Mississippi's path, redirecting it along its current channel. It's helpful to keep this change in direction in mind as you drive around, especially if you use the river as a point of reference, like I do. Between Rapids City and Muscatine, Iowa, if the river is on your right, you're heading west, not south.

In the nineteenth century, the cities along this part of the river grew quickly, thanks to booming factories that lined the river. Most of those factories closed years ago, and the cities of this region have been converting the old industrial tracts into open spaces for recreation. You'll find many places around here to enjoy the river.

HIGHLIGHTS

The Great River Trail runs over sixty miles along the Mississippi River from Sunset Marina in Rock Island to Savanna. The trail runs through densely populated cities, small towns, and remote areas where you may not see another person for some time. Most of the trail follows a separate, paved path, but in a few places it runs along the shoulder of State Highway 84. The stretch through

Moline is especially scenic (and popular). There are multiple places to access the Great River Trail. The southern end is at Sunset Marina in Rock Island, but you'll also find places to park and ride the trail along River Drive in Moline.

Illiniwek Forest Preserve offers an escape into the woods just a few miles north of the city. Five miles of trails wind around the area. One short trail ascends from the parking lot on the bluff side of the road through upland forests to an overlook of the river. The Prairie Trail runs for a mile along restored grasslands. The preserve also manages a campground. Illiniwek Forest Preserve is just north of the Village of Hampton along Illinois Highway 84. The hiking trails and forest are on the bluff side of the highway, whereas the campground is next to the river.

For sixty years, Republic Steel Works operated a huge factory on Sylvan Island. After they closed in 1956, nature gradually reclaimed the land. Most of the structures are now long gone, but as you wander the park's thirty-seven acres, you'll find places where the old concrete foundation walls still stand. Today, Sylvan Island is a city park blanketed in forest. A mile-plus-long trail winds around the island and is a terrific way to pass an afternoon and get an intimate look at how the natural world adapts to an area after heavy industry leaves.

Sylvan Island is south of central Moline. Follow River Drive south to 1st Street and turn right. At the end of the road, turn right and follow the road to the parking lot. Walk across the bridge to enter the park.

Black Hawk State Historic Site occupies two hundred prominent acres atop a bluff near the confluence of the Rock and Mississippi Rivers. In the eighteenth century, the Sauk and Meskwaki Peoples built a village called Saukenuk that served as their home until the US government forced them out after the Black Hawk War. Their history is the central story featured in the John Hauberg Museum.

The Rock River Trail runs a mile along the bluff next to the museum and features several interpretive signs describing the area's history. Across 46th Avenue, Black Hawk Forest occupies the eastern half of the site and features an upland forest dominated by oak trees. Wildflowers pop in spring. Avid bird-watchers have observed 175 different avian species in the park. The 1.4-mile Black Hawk Trail begins at the nature center and loops through the forest.

Black Hawk State Historic Site occupies part of the southern end of Rock Island. From central Rock Island, take US Highway 67 (11th Street) south for about three miles. Turn left on 46th Avenue. The parking lot for the Hauberg Museum, park office, and Rock River Trail will be on the right. Turn left to visit the nature center and walk the Black Hawk Trail.

CONTACT

Illiniwek Forest Preserve
836 State Avenue
Hampton, IL 61256
(309) 496-2620

Great River Trail

Sylvan Island
2nd Street at 1st Avenue
Moline, IL
(309) 524-2424

Black Hawk State Historic Site
1510 46th Avenue
Rock Island, IL 61201
(309) 788-0177

LOUD THUNDER FOREST PRESERVE

LOUD THUNDER FOREST Preserve sprawls over 1,480 acres of rolling hills along the Mississippi River. Rock Island County manages the park primarily for recreation, which is one reason you'll find five separate campgrounds with 140 individual sites. Most of the property consists of dense upland forests, but you'll also find a narrow strip of bottomland forest and access to the main channel.

HIGHLIGHTS

Twelve miles of trails run through the park, the longest of which cut through the upland forests and are managed for both hiking and horseback riding. The eastern portion of the Hauberg Trail follows the river closely, passing through a bottomland forest with a thick understory. It's a muggy hike on a summer day, but the canopy shields the sun; expect a few hills. Park at the boat ramp; access this trail from the east side of the campground. From the trailhead to the spot where the trail dips down next to the river is about a mile (one way).

CONTACT

Loud Thunder Forest Preserve
19406 Loud Thunder Road
Illinois City, IL 61259
(309) 795-1040

Hiking in the floodplain forest at Loud Thunder Preserve

DIRECTIONS

From Andalusia, follow State Highway 92 for five miles, then turn right on Loud Thunder Road. The road to the campground will be about a mile on the right; the road to the park office is another mile down the road and will be on the left.

KIBBE LIFE SCIENCES STATION

Upland forest at Kibbe Life Sciences Station

IN 1964, Dr. Alice Kibbe donated 115 acres in Hancock County, Illinois, to Western Illinois University (WIU). Dr. Kibbe was an esteemed botanist at Carthage College and regularly took her students to the site for research, education, and the chance to be outside for a while. Today, the site has grown to 222 acres and is called the Alice L. Kibbe Science Research Station. The Illinois Department of Natural Resources manages another 1,458 acres adjacent to Kibbe (Cedar Glen Natural Area and Mississippi River Sand Hills Nature Preserve), which together form a nice cluster of conservation lands along the Mississippi River in west-central Illinois.

HIGHLIGHTS

Although the site's main purpose is education and research for WIU students, the hiking trails are open to the public. The trails are well tended and pass through upland deciduous forests (mostly oak with hickory, sugar maple, and basswood) with a few hills. Spiderwebs sometimes span the trail in the deep of the forest, and birds are abundant. There's also a trail around Cedar Glen, which is a section of tall-grass prairie in the middle of the site. (Note that Cedar Glen is closed to public access from November 1 to March 1 to give resident bald eagles some peace and quiet.) You can download a geo-referenced map of the hiking trails from the Kibbe website.

CONTACT

Kibbe Life Sciences Station

(309) 298-2045

DIRECTIONS

Access the station from State Highway 32 (Warsaw Road) near Warsaw. From US Highway 136 at Hamilton, turn south on Highway 32; the entrance is about five miles on the left at the top of a hill. When you get onto the property, turn on either of the first two gravel roads and park in the signed gravel lot near the student dormitory.

TWO RIVERS NATIONAL WILDLIFE REFUGE

The Brussels Ferry connects Two Rivers NWR.

TWO RIVERS NATIONAL Wildlife

Refuge conserves 9,200 acres of critical wetlands for waterfowl and other life at the scenic confluence of the Illinois and Mississippi Rivers. Wetlands abound on refuge lands, but you'll also find scenic bluffs and patches of prairie. The refuge is a great place for bird-watching, especially during migration season, but a lot of birds call the refuge home in summer, too. The refuge manages properties around the confluence on both sides of the Illinois River and along the Mississippi.

HIGHLIGHTS

Stop in to the refuge visitor center at the Calhoun Division. There are several places to observe wildlife along the roads nearby and a boat ramp to put in on Swan Lake. The Wildlife Haven and Prairie Adventure Trails are each one-half mile long and each loops around grasslands near the visitor center. If you're up for a longer walk, hike the top of the Swan Lake levee, which runs along the Illinois River. If you hike to the end and back, it's a twelve-mile trip.

Across the Illinois River, Gilbert Lake is a rich backwater wetland and forest habitat. A three-mile (one-way) hiking trail runs through the area. The Gilbert Lake Trail is on the other side of the Illinois River from the Calhoun Division. Take the Brussels Ferry across the Illinois River and go left on State Highway 100. Take the first left (at the sign) and follow the gravel road to the parking lot.

CONTACT

Two Rivers National Wildlife Refuge
364 Wildlife Conservation Road
Brussels, IL 62013
(618) 883-2524

DIRECTIONS

The visitor center is in Calhoun County. From Grafton, go north on State Highway 100 and take the Brussels Ferry (free) across the Illinois River. Continue on Illinois River Road for four and one-half miles to Hagan Road. Turn right and follow the road to the visitor center.

PERE MARQUETTE STATE PARK

Fall in Pere Marquette State Park

IT'S NOT QUITE on the Mississippi River, but Pere Marquette State Park is just a few miles upriver from where the Illinois River merges with the Mississippi, and it's a gem. That's good enough for me. The park conserves eight thousand acres of diverse habitats along the Illinois River that are also common along the Mississippi: upland deciduous forests, bottomland hardwood forests, and floodplain wetlands. The Civilian Conservation Corps built a cluster of beautiful cabins in the 1930s (which have been updated), and the main lodge has a restaurant. The state park also manages a campground.

HIGHLIGHTS

Twelve miles of trails work their way through the woods. Most of the hikes involve fairly steep ascents, and the trails can hold the moisture well after a good rain. The Twin Mounds Trail climbs from the floodplain to the top of a bluff, so the reward is a splendid view of the Illinois River valley.

If you brought a boat with you, there's a boat ramp across the highway from the visitor center. The Illinois River has a weak current here so it's entirely possible to paddle upstream with about the same amount of effort as paddling downstream, but you will need to watch for barge traffic.

CONTACT

Pere Marquette State Park
13112 Visitor Center Lane
Grafton, IL 62037
(618) 786-3323

DIRECTIONS

The park is north of Grafton. Follow State Highway 100 for about six miles to the park entrance.

JOHN M. OLIN NATURE PRESERVE

Waterfalls at Olin Preserve

OWNED AND MANAGED by The Nature Institute, the John M. Olin Nature Preserve offers scenic hikes through upland forests and along rocky streams in dense woods. The preserve is 150 feet above river level and along and behind bluffs that line the Mississippi. As you might expect, the woods and streams attract a lot of birds and other animals.

HIGHLIGHTS

Several trails, which roam down to the stream and back up, loop through the area. The stream cuts through a narrow valley, running across a limestone bed and down a small waterfall at the far end of the trail. A short walk from the parking lot to an observation deck delivers good views of the river. You can also walk around the area where the staff and volunteers are restoring native prairie. The preserve is closed to the public from mid-November to mid-March.

CONTACT

The Nature Institute
 2213 South Levis Lane
 Godfrey, IL 62035
 (618) 466-9930

DIRECTIONS

From downtown Alton, take Alby Street north to 20th Street. Turn left, then turn right on Belle Street. After it merges with State Street, turn left on West Delmar Avenue. After a mile, turn left onto Levis Lane and follow it for one-half mile to South Levis Lane. Turn left and follow the road to the preserve entrance.

MCT CONFLUENCE TRAIL/SAM VADALABENE BIKE TRAIL

Biking along the Mississippi near Alton, Illinois

THE MCT CONFLUENCE Trail runs about twenty miles along the Mississippi River from the McKinley Bridge at Venice to Alton. Most of the trail is on a dedicated path and is paved.

HIGHLIGHTS

The stretch from the Mel Price Lock and Dam into Alton runs on top of the Mississippi River levee and has nice views of the river, bridge, and dam, but can get breezy. When you get to the end of the MCT Confluence Trail, you can continue along the Sam Vadalabene Bike Trail and ride for another twenty miles to Pere Marquette State Park. (You'll have to ride a couple of miles on roads to get between the two trails.) This route is one of the most scenic stretches of the Mississippi. Tall bluffs rise next to the trail, and the views of the river are terrific. Take a detour though the Village of Elsah for a step (peddle) back in time. The southern trailhead is the parking lot along State Highway 100 next to the bluff with the Piasa bird painted on it. You can also park in Elsah and Grafton. The trail ends at Pere Marquette State Park.

CONTACT

MCT Confluence Trail
(618) 797-4600

DIRECTIONS

The easiest places to park and access the MCT Confluence Trail are at Russell Commons Park in Alton (along State Highway 143 just below the Clark Bridge) and the Old Chain of Rocks Bridge. Other access points with parking include the National Great Rivers Museum at the Melvin Price Locks and Dam and the Lewis and Clark Interpretive Center in Hartford.

CHAIN OF ROCKS

THE LAST SET of rapids on the Mississippi—the Chain of Rocks—rolls over rocks just north of St. Louis. There are a couple places to take in views of the rapids.

HIGHLIGHTS

The best place to start is at the Old Chain of Rocks Bridge, where you can watch the rapids from on high. The structure once carried traffic for Route 66, but many drivers were terrified to drive across it because it made a sharp 22-degree turn midriver. The bridge closed to auto traffic in 1970 after a replacement opened. Extensive rehabilitation converted the bridge into a path for bicycles and hikers. The views from the bridge are fantastic; on a clear day, you can see downtown St. Louis. If you want to hike through the bottomland forests under the bridge and walk to the river, look for the trailhead to the right of the gate.

For a closer look at the rapids, when you leave the parking lot, take the first right and follow the road until it ends at another parking lot (and a popular place to fish). You'll be at river level next to the rapids and can walk around to get different views.

CONTACT

For information about the bridge, contact Great Rivers Greenway at (314) 436-7009.

Chain of Rocks in winter

DIRECTIONS

From Interstate 270, go south on State Highway 3. Turn right on Chain of Rocks Road and follow the road until it ends at the parking lot for the bridge. Part of the road passes over the Chain of Rocks Canal on a one-lane bridge; the stoplight may take a while to turn green, but it will eventually turn! You can also bike to the bridge. In Missouri, the Mississippi River Greenway connects to the bridge, as does the Mississippi Confluence Trail in Illinois.

STEMLER CAVE WOODS

Sinkhole at Stemler Cave Woods

STEMLER CAVE WOODS is one of the places along the Mississippi where you'll find a great example of karst topography among the bluffs. In these areas, rain scours holes in easily erodible rocks. Over time, water carves out caves, sinkholes, and other gaps in the rocks. Stemler Cave Woods preserves one section of karst topography just southeast of St. Louis that also happens to have a stand of old-growth, upland forest, mostly hickory with several species of oak (white, red, and black). In the preserve, you'll also find a couple patches of native prairie, and areas where restoration of native prairie is underway.

HIGHLIGHTS

The namesake cave isn't open to the public, but you can walk around the woods on two miles of trails, some of which are marked with interpretive signs. The sinkholes are pretty cool, especially a particularly wide one that is still growing. It's an easy hike through the woods, with a few gentle hills and plenty of shade. I suggest taking a picture of the trail map with your phone camera before you start, as it's easy to get lost wandering the trails (at least it was for me!).

CONTACT

Stemler Cave Woods
2200 Stemler Road
Columbia, IL 62260
(618) 295-2877

DIRECTIONS

From downtown St. Louis, cross the river on Interstate 55/64 and exit at Illinois Highway 3 (the first exit). Follow Highway 3 south for three miles to State Highway 157 and turn left. After two miles, turn right on Triple Lakes Road and follow it for six and one-half miles. At Stemler Road, turn right. The small parking lot is on the left after a half-mile.

FULTS HILL PRAIRIE NATURE PRESERVE AND KIDD LAKE MARSH NATURAL AREA

HEADING SOUTH FROM St. Louis, Bluff Road passes through the floodplain with limestone-faced bluffs often coming right to the edge of the pavement. Although you'll drive by a lot of floodplain farms, two adjacent state preserves offer a good chance to get outside and walk around. Fults Hill Prairie Nature Preserve conserves 532 acres of bluff territory that include upland oak-hickory forest and hill prairie. Kidd Lake Marsh conserves a patch of wetlands in the floodplain that attracts waterfowl during much of the year.

Uphill hike at Fults Hill Prairie

HIGHLIGHTS

A one-and-one-half-mile trail loops up and around, then back down, Fults Hill. Take the stairs to get started. You'll be hiking uphill for a bit (wildflowers often line the trail), but there are places to stop and enjoy the wide views of the floodplain and bluffs from a hill prairie or small savanna. At the top, the trail continues through the woods, then loops back down to the parking lot. There are no trails at Kidd Lake, but you can drive around the perimeter to observe wildlife.

CONTACT

Fults Hill Prairie Nature Preserve
(618) 826-2706

DIRECTIONS

From downtown St. Louis, cross the river on Interstate 55/64 and exit at Illinois Highway 3 (the first exit). Follow Highway 3 south for about twenty-two miles to Waterloo, turn right onto State Highway 156, then go west on Lakeview Road (also called Maeystown Road). After passing through the Village of Maeystown, turn left on Bluff Road. From Fults, the parking lot is 1.6 miles on the left. Fults Hill is about an hour's drive from downtown St. Louis. Kidd Lake Marsh is just down the road from Fults Hill. Turn left when leaving the parking lot; the marsh will be on the right.

MIDDLE MISSISSIPPI RIVER NATIONAL WILDLIFE REFUGE

The Middle Mississippi from Fountain Bluff

BELOW ST. LOUIS, the flow of the Mississippi is unimpeded by dams, although levees have narrowed the channel and cut it off from much of its traditional floodplain. Congress created the Middle Mississippi River National Wildlife Refuge in 2000 to conserve some of the remaining parts of the river's world that provide critical habitat for birds and other creatures.

HIGHLIGHTS

The refuge has seven divisions, and most of the protected areas are islands. You'll need a boat to visit them. Wilkinson Island, however, is accessible by car (but subject to seasonal flooding). The center trail at Wilkinson Island runs 1.4 miles (one way) from the parking area and passes through typical bottomland forests that are popular with birders. Farther down Levee Road, you'll come to another pull off, where you can access the south trail, which is about a mile round-trip.

CONTACT

Middle Mississippi River National Wildlife Refuge
(573) 847-2333

DIRECTIONS

From Chester, take State Highway 3 south for about thirteen miles to Jones Ridge Road and turn right. After two miles, turn right onto Levee Road (which runs on top of a tall levee, hence the name). The parking lot for the center trail will be just on your left; you'll have to drive down off the levee, which is a bit steep. To reach the area for the south trail, turn right on Levee Road and drive two miles, then head down off the levee and park.

PINEY CREEK RAVINE STATE NATURAL AREA

PINEY CREEK RAVINE is a wilderness oasis hidden among the corn and soybean fields of Southern Illinois. The creek cut a ravine through the limestone bedrock and still flows over (and erodes) that limestone. In this small area (two hundred acres), the habitat changes considerably from the upland forest at the trailhead to the forested areas along Piney Creek. The oaks give way to shade- and moisture-loving ferns and mosses. Wildflowers bloom from spring through fall, and short-leaf pines even find the place to their liking, one of just two locations in Illinois where they are native. Exposed rock reveals layers of time, which roll like waves across the faces of the bluff.

Piney Creek Ravine

HIGHLIGHTS

From the parking lot, follow a mowed path between a row of trees to reach the trailhead. The trail then descends into the ravine and follows the creek for much of its route. The path can be slippery, especially when it passes over rocks.

Although the natural features of Piney Creek Ravine offer good reasons to visit, the natural area also preserves the largest collection of Indigenous rock art (petroglyphs) in Illinois. Native Americans created the artwork between 1,500 and 1,000 years ago, scientists estimate. In the past century or so, non-Indigenous People have added their carvings to the wall, some of them fairly recently, so you'll need a good eye to distinguish the old art from the recent carvings.

CONTACT

Piney Creek Ravine State Natural Area
2280 Piney Creek Road
Campbell Hill, IL 62916
(618) 826-2706

DIRECTIONS

To reach the parking lot from Chester, follow State Highway 3 south for eleven miles to Hog Hill Road. Turn left and follow it to Rock Crusher Road; turn left. Look for the sign for the natural area and turn left on Piney Creek Road. The parking lot will be on the right.

SHAWNEE NATIONAL FOREST

LaRue Swamp at Shawnee National Forest

SHAWNEE NATIONAL FOREST spreads across 289,000 acres of Southern Illinois from the Ohio River to the Mississippi. Much of the land was originally thick deciduous forests that grew over the rolling Shawnee and Ozark Hills. The glaciers didn't get this far south, so the land is rugged, dotted with weathered domes of limestone, sandstone, and shale. Thick forests cover the hills and valleys today. Oaks are common, but you'll find different types depending on how moist an area is. In the driest sites, post and blackjack oaks do well, whereas in the bottoms, black, white, and northern red oak do best. Most of it is second growth.

Euro-American settlers cleared much of the land in the late-nineteenth and early twentieth centuries, but the soil proved inadequate for most crops. Many of the farmers gave up and sold their land to the federal government in the 1930s, which assembled it into a national forest and has been gradually restoring native habitats since. Within the boundary of Shawnee National Forest, you'll find impressive ecological diversity: upland deciduous forests, bottomland hardwood forests, cypress swamps, and prairie.

HIGHLIGHTS

This guide focuses on the areas near the Mississippi River, but there is much more to explore in the rest of the national forest and Southern Illinois. If you have time, visit Giant City State Park, the Garden of the Gods

Recreation Area, and the cypress swamps along the lower Cache River. If you're feeling ambitious, the river-to-river trail runs 160 miles from the Ohio River to the Mississippi, although some parts of the trail follow the shoulders of local roads. There are multiple campgrounds throughout the national forest, and you'll find a lot of cabins for rent by mom-and-pop owners, plus many small wineries.

The areas near the Mississippi River have plenty to offer as well. LaRue-Pine Hills includes wetlands, prairie, and forests, all in and around a long row of bluffs built from four-hundred-million-year-old limestone. There are a few good ways to go deeper into the area. Inspiration Point Trail runs on top of the bluff and leads to overlooks with remarkable views of the river valley. If you drive to the upper parking lot, it's a shorter, flat hike to the overlook, but you can also park in the lot at floodplain level and hike uphill. The entire length of the trail between the two parking lots is three-quarters of a mile.

To reach the Inspiration Point Trail from Chester, drive south on State Highway 3 for thirty-seven miles. After crossing the Big Muddy River, turn left on Muddy Levee Road (a gravel road). When it dead-ends, turn left on LaRue Road, then take the next right. The lower parking lot will be on your right, or keep driving uphill to reach the upper lot.

Back in the floodplain, you can drive or walk around the perimeter of the wetlands that make up Otter Pond Research Natural Area. From the parking lot for Inspiration Point, head south on LaRue Road. The stretch of LaRue Road from Muddy Levee Road south has earned the nickname Snake Road. Two times a year (March 15 to May 15 and September 1 to October 30), 2.8 miles of the road are closed to all vehicle traffic so snakes can migrate between their summer homes in the swamps and their winter homes next to the bluffs. It's a fun time to walk the road and look for snakes, but keep your distance from them. Venomous cottonmouths are common, and although they aren't aggressive, they will strike if you get too close. Snake Road runs south of Muddy Levee Road. You can access it from either end, but the easiest access is just south of Muddy Levee Road, where you'll find a small parking lot.

A little farther up the road, the Little Grand Canyon is another rewarding place to hike. The trail (three miles round-trip) dips into a deep canyon (deep for the Midwest) along a stream. The hike passes over rock ledges and along the tree-lined stream. The hike is moderately difficult because of the elevation changes (some of it up or down those ledges) and for areas where wet patches can make the path slippery. For most people, a complete loop takes about three hours to complete, so bring water. You can also hike to a couple of overlooks from the parking lot, if you just want a quick look at the canyon.

To reach Little Grand Canyon from Chester, follow State Highway 3 for twenty-four miles to State Highway 149. Turn left, then turn right on Grimsby Road. At Sand Ridge, turn left on Town Creek Road and follow it for four miles to Maple Spring Road. Turn right, and stay on Maple Spring Road for about a mile, then turn left on Hickory Ridge Road. After about five miles, you'll see the entrance to the parking lot for Little Grand Canyon.

CONTACT

Shawnee National Forest Headquarters
50 Highway 145 South
Harrisburg, IL 62946
(618) 253-7114 or (800) 699-6637

HORSESHOE LAKE STATE FISH AND WILDLIFE AREA

Horseshoe Lake

SOUTHERN ILLINOIS' HORSE-SHOE Lake and Horseshoe Lake by St. Louis are both old channels of the Mississippi. The lakes were part of a meander that the river eventually cut through, leaving behind an oxbow-shaped pool that was connected to the main channel only during periods of high water. The Horseshoe Lake in Southern Illinois covers 2,400 acres of beautiful cypress-tupelo swamp that is covered with fields of lotus by summer. Birds are abundant, especially during migration seasons. There's a campground, if you'd like to stick around for a night or two.

HIGHLIGHTS

There are no hiking trails, but you can drive (or bike) around the area and watch for wildlife. There are also a couple of boat ramps where you can put in for a paddle.

CONTACT

Horseshoe Lake State Fish and Wildlife Area

21759 Westside Drive
Miller City, IL 62962
(618) 776-5689

DIRECTIONS

Take State Highway 3 south to Olive Branch. Turn right on Miller City Road; roads enter the area from the left.

MISSOURI

THE MISSISSIPPI RIVER changes and grows as it passes along the eastern border of Missouri. Big tributaries feed the Mississippi, so it carries increasingly larger volumes of water: the Des Moines, Missouri, Illinois, Kaskaskia, and Ohio Rivers. The bluffs that have lined the Mississippi since the Twin Cities lose height until they finally end and the Mississippi enters the wide plain known as the delta or the Mississippi Embayment. The dams end at St. Louis, so the river returns to a free-flowing state. As you head south, the warm days linger longer and cypress trees show up in the river's wetlands. From Missouri, you can visit the Upper, Middle, and Lower Mississippi without leaving the state.

This is the Mississippi that sparked the imagination of Samuel Clemens, that nurtured thousands of years of Indigenous communities, that inspired enslaved people to dream of freedom, that fueled the growth of the Gateway to the West, St. Louis. It's also an area where the conflicts between our many uses of the river are hard to ignore. Levees have narrowed the river's channel and corn and soybean fields have replaced bottomland forests. Navigation dams enable bulk transportation but alter the flow and rhythms of the river's world and trap sediment that fills in wetlands. Docks and factories line the river around St. Louis.

And yet. Life still thrives along the river. It may not be as abundant as it was before we altered the river, but it's still there and still depends on the river. Remote places bustling with life are easy to find, even in and around the big cities. Multiple conservation areas protect wetlands and forests for future generations. The river is still a substantial, life-generating force.

Missouri has more public lands than I can include, but the places listed offer easy access and a chance to experience the different parts of the river's world. You won't have trouble finding a place to stay or eat. Storied Hannibal is a good place to base in the northwest region, and St. Louis, of course, offers an abundance of options. In the southwest region, historic Ste. Genevieve and Cape Girardeau are excellent places to stay for a few days.

Whether you want to get to know the Mississippi by car, bike, boat, or on foot, the sites in Missouri can accommodate you. Many places offer easy hikes on flat trails through bottomland forests, whereas at others you'll find extensive wetlands that attract thousands of birds at certain times of year that you can observe from your car. Still, I think you'll find it hard to resist the temptation to get out and wander around.

JULIAN STEYERMARK WOODS CONSERVATION AREA AND LOVER'S LEAP

JUST NORTH OF downtown Hannibal, Steyermark Woods Conservation Area offers a pleasant place to hike through upland forest growing around limestone outcroppings. Common trees include basswood, black walnut, sugar maple, and several species of oak. A few pawpaw trees grow in the understory, and the wildflowers pop up all over the forest floor, especially in spring. The park's namesake, Dr. Julian Steyermark, devoted his career to studying and identifying plants. He collected more than one hundred thousand specimens from around the world and was the first to describe nearly three thousand plants. His book *Flora of Missouri* is still a go-to reference.

Steyermark Woods

HIGHLIGHTS

A wide, 1.3-mile trail winds through the woods. For an eagle's-eye view of the Mississippi's main channel and the surrounding area, drive to Lover's Leap on the southern end of Hannibal.

CONTACT

Julian Steyermark Woods Conservation Area

County Road 410 East
Hannibal, MO 63401
(573) 248-2530

DIRECTIONS

To reach Steyermark Woods, drive north on US Highway 61 to Missouri Highway 168. Turn right. After two miles, turn right (east) on County Highway 410. After a mile, look for the pull-off where you can park.

To reach Lover's Leap, follow State Highway 79 (S. 3rd Street) south from downtown. The entrance is on the left, a little more than a mile south of Broadway.

MISSISSIPPI RIVER WATER TRAIL

Along the Mississippi River Water Trail

ONE OF THE best ways to explore the places along the Mississippi River is by getting directly on the water. The Mississippi River Water Trail Association works with the US Army Corps of Engineers to promote and maintain 121 miles of the Mississippi River as a water trail. The trail begins just south of Hannibal at Lock and Dam #22 and ends at the St. Louis riverfront.

HIGHLIGHTS

The route includes two locks (that are free to pass through), the rapids called the Chain of Rocks (which are navigable only at higher water levels) small river towns, undeveloped islands, hardwood forests, and majestic limestone-faced bluffs. Some sections are so remote that you may not see another person or boat for hours.

There are many options for day trips (such as circumnavigating Cuivre Island) as well as point-to-point trips that could last a few hours or several days. The sandbars and islands offer some of the most scenic camping in the Midwest. If you're interested in paddling along this route, I suggest looking over the map and itineraries described on the water trail's website. Please also read the tips on the website for how to paddle safely on the Mississippi: mississippiriverwater-trail.org/safety.

CONTACT

Mississippi River Water Trail
301 Riverlands Way (mailing address)
West Alton, MO 63386

DIRECTIONS

The trail begins at Lock and Dam #22 at Saverton, Missouri, and runs 121 miles to the St. Louis riverfront. There are multiple places to access the trail in between.

TED SHANKS AND DUPONT RESERVATION CONSERVATION AREAS

A FEW MILES south of Hannibal, Ted Shanks and DuPont Reservation Conservation Areas offer a lot of space and wetland habitats for waterfowl. Stretching over nine miles of Mississippi River shoreline, the conservation areas feature marsh and sloughs, plus some bottomland and upland forests. During migration season, the areas fill with birds.

HIGHLIGHTS

You can observe some wildlife by driving the road that cuts through Ted Shanks Conservation Area, but I prefer to walk along the levee. If the river's not too high, you can also dip down off the levee into the floodplain forest.

DuPont Reservation Conservation Area is adjacent to Ted Shanks CA; it conserves upland forest for the most part, but also includes a boat ramp on the main channel and a small campground (primitive camping only).

CONTACT

Ted Shanks and DuPont Reservation Conservation Areas
  (573) 248-2530

Wetlands at Ted Shanks

DIRECTIONS

Ted Shanks Conservation Area is seventeen miles south of Hannibal. Follow Missouri Highway 79, then go east on County Road TT. Turn right to tour the refuge.

To reach the boat ramp and campground at DuPont Reservation from Ted Shanks CA, stay left at the entrance to Ted Shanks CA and follow the road around to the boat ramp and campground.

CLARENCE CANNON NATIONAL WILDLIFE REFUGE

Spring flooding at Clarence Cannon NWR

WETLANDS ARE THE focus at Clarence Cannon National Wildlife Refuge. Much of the refuge's three thousand acres includes marshes, ponds, and sloughs, with some bottomland forest, too. The refuge is a popular spot for birding, so expect waterfowl, especially during migration season, but also bald eagles and other birds of prey.

HIGHLIGHTS

If you've got some time, hike the four-mile Unit 7 Trail (catchy name!) through bottomland forest and past some marshes. The path is wide and well maintained. Otherwise, take a slow drive through the refuge. There are multiple places to pull over and observe. If you're going to visit in spring, keep in mind that the refuge floods when the Mississippi is high, so some (or all) of the roads might be closed.

CONTACT

Clarence Cannon National Wildlife Refuge

37599 Pike 206
Annada, MO 63330
(573) 847-2333

DIRECTIONS

From State Highway 79 at Annada, follow Pike County Road 206 for a mile to the refuge office.

B. K. LEACH MEMORIAL CONSERVATION AREA

B. K. Leach Memorial CA

B. K. LEACH Memorial Conservation Area conserves critical wetland habitats for migratory animals and permanent residents of the Mississippi valley. The state pieced together the property via multiple land purchases beginning in 1985, and again after the flood of 1993 broke through a nearby levee and flooded the area. You'll find marshes of varying maturity, backwater sloughs, and ponds. Spring and fall attract the greatest variety of birds, but many stick around all year. Muskrats and beavers are among the other wildlife you may spot during a visit.

HIGHLIGHTS

The conservation area is split between three separate parcels, but the main one is the easiest to access. If you follow B. K. Leach Road to the end, you'll find a parking lot and access to a service road that loops around wetlands. You are welcome to walk the road. Otherwise, drive slowly and pull over when something catches your eye.

CONTACT

B. K. Leach Memorial Conservation Area
(573) 898-5905

DIRECTIONS

To reach B. K. Leach CA, take State Highway 79 south from Elsberry for three miles. Turn left (east) on County Highway M and go another three miles. To reach B. K. Leach Road, turn right on Marre Road (County Highway 939), then turn left after a mile.

UPPER MISSISSIPPI CONSERVATION AREA/ DRESSER ISLAND

Dresser Island

DRESSER ISLAND IS one of the few undeveloped Mississippi River islands that you don't need a boat to visit. The island is managed as part of the Upper Mississippi Conservation Area, a partnership among the Missouri Department of Conservation, the US Fish and Wildlife Service, and the US Army Corps of Engineers. Bottomland forests cover much of the island, but you'll also find backwater sloughs and views of the main channel. Birds enjoy the island, as do muskrats and other animals.

HIGHLIGHTS

The island is open to hunting and fishing, but typically doesn't draw a lot of visitors. It's easy to spend a couple of hours wandering around, even without well-groomed trails. From the parking lot, walk across the bridge onto the island.

CONTACT

Upper Mississippi Conservation Area/ Dresser Island

(636) 441-4554

DIRECTIONS

From Alton, take US Highway 67 into Missouri (across the Clark Bridge), then turn right on State Highway 94. Follow the highway for about five miles, passing through West Alton and around a couple of bends. The second time the highway makes a sharp turn to the left, drive straight into the parking lot for the conservation area.

THE MISSISSIPPI RIVER/ MISSOURI RIVER CONFLUENCE

Confluence of the Mississippi and Missouri Rivers

JUST NORTH OF St. Louis, the two longest rivers in North America become one. The brown current of the sediment-rich Missouri River merges with the less opaque waters of the Upper Mississippi, and it takes a few miles for their waters to fully mix. Historically, the area where the rivers meet was rich with prairies and marsh, with some bottomland hardwood forest and sandbars, but agricultural and industrial development ate into much of it. The confluence is a dynamic area and has shifted across time. Today's confluence, for example, is about three miles south of where it was when Lewis and Clark began their expedition up the Missouri River in 1804. After the Great Flood of 1993 (and subsequent extensive flooding), some of that land has returned to a more natural state. We are lucky now to have multiple places to enjoy time around the confluence.

HIGHLIGHTS

When the US Army Corps of Engineers built the billion-dollar Melvin Price Lock and Dam, they agreed to restore wetlands and woods as mitigation for the massive project. The result is the Riverlands Migratory Bird Sanctuary, which covers 3,700 acres, about a third of which is wetlands. The sanctuary includes a short hiking trail through an area where native prairie is being restored, a hiking trail on Ellis Island, and plenty of places to pull over to observe wildlife. Birds are especially abundant.

Given the abundance of birds at the sanctuary, it's no surprise that the Audubon Society operates an education center in the area. The Audubon Center at Riverlands features exhibits on native wildlife and strategically positioned viewing scopes, and offers nature-themed programs throughout the year, including programming featuring bald eagles in winter. From Alton, take US Highway 67 across the river, then turn left onto Riverlands Way. Take the first left to park at the trailhead for Ellis Island, or continue straight to the Audubon Center and the prairie hike.

Just down the road from Riverlands, Edward "Ted" and Pat Jones Confluence Point State Park offers visitors a close encounter with the confluence. The park occupies the very spot where the two rivers come together. You can walk onto the narrow slice of land at Confluence Point and have the Mississippi on one side and the Missouri on the other. The confluence is a short quarter-mile walk from the parking lot. The road to the parking lot passes through wetlands in varying stages of restoration; they attract a lot of birds. To reach the park from the Audubon Center, continue on Riverlands Way until you see the sign for Confluence Point State Park. Turn right and follow the gravel road about four and one-half miles to the parking lot.

On the other side of the Missouri River, Columbia Bottom Conservation Area offers more chances to get out around the confluence. At one time, the city of St. Louis considered building an airport at this site, but, lucky for us, flooding and other factors made that plan unworkable. The conservation area covers four thousand square miles, some of which are still farmed. The park's roads and trails took quite a hit in 2019 when high floodwaters covered the area for weeks, and some roads remain closed.

The easiest way to visit is to follow the gravel road around to the boat ramp and back. The road passes several wetlands. From parking lot O, you can follow a short trail down to the riverfront and walk along the shoreline. The road to the confluence viewing platform is closed, but from parking lot L you can walk to it (one mile, one way). Once you reach the confluence, you can hike through bottomland forests if you head downriver. The river has erased much of the trail that used to run through there, so it can be a little work to get around.

To reach Columbia Bottom Conservation Area from Riverlands (a thirty-minute drive), go back to US Highway 67 and head south. Exit at New Jamestown Road and turn left onto New Jamestown Road. When the road ends, turn right on Bellefontaine Road. After a mile, turn left on Spanish Pond Road and follow it around as it becomes Strodtman Road. After the road descends into the floodplain and becomes Columbia Bottom Road, the entrance to the conservation area will be on the left.

CONTACT

Riverlands Migratory Bird Sanctuary
301 Riverlands Way
West Alton, MO 63386
(636) 899-2600

Audubon Center at Riverlands
301 Riverlands Way
West Alton, MO 63386
(636) 899-0090

Edward "Ted" and Pat Jones Confluence Point State Park
1000 Riverlands Way
West Alton, MO 63386
(636) 899-1135

Columbia Bottom Conservation Area
801 Strodtman Road
St. Louis, MO 63138
(636) 441-4554

ST. LOUIS RIVERFRONT

Cobblestone levee along the St. Louis riverfront

IT'S SURPRISINGLY DIFFICULT

to get near the river that gave life to St. Louis, but luckily we have two good options: a national park and a bike trail.

HIGHLIGHTS

The easiest place to access the river is by visiting Gateway Arch National Park. Although most people visit the park to tour the 630-foot-tall steel monument, the park borders the Mississippi and offers good views of the main channel as well as nicely mani-cured park grounds to walk around. Gateway Arch National Park is on the west side of downtown; you'll need to park in one of the many parking garages nearby and walk a couple of blocks to the entrance.

The Mississippi River Greenway provides more access, with fifteen miles of paved trail from just north of the Arch to the Chain of Rocks Bridge. The trail parallels the river and passes through industrial areas, but you'll also find pockets of willows and some wild-life. I've seen bald eagles a few times along the trail. There's a small parking lot at the Biddle Street Trailhead (1 Biddle Street). You can also park anywhere around the Arch or Laclede's Landing and ride to the trailhead.

CONTACT

Gateway Arch National Park
(314) 655-1600
Mississippi River Greenway
(314) 436-7009

JEFFERSON BARRACKS PARK

CONTACT

Jefferson Barracks Park
    251 Cy Road
    St. Louis, MO 63125
    (314) 615-4386

DIRECTIONS

Jefferson Barracks Park is about fifteen minutes by car from downtown St. Louis. Take Interstate 55 south to the Germania Avenue Exit. Turn left, then turn right on Ivory Street (it becomes Lemay Ferry Road), then, after crossing the bridge, take a quick left onto River City Casino Boulevard. Turn right onto South Broadway (Missouri Highway 231) and follow it for a little over a mile to the park entrance.

SOUTH OF DOWNTOWN, Jefferson Barracks Park sits atop the river bluffs and is part historical site, part urban park

HIGHLIGHTS

Within the park, you'll find several small museums related to the site's history as a US military installation (including one dedicated to the Civil War), but it's also a beautiful park with overlooks of the Mississippi and room to picnic and spread out. The Mississippi River Greenway Trail, which begins at River City Casino, runs through the park and comes with good river views.

CLIFF CAVE PARK

Hiking at Cliff Cave Park

LOCATED IN THE southern suburbs of St. Louis, Cliff Cave Park is a fine place to pass some time outside, whether you want to rest next to the river or explore the upland bluffs and forests.

HIGHLIGHTS

The namesake cave is closed (and access blocked by a gate), but the park offers good views of the main river channel and hiking through upland forests. Another branch of the Mississippi Greenway bike trail runs through Cliff Cave Park. The Greenway includes 4.7 miles of paved path in the floodplain and another two miles that head up into the bluffs and to Telegraph Road. The River Bluff Trail runs a mile through upland forests; Spring Valley Trail covers three miles and comes with some minor elevation changes.

CONTACT

Cliff Cave Park
806 Cliff Cave Road
St. Louis, MO 63129
(314) 615-4386

DIRECTIONS

You can drive to the park in about twenty-five minutes from downtown St. Louis. Take Interstate 55 south to Interstate 255 east. Exit I-255 at Telegraph Road (State Highway 231) and go south. After driving about two and one-half miles, look for the park entrance on the left.

MAGNOLIA HOLLOW CONSERVATION AREA

Magnolia Hollow in fall

MAGNOLIA HOLLOW CONSERVATION

Area covers 1,700 acres along Establishment Creek where it meets the Mississippi and offers good hiking through a diverse mix of trees and plants in upland and bottomland forests.

HIGHLIGHTS

The conservation area maintains an overlook of the Mississippi and adjacent bottomlands, and there are also several miles of trails and roads on which to wander through the woods. Fall colors are often terrific, and spring wildflowers dot the forest floor. You may even come across orchids in the hollow.

CONTACT

Magnolia Hollow Conservation Area
(573) 290-5730

DIRECTIONS

Magnolia Hollow is about ten miles north of Ste. Genevieve. From Interstate 55, exit at Bloomsdale and head east. Take US Highway 61 south for a mile to County V and turn left (east). After a mile, turn left on Magnolia Hollow Drive and follow it to the entrance.

SEVENTY-SIX CONSERVATION AREA

Seventy-Six Conservation Area

YOU WON'T SEE much evidence of the town today, but a community known as Seventy-six prospered along the banks of the Mississippi at the site where the conservation area is now. The town peaked in the nineteenth century, but by the 1950s not much remained, especially after the post office and general store closed. The Missouri Department of Conservation purchased the area in 1991. Most of the area today consists of upland forests on bluffs and hills.

HIGHLIGHTS

You can hike a three-mile trail atop the bluff through oak-hickory forests that sometimes abut steep hollows. The trail rolls up and down with the hills, and although you may not catch sight of the river, the views are still good. There's another, shorter, trail that runs next to the river.

CONTACT

Seventy-Six Conservation Area
(573) 290-5730

DIRECTIONS

The conservation area is about twenty miles southeast of Perryville. From Perryville, take US Highway 61 south for about six miles. Turn left (east) onto County Highway D. After passing through Brazeau, County D will end at a gravel road. Follow that gravel road into the conservation area.

TRAIL OF TEARS STATE PARK

Hiking at Trail of Tears State Park

TRAIL OF TEARS is a specular park that conserves 3,400 acres of important habitat along the Mississippi River while also preserving the memory of a tragic event in US history. In the winter of 1838–39, thousands of Cherokee People crossed the Mississippi in nine groups at this site. Forced out of their homes in the southeastern United States, many died as they walked to Oklahoma Territory.

HIGHLIGHTS

Stop in to the visitor center to read more about the Trail of Tears and other Indigenous People who had lived in the area for generations and for maps of hiking trails. The park conserves steep bluffs and rolling hills along the Mississippi River. Upland deciduous forests cover the blufftops, whereas small areas of bottomland forest inhabit the spaces at river level. In Indian Creek Wild Area, in the northern section of the park, you'll find oak and hickory trees at the higher elevations and sweetgum and willow closer to the creek. At Vancil Hollow (in the middle of the park), though, you'll see trees such as American beech, magnolia, and tulip poplar growing among thick carpets of ferns. The park is a great place to view fall colors and wildflowers in spring.

Fourteen miles of trails offer access deep into these forests. Expect elevation changes and trails that are sometimes bordered by steep drop-offs. The Peewah Trail runs about eight miles through the park; the east loop includes several spots with dramatic overlooks of the river from the blufftop. There's a campground next to the river.

CONTACT

Trail of Tears State Park
429 Moccasin Springs
Jackson, MO 63755
(573) 290-5268

DIRECTIONS

The park is twelve miles north of Cape Girardeau. From Interstate 55, exit at Jackson and follow US Highway 61 south for a mile to County Highway Y. Turn left (east) and stay on County Y for seven miles until you reach County V. Turn right (east) on County V and follow it three miles, then turn left (north) onto Missouri Highway 177. After one-quarter mile, turn right into the park.

CAPE GIRARDEAU AREA

Mississippi River from Cape Rock Park

CAPE GIRARDEAU SITS in the sweet spot of a big bend in the Mississippi. The river played a big role in the city's early development and is still a source of pride today, even if a big flood wall separates it from the city. You can pass through the flood wall at the foot of Broadway to get next to the river.

HIGHLIGHTS

The city maintains a 1.25-mile-long walking path along the river. In addition, you'll find a few areas north and south of the city that get you deeper into the river's world.

Just north of the city, you'll find three small, adjacent parcels: Juden Creek Conservation Area (managed by the state of Missouri), Twin Trees Park (managed by Cape Girardeau), and Kelso Sanctuary (owned by the Missouri Birding Society but managed by Southeast Missouri State University). A trail—much of it atop a ridge—passes through all three areas and offers a hike through stands of American beech, trees that do well only in a few parts of the Mississippi valley, like here.

If you're near the parks just mentioned, swing by Cape Rock Park for a view of the river from a bit higher up. It's just a mile from the conservation areas.

CONTACT

Juden Creek Conservation Area
(573) 290-5730

Kelso Sanctuary
(573) 651-2170

Twin Trees Park
1 East Cape Rock Drive
Cape Girardeau, MO 63701
(573) 339-6340

Cape Rock Park
10 East Cape Rock Drive
Cape Girardeau, MO 63701
(573) 339-6340

DIRECTIONS

Juden Creek CA is about four miles north of downtown Cape Girardeau. Follow State Highway 177 north (it is called North Sprigg Street in the city, then Lexington Avenue and Big Bend Road). Turn right on old Missouri Highway V, then right on Cape Rock Drive. The parking lot and trailhead will be the first right, about one-third mile after you turn (the street address is 1 East Cape Rock Drive, but online maps may incorrectly guide you to a parking lot on the left; keep going until you reach the first parking lot on the right).

To get to Cape Rock Park from the parking lot at Juden Creek CA, drive one mile south along East Cape Rock Road.

BIG OAK TREE STATE PARK

THEY SEEM ENTIRELY out of place today, but the swamps and dense, wet forests preserved at Big Oak Tree State Park used to be the norm in this part of the Mississippi River's floodplain. In the early 1900s, timber companies moved in to harvest the trees, then people formed drainage districts to dry out the land. This little patch of a thousand acres is all that remains of the swamps and forests that developed over hundreds of thousands of years.

It's a remarkable transition, therefore—breathtaking, even—to drive through miles of farm fields, and then turn into the park and watch the light dissipate under the canopy of old-growth trees. The park is known for the towering oak and hickory trees that lord above everything else, but it also preserves cypress swamp and other wetlands. The park is a haven for birds, frogs, snakes, and other animals that rely on wetlands and bottomland forests for their survival.

Big Oak Tree State Park boardwalk

CONTACT

Big Oak Tree State Park
13640 S. Highway 102
East Prairie, MO 63845
(573) 649-3149

HIGHLIGHTS

The chief attraction is a walk along the boardwalk that passes the old trees. In spring, the forest floor usually floods, but it dries out in summer. Don't stop there, though. Continue on the park road to the cypress swamp. In spring and summer, it teems with life. A one-mile trail loops around it. If you've got the time, hike the 1.4-mile trail through the bottomland forest that runs between the boardwalk and the cypress swamp trail.

DIRECTIONS

The park is about eighteen miles south of East Prairie. If you're heading south on Interstate 55, exit at State Highway 80 and follow it through East Prairie. After passing through town, turn right (south) on Missouri Highway 102. Follow it for eleven miles to the park entrance.

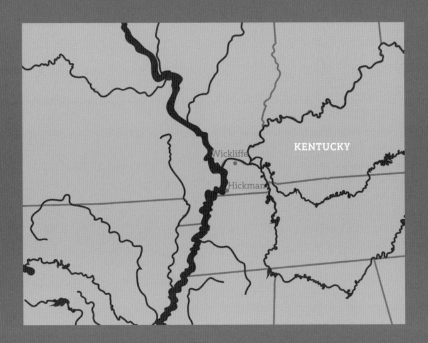

Wickliffe

Hickman

KENTUCKY

KENTUCKY

KENTUCKY MAY ONLY border the Mississippi River for sixty miles, but the areas along the river are remote and diverse. Dense floodplain forests run along the river and below tall bluffs. Two-lane roads wind their way through small towns and under canopies of deciduous trees. And the Mississippi has played a prominent role in shaping the state's history—and its shape.

South of the Ohio River, the Mississippi makes a dramatic loop called the New Madrid Bend (or the Kentucky Bend, if you live on the river's east bank). As surveyors worked their way west to map the boundary between Tennessee and Kentucky, they intended to draw a straight line at 36 degrees, 30 minutes

north latitude. They messed up when they reached the Tennessee River, though, so the boundary between the states jumped north about seventeen miles of the intended line. Not content to make just one mistake, the surveyors failed to notice that their boundary cut a line directly through a Mississippi River meander. That line would have consequences.

The land inside the meander amounted to seventeen and one-half square miles encircled by forty miles of river shoreline. Until 1848, Tennessee insisted that those seventeen and one-half square miles were part of its Obion County. Kentucky eventually won the dispute, and the land merged with

Kentucky's Fulton County. The area is a geographic oddity. It has no land connection to the rest of Fulton County, or any part of Kentucky. The area has been variously called Madrid Bend, Kentucky Bend, and Bessie Bend (after nearby Bessie, Tennessee). The killjoys at the US Census Department call it "West Census County Division." The fun people just call it "Bubbleland."

Bubblelanders were (and still are) mostly farmers. At first, most people grew corn and wheat, but cotton was the dominant crop before the Civil War. Just about every farm that was next to the river had a landing for steamboats, and many of them sold wood from their forests to refuel the boats: Watson's Landing, Harris's Landing, Compromise, Noland's Landing, Kentucky Point, Carrigan's Flat, Adam's Landing, Moss Landing, State Line Landing. The narrowest point in the bend is just one-half mile wide, so at one time, a steamboat passenger could disembark at the state line on one side of the bend, get a night's sleep, then board the same steamer on the other side of the bend and continue their trip.

The population peaked in the late-nineteenth century at just over three hundred people, many of them sharecroppers. Changes in agriculture and repeated flooding eventually took a toll on Bubbleland. In 1937, a levee break flooded the peninsula and left behind blue holes and piles of sand. The area has flooded multiple times since then.

Bubbleland, today, is a handful of houses, a cemetery, and a few thousand acres of cultivated land surrounded by tall levees meant to keep that pesky Mississippi River from flooding it again. The dozen or so remaining residents might be more isolated today than they were in the nineteenth century.

New Madrid (Missouri) is the closest city, but you need a boat to get there, and ferry service ended long ago. The only land route into the area is via Tennessee State Road 22. Bubblelanders get their mail twelve miles away at Tiptonville, Tennessee, which is also where the nearest grocery store and health care facilities are. To vote, residents have to drive forty miles to Hickman, Kentucky, passing through Tennessee before re-entering Kentucky. Their children go to school in Lake County, Tennessee. Life in Bubbleland now requires a lot of driving.

There's no population center in Bubbleland, and the biggest communities near the Mississippi River in Kentucky—Wickliffe, Columbus, Hickman—count two thousand or fewer residents. You won't find many places to stay near the river, but Columbus-Belmont State Park has a campground, and you'll find some accommodations around Reelfoot Lake (but in Tennessee). Otherwise, Paducah is about thirty-five minutes from Wickliffe, and you can get from Mayfield, Kentucky, to Hickman in about forty-five minutes.

Sure, Kentucky may have fewer places to visit along the Mississippi than other states, but the Great River Road through the state is a pleasure to drive. Roll down the car windows and unwind as the road passes through woods, farm fields, and small towns.

COLUMBUS-BELMONT STATE PARK

Mississippi River from Columbus-Belmont State Park

COLUMBUS-BELMONT STATE PARK occupies the site about where the old village of Columbus once stood, a place that had a busy steamboat port. During the Civil War, the Confederate army fortified the area under the direction of General Leonidas Polk, who commanded up to thirteen thousand soldiers and ten thousand enslaved Black people. They ultimately abandoned the fort in March 1862, and the Union army moved in. They used Columbus as a base to coordinate the movement of goods and soldiers farther south.

After the Civil War, increasing business from railroads kept Columbus prospering, at least until 1927. The Great Flood that year devastated the town. The river's swollen currents eroded shorelines around town and swallowed the town's entire business district. After the waters receded, Columbus rebuilt on a bluff one-half mile away and 140 feet above the water. The Red Cross spent $87,710 to help people move who couldn't afford to do so themselves. The park today is a mix of upland and bottomland deciduous forests. The park maintains a campground and several places to enjoy a picnic meal.

HIGHLIGHTS

The state park's museum and plaques recount the area's history. You can also hike a two-and-one-half-mile trail through the upland forests and past some of the Civil War fortifications and enjoy magnificent views of the main channel.

CONTACT

Columbus-Belmont State Park

350 Park Road

Columbus, KY 42032

(270) 677-2327

DIRECTIONS

The state park is eighteen miles south of Wickliffe. From State Highway 123, turn right on Back Street and follow it around a curve. Turn right on Carrington Street and follow it to the park entrance.

DORENA-HICKMAN FERRY

I KNOW. This isn't a park, but the ferry between Kentucky and Missouri is still a fun way to get on the river and to see its world from the middle of the main channel.

HIGHLIGHTS

The ride lasts about fifteen minutes, and you'll pay a fee that varies with the size of the vehicle you're driving. (The ferry also charges a small toll to transport people on foot, horseback, or bicycle.) If you keep your ticket, your toll will be cut in half for the ride back across the river. The ferry sometimes closes during periods of especially high or low water, so check in advance if you're hoping to ride it.

CONTACT
Dorena-Hickman Ferry
  (731) 693-0210

DIRECTIONS

You'll find the ferry landing at Hickman Harbor between a couple of docks, at the foot of Highway 1354 (Hickman Ferry Crossing). If you're driving north on Highway 94 (the Great River Road), make a left turn onto Highway 1354.

REELFOOT NATIONAL WILDLIFE REFUGE

A SERIES OF monster earthquakes created Reelfoot Lake (see the Tennessee chapter for more background about the lake), and the surrounding areas remain important habitats for birds and other wildlife. Reelfoot National Wildlife Refuge conserves two thousand acres on the northern side of the lake. In winter, bald eagles, waterfowl, and other migratory birds fill the refuge's wetlands and forests. Some of the refuge land is in Kentucky; the rest of the property and the visitor center are in Tennessee. Spring and fall are ideal times to visit, not just because it won't be stifling hot, but also because that's when the greatest variety of birds is present.

HIGHLIGHTS

Stop at the visitor center to find out what animals are active, then you can walk a mile-long loop trail that passes grasslands and a couple of small lakes.

The refuge's auto tour winds for three and one-half miles through bottomland hardwood forest and is another good place to watch for birds.

Hike the Grassy Lake Trail (one mile), which is part gravel and part boardwalk, for a stroll around a bottomland forest. Head north on Highway 157 to Walnut Logging Road, and turn left. Follow the road for about two miles to the trailhead.

The refuge includes a lot of water, and not just on Reelfoot Lake proper, and the refuge staff encourages paddling on those waters. There are three designated water trails; each is open from spring through fall. Spring is the best time to paddle, as water levels are usually higher and the vegetation hasn't yet gotten too thick to block passage. Refuge staff lead guided canoe trips on weekdays from mid-March through May, but you must call ahead to reserve a spot.

The Glory Hole Trail on Grassy Lake is the longest route at three-and-one-half miles. If you are paddling with children, the West Boat House Trail (one-and-one-half miles) is the easiest. The refuge does not rent canoes or kayaks, but you are welcome to bring a boat and explore the trails on your own. If you do, take a few steps to prepare, including checking the weather before you set out, bringing drinking water, and knowing where you're going.

CONTACT

Reelfoot National Wildlife Refuge
   4343 Highway 157
   Union City, TN 38261
   (731) 538-2481

DIRECTIONS

The visitor center is fourteen miles from Hickman. Take State Highway 94 west to State Highway 311, which becomes Tennessee State Highway 157. The visitor center is on the right.

TENNESSEE

THE MISSISSIPPI RIVER corridor in Tennessee offers a study in contrasts, from the agricultural fields in the northeast to the bustling city streets of Memphis, from the lowlands next to the main channel to the tall loess bluffs that rise above it. The meandering river channel plays tricks with our bureaucratic desire to establish firm boundaries. From Fort Pillow State Park, you can walk from Tennessee into Arkansas without getting wet; the shifting river channel left a portion of Arkansas stranded on the east bank.

Thick bottomland forests and swamps spread out over the lowlands, regenerating after generations of logging and development for agriculture. Tall hills built from fine, wind-blown particles (instead of rock, like the bluffs of the Upper Mississippi) line the Mississippi along Tennessee, broken up only when another river cuts through them. Before Euro-American settlement, grasslands covered these hills, but today they are thick with forests.

Tennessee's stretch of Mississippi River offers a pleasing mix of habitats and isolation. But even metropolitan Memphis offers natural spaces that preserve some of the river's traditional world. Dyersburg is a good place to base in the northern region. In southwest Tennessee, Memphis offers the best options for places to stay and eat.

Many of the public lands along the Mississippi in Tennessee are a short drive from Memphis, but once you leave the blacktop behind, and as the gravel roads narrow and go deeper into the forest canopy, the city will feel as far away as the moon. From the thick bottomland forests of Chickasaw National Wildlife Refuge to the rolling hills of Meeman-Shelby Forest State Park, you won't have any trouble finding places to go deep into the river's world.

REELFOOT LAKE

Cypress trees at Reelfoot Lake

IN DECEMBER 1811, a powerful earthquake shook the ground in the middle of the night, terrifying residents of New Madrid, Missouri, and surrounding areas. More earthquakes followed, which reshaped the land and the Mississippi River. On January 23, naturalist John J. Audubon was riding through the countryside just north of Tennessee's Reelfoot Creek. He wrote in his book *Delineations of American Scenery and Character* that he: *saw a sudden and strange darkness rising from the western horizon . . . . I heard what I imagined to be the distant rumbling of a violent tornado. . . . I thought my horse was about to die and would have sprung from his back had a minute more elapsed, but at that instant all the shrubs and trees began to move from their very roots. The ground rose and fell in successive furrows like the ruffled waters of a lake.*

Before the quake struck that day, Reelfoot Creek flowed through forests of deciduous trees and cypress swamps. The January 23 tumult and subsequent earthquakes, though, moved sand and dirt into a dam that blocked the flow of the stream, and the ground sank. Reelfoot Creek became Reelfoot Lake. The lake grew to twenty miles long and six miles wide. Sedimentation has since reduced the size of the lake, but it still spreads out over fifteen thousand acres in northwest Tennessee. Many of the trees that formed the old forest are still present in the lake, just as stumps below the waterline. The deepest point in the lake measures twenty feet, but the water averages about five to eight feet in depth. Today, the lake is eleven miles long and cut off from the flow of the Mississippi River by levees. Its forests and wetlands provide a rich habitat for birds and many other species. The state park manages a campground and rents out a few large, modern cabins.

HIGHLIGHTS

Stop at the visitor center in Reelfoot Lake State Park to read about the lake's formation and ecology. A boardwalk and trail pass through a cypress swamp from the visitor center and include observation decks with good views of the lake. Park staff regularly lead interpretive tours, including guided walks in winter to spot bald eagles.

If you have a boat with you, there are multiple boat ramps to put in and paddle around. The park and some local outfitters also rent canoes and kayaks.

Reelfoot Wildlife Management Area (WMA) is northwest of the state park and is less developed. At the end of Carrington Road, you'll find a small parking lot and a mile-long trail through the woods.

CONTACT

Reelfoot Lake State Park
2595 Highway 21 East (Visitor Center)
Tiptonville, TN 38079
(731) 253-9652

Reelfoot Wildlife Management Area
(731) 423-5725

DIRECTIONS

To get to the state park visitor center from Tiptonville, take State Highway 21 east for about two miles. The WMA is about three miles from Tiptonville. Take State Highway 22 north from town, then continue north on State Highway 78. Look for signs directing you to the WMA; any of several eastbound roads will get you there.

CHICKASAW NATIONAL WILDLIFE REFUGE

Chickasaw NWR

SPRAWLING OVER twenty-five thousand acres, Chickasaw National Wild-life Refuge—part of the territory where the Chickasaw People once lived—offers critical habitat for wildlife, especially for migrating waterfowl. In winter, thousands of gadwalls, mallards, northern pintails, and other birds inhabit the refuge. Egrets, herons, and other wading birds and shorebirds live in the refuge most of the year.

You'll find a range of habitats in a fairly compact area, from cypress-tupelo swamps to bottomland hardwood forest to upland forest to sandbars. The refuge includes eight miles of Mississippi River shoreline, although much of that is accessible only by boat.

The Park Service manages most of the refuge for habitat conservation rather than for recreation, so camping is prohibited. Most of the hiking trails are geared for hunters, but anyone is welcome to walk them. Gravel roads are the main way to get around the refuge, and they are generally well maintained.

HIGHLIGHTS

The Barr Road Trail offers a unique experience for the area. The trail passes over an old sandbar that is gradually becoming covered with vegetation. It's also the highest bit of ground, which is why a small community used to call it home. (They're the ones who planted the pine trees.) Some of the trail passes over a sandy base with a lot of prickly pear cacti; at other times, it goes through deciduous forest. The trail ends at a back channel of the Mississippi. It's about three and one-half miles round-trip to the back channel. In some places, poison ivy covers the path, so it is nearly impossible to avoid. If you are allergic, bring shoes and pants you can change into after the hike. Also, bring plenty of water and a hat, as long stretches of the hike are in open sun.

For a close-up view of the main channel, stop at the Ed Jones Boat Ramp on Hales Point Barr Road. You can also get to the main channel of the Mississippi by following Morris Road in the southern part of the refuge until it dead-ends, then walking a few feet through an opening between the trees.

The Wardlows Chute Boat Ramp offers access to a lake and lovely cypress swamp.

DIRECTIONS

The refuge is west of the towns of Halls and Ripley. State Highway 88 from Halls leads directly to the refuge.

The Barr Road trailhead is located at the end of Barr Road in the northwest corner of the refuge. Follow State Highway 88 toward the river; after passing Dee Webb Road, continue on Hales Point Barr Road until it ends at JD Smith Road. Turn right and follow it up and around. When you get to Barr Road, turn right, then right again. Park on the side of the road where it ends; you'll see the trailhead across the road from a farm. If you follow these directions, you'll pass the entrance to the Ed Jones Boat Ramp.

To reach Wardlows Chute Boat Ramp, continue south on Barr Road for about three and one-half miles. If you're going on to view the main channel of the Mississippi from the end of Morris Road, continue on Barr Road until it ends at Watkins Road. Turn right, then turn right again on Morris Road and follow it until it ends (about two and one-half miles).

CONTACT

Chickasaw National Wildlife Refuge
1505 Sand Bluff Road (Refuge Office)
Ripley, TN 38063
(731) 635-7621

FORT PILLOW STATE HISTORIC PARK

Sunset over the Mississippi from Fort Pillow

HIGH ON TOP of the loess bluffs west of Henning, you'll find clear views up and down the Mississippi River. That's one reason Confederate troops under the command of General Gideon Pillow built a fort at the top. The Confederates abandoned the fort the next year, and Union forces later occupied it. On April 12, 1864, Confederate General Nathan Bedford Forrest led a surprise attack on the fort that overwhelmed the Union troops. When the Union refused to surrender, Confederate forces hit them hard, killing 40 percent of the 557 Union soldiers. Three-quarters of the 262 Black Union soldiers died or suffered severe wounds. It turned out to be only a fleeting victory though, as Union forces soon seized full control of the Mississippi valley.

The park features a lot of exhibits on the area's Civil War history, but it is also a beautiful spot along the Mississippi. The park borders the main channel of the river, and although most of the land is upland forest, there are some areas of bottomland hardwood and small patches of wetlands. The park maintains a cozy campground among the trees of the upland forest.

HIGHLIGHTS

Tour the museum for a recounting of the site's Civil War history, then pick a trail to hike. You have twenty miles of paths to choose from. From the visitor center, the yellow and red trails weave through upland forest to a restored part of the fort.

The blue (Chickasaw) trail runs through upland forest to a beautiful overlook of the Mississippi's main channel. The overlook is a delightful spot to watch the sunset, but bring a headlamp or flashlight to help you find your way back. After the overlook, the trail passes an old cemetery, then dead-ends. If you walk the entire trail, it's four miles round-trip, but it's about half as long if you start from the campground.

CONTACT

Fort Pillow State Historic Park
3122 Park Road
Henning, TN 38041
(731) 738-5581

DIRECTIONS

Fort Pillow is about a thirty-minute drive west of Henning. From US Highway 51, go west on State Highway 87 for about seventeen miles to the park entrance.

LOWER HATCHIE NATIONAL WILDLIFE REFUGE

FOUNDED IN 1980 to conserve habitat for migrating waterfowl, the refuge today covers nearly ten thousand acres along the confluence of the Hatchie and Mississippi Rivers in several parcels, the largest of which is right at the confluence. Although there's a lot of bottomland hardwood forest, the refuge also offers access to swamps, sandbars, lakes, and the main channel of the Mississippi. The best time to observe migrating birds is in fall just before the refuge closes (November 15) and again in spring after it reopens (March 15), assuming the refuge isn't flooded.

HIGHLIGHTS

Stop at the observation deck near the refuge office to see who's hanging out below.

There are two good places to get to the river's main channel when the river is below twenty feet on the Memphis gauge. Either would be a pleasant spot for a picnic lunch. Follow the road until it ends and then walk the path down to the river. Even better, backtrack about a quarter mile to another trailhead and walk a quarter mile through the floodplain forest. The trail ends at one of the most beautiful stretches of beach you'll find anywhere. When the river gets down to about twelve feet on the Memphis gauge, a nice gravel bar opens up.

On the way back out to the main road, stop at the Champion Lake Boat Ramp along State Highway 87. It's a good place to paddle if you brought a boat with you, but the views of cypress-tupelo swamps are good, regardless.

Gravel bar and beach at Lower Hatchie NWR

CONTACT

Lower Hatchie National Wildlife Refuge
234 Fort Prudhomme Drive
Henning, TN 38041
(731) 738-2296

DIRECTIONS

To reach the refuge office, overlook, and hiking trails, take State Highway 87 for two miles past the entrance to Fort Pillow and turn left onto the entrance road.

MEEMAN-SHELBY FOREST STATE PARK

A SHORT DRIVE north of Memphis, Meeman-Shelby Forest State Park is another gem in the park system along the Mississippi River. The park conserves extensive stands of upland forests on the ridges of the loess hills known as the Chickasaw Bluffs. The park's thirteen thousand acres also include a couple of lakes, an atmospheric stretch of bottomland hardwood forest with wetlands mixed in, and access to the main channel of the Mississippi. Given the variety of habitats, it's no surprise that the park supports a diverse group of plant and animal life, especially birds. Fall colors can be striking in the park's forests. The park's campground is in a shaded upland forest; the park also rents a few large cabins.

Winding road through floodplain forest at Meeman-Shelby Forest State Park

the end of the road is a popular spot to enjoy watching the sun set over the river.

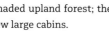

HIGHLIGHTS

The park's twenty miles of trails offer some good choices for getting into the forests and around wetlands. The Chickasaw Bluff (eight miles) and Woodland Trails (three and one-half miles) stick mostly to the upland forests. Blooming plants are abundant in spring, and fall colors can be spectacular. If you want to bike through the forest, the park maintains a five-mile paved path.

It's a seven-mile drive from the visitor center to the boat ramp on the Mississippi, but you won't mind taking your time as you wind your way under the thick canopy of the floodplain forest, where you'll probably also see wildlife along the edges. The boat ramp at

CONTACT

Meeman-Shelby Forest State Park
910 Riddick Road
Millington, TN 38053
(901) 876-5215

DIRECTIONS

From Memphis, take US Highway 51 north for seven miles. Go left (north) on State Highway 388 for seven miles. Turn left on Locke Cuba Road, then right on Bluff Road. The park entrance is three-quarters of a mile on the left.

OLD FOREST STATE NATURAL AREA AT OVERTON PARK

Hiking at Old Forest SNA

WHO WOULD HAVE thought you could find a patch of old-growth deciduous forest in the middle of a big American city? And, yet, that's exactly what the Old Forest Area at Overton Park is.

Walking the network of trails (there are many), the park feels bigger than 126 acres. The dense canopy and vegetation knock down the heat of the day considerably, and the forest buffers most of the city's noise. It's a rewarding place to wander in search of flowers, birds, or peace and quiet.

HIGHLIGHTS

There are slight elevation differences throughout the forest that change the makeup of the plants. On the low ridges, tulip poplar is common, along with eleven different species of oak, including southern red oak. In the lower elevations, you'll see stands of cherrybark oak and sweet gum. And in the understory, dogwood, redbud, hop hornbeam, red maple, and pawpaw do well. You'll see some big oaks in the forest, but trees account for only 20 percent of the plant life. Eight species of grapes grow in the forest, and catbriers and poison ivy are also abundant. Common ground cover plants include celandine poppy, mayapple, tooth-wort, and wild ginger.

CONTACT

Old Forest State Natural Area at Overton Park
1914 Poplar Avenue
Memphis, TN 38104
(901) 214-5450

DIRECTIONS

The park is just a ten-minute drive east of downtown Memphis. Poplar Avenue runs from downtown and along the southern boundary of Overton Park. Old Forest is in the middle. Turn left onto Veterans Plaza Drive and follow the signs to the parking lot.

Pawpaw tree

Pawpaw

If you're hiking in a floodplain forest in late August or September, you may get lucky and stumble across the largest fruit native to North America—the pawpaw. The pawpaw is a deciduous understory tree, rarely taller than thirty or forty feet, that grows mostly in the eastern half of the country (even into parts of Ontario), including along the Lower Mississippi River.

These trees prefer areas where the soil drains relatively quickly, and they need little sun, at least to get started; pawpaw seeds can germinate in deep shade. Pawpaws now grow in some upland forests, too. A single pawpaw will grow into a cluster of genetically identical trees by sending out rhizomes that sprout new trunks. The pawpaw's leaves, branches, and bark contain acetogenins, chemicals that act as natural insect repellents and give off a distinct scent.

Pawpaws need pollen from an unrelated tree to produce fruit, so they get a helping hand from pollinators that includes flies and beetles. The oval-shaped fruit ripens from mid-August into September (which is why the Shawnee People call September the month of the pawpaw moon), often forming in clusters. The fruit has a smooth texture, with hints of banana and kiwi and just a little sweetness. Pawpaws begin to ferment within a couple of days of being picked, so the only way to extend their shelf life is by drying, freezing, or canning them.

We may not be too familiar with pawpaws today, but they were a dietary staple for many Indigenous People (who also used the tree's inner bark to weave ropes and nets). Pawpaws were also an important food for many enslaved Blacks in the South. With today's focus on eating more locally grown foods, pawpaws may again become part of our diets.

MEMPHIS RIVERFRONT

Memphis riverfront

MEMPHIS HAS BEEN working hard to create open, welcoming spaces along its riverfront, and there's much to admire even as some of the work continues. Memphis completed a major renovation of Tom Lee Park in 2023 and may also make some changes to the attractions on Mud Island in the near future.

HIGHLIGHTS

The Tennessee Welcome Center sits right on the river just south of the Hernando de Soto Bridge and is a good place to start a visit and get the status of the riverfront projects.

Mud Island features a park, an amphitheater, a boat ramp, and expansive views of the river. You can walk there by crossing the skybridge from downtown (enter from 125 N. Front Street) or drive and park on the island. Just south of the Welcome Center, Fourth Bluff Park offers green space along Wolf River Harbor, a bike share station, historic markers, and good views.

One-half mile south of Fourth Bluff Park, Beale Street Landing is the main stop for touring riverboats, but the platforms also offer some of the best views of Memphis, the river, and its bridges. Tom Lee Park covers a large swath of the riverfront south of Beale Street Landing. The city's ambitious renovation includes better connections to adjacent neighborhoods, open green spaces, plazas for public events, and recreating native habitats. Several small parks along the blufftop offer pleasant places to rest for a moment and enjoy good views of the river.

If you have time for just one stop along the Memphis riverfront, walk the spectacular Big River Crossing. Nearly a mile from end to end, it's the longest pedestrian crossing over the Mississippi River. The trail runs along the Harahan Bridge, which is still an active railroad bridge, and the views are inspiring. From the Arkansas side, you can continue biking along the Big River Trail (see the Arkansas chapter). You'll find bike share stations on both sides of the bridge.

DIRECTIONS

Riverside Drive parallels the Mississippi River. The Tennessee Welcome Center is at the north end, just below Interstate 40 and the Hernando de Soto Bridge. If you just want to walk the Big River Crossing, park either along Channel 3 Drive west of Riverside Drive or in the lot at Martyrs Park (take the first right from Channel 3 Drive after Founders Drive). If you're on the Arkansas side, look for the parking lot on Dacus Lake Road (take Exit 1 from Interstate 55).

CONTACT
Tennessee Welcome Center
119 Riverside Drive
Memphis, TN 38103
(901) 543-6757

T.O. FULLER STATE PARK

the late 1800s, but his public service ended when white politicians disenfranchised Black voters at the end of the nineteenth century. Fuller moved to Memphis in 1900 and got hired as minister at First Baptist Church. Soon after that, he accepted the job of principal at Howe Institute, a private school and one of just two grade schools for Black children in Memphis. He was also a successful entrepreneur and nurtured other Black-owned businesses, wrote books about African American history, and served as editor for a literary publication called the *Signal*.

When the CCC was remaking the park, workers uncovered evidence of an old Native American village while excavating for a swimming pool. Archaeologists subsequently determined that Indigenous North Americans began living at the site about 1,100 years ago, and it was probably one of the communities Hernando de Soto's army ransacked.

The county sold the park to the state of Tennessee for a dollar in 1949, and the state park today covers 1,138 acres. The park manages a campground, swimming pool, hiking trails, and picnic areas. Several miles of trails pass through the beautiful upland deciduous forests of the Fourth Chickasaw Bluff. The park is restoring the former golf course (it closed in 2011) to native grassland as well as restoring some wetlands. The adjacent Chucalissa archaeological site, which the University of Memphis manages as the C.H. Nash Museum, is within the park's boundaries. On weekends, the park can get busy, but it is a peaceful place in spite of its proximity to a big city.

WHEN THE PARK was established in 1933 as Shelby City Negro State Park, it was one of only two state parks in Tennessee that welcomed African Americans. During the Depression, workers from the Civilian Conservation Corps (CCC) transformed the park with new buildings, roads, and plantings. In 1942, the county renamed the park for Dr. Thomas Oscar Fuller. Dr. Fuller won election to public office in his native North Carolina in

HIGHLIGHTS

The interpretive center includes exhibits on the park's native plants and animals as well as displays on the park's history, including a profile of Boxtown, a community of newly emancipated Blacks who lived nearby after the Civil War.

The park offers several good hikes. The Discovery Loop Trail winds four miles through upland forest with some minor elevation changes and passes the Chucalissa site and wetlands. If you just want to walk around the Chucalissa site, you can follow a three-quarter-mile loop trail.

The Initiation Loop covers two and one-half miles through upland forest and is a bit more work than the other trails: it runs from the top of the bluff to the floodplain, so the elevation changes four hundred feet along the route.

The park resurfaced the former golf course paths with a material made from recycled tires, so it's easy on the feet and legs. The trail runs 2.9 miles through prairie restoration, a pond, and some upland forest.

CONTACT

T.O. Fuller State Park
1500 W. Mitchell Road
Memphis, TN 38109
(901) 543-7581

DIRECTIONS

It takes about twenty minutes to drive to T.O. Fuller State Park from downtown Memphis. Take Interstate 40 east to Interstate 240/Interstate 69 south, then exit to Interstate 55 north. Exit at US Highway 61 and go south. Turn right on East Peebles Road, and continue on the same road as it turns south and becomes Weaver Road. After a mile, turn right on West Mitchell Road, and after another mile, turn right into the state park.

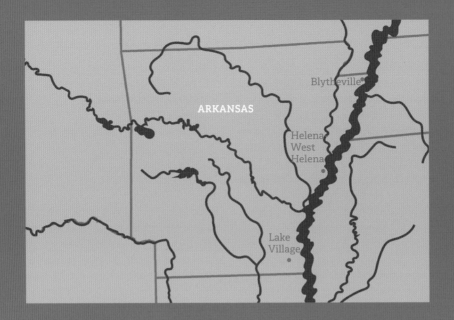

ARKANSAS

THE RIVER'S WORLD in Arkansas offers a wonderful variety of ecosystems that are often spectacular, even if there are fewer of them than in other states. In the northeast corner of the state, upland forests run along the spine of Crowley's Ridge. Tributaries of the Mississippi—the White, Arkansas, and St. Francis Rivers—bring together thousands of acres of dense bottomland hardwood forests. Buck and Choctaw Islands feature the variable worlds of low-lying land in the middle of the river. Remnants of the Grand Prairie survive in central and southeast Arkansas.

And one of the biggest oxbow lakes in the country draws recreational users as well as wildlife enthusiasts. A mix of federal, state, and local conservation lands preserves vital spaces for migratory and native life. Although it's possible to see some of these places in an hour or two, most will beckon you to stick around longer, much longer, to get to know them in depth.

When you're traveling along the Mississippi River through Arkansas, several communities would serve well as a place to base, including Blytheville, West Memphis, Helena-West Helena, and Lake Village.

You'll find plenty of wild spaces near the Mississippi River in Arkansas, especially along the lower reaches of its tributaries, including two large islands that don't get a lot of visitors. Arkansas also offers miles of scenic bike trails along the Mississippi, with plans to expand them in the coming years.

BIG RIVER TRAIL

Big River Bike Trail

SOMEDAY, WE'LL BE able to ride a bike (or walk) hundreds of miles atop Mississippi River levees, but for now, we can enjoy a seventy-mile segment from West Memphis to Marianna. This is a remote section of Arkansas, so cell service is spotty. If you want to bike the entire path, you'll encounter a couple of gates that appear to block access, but it's okay to lift your bike up and over to continue riding. The entire route from West Memphis to Marianna is open for public use.

HIGHLIGHTS

The crushed gravel trail passes agricultural fields, floodplain forests, and wetlands and always parallels the Mississippi River. You'll find trailheads at the foot of the Big River Crossing in West Memphis and in Marianna, but you can access the trail from several other spots as well. If you're not feeling up to a seventy-mile trip, the loop through West Memphis north of Big River Crossing runs seven miles.

CONTACT

Big River Bike Trail
(870) 732-7587 (West Memphis Convention and Visitors Bureau)

DIRECTIONS

In West Memphis, take Exit 1 from Interstate 55 and park at the lot for Big River Crossing on Dacus Lake Road.

ST. FRANCIS NATIONAL FOREST AND MISSISSIPPI RIVER STATE PARK

Mouth of the St. Francis River

THE LAST MILES of the St. Francis River run through what is now St. Francis National Forest and Mississippi River State Park. The federal government and the state of Arkansas cooperate to manage the area. Arkansas manages the recreational areas within the forest. Most of the area is bottomland hardwood forest, but you'll also find sandy shorelines, sandbars, and wetland habitats. Crowley's Ridge also runs through the park along the southwestern sections, so the landscape changes to upland forests along the ridge.

The roads are often unmarked, but it's hard to get too lost as there just aren't that many roads through the forest. The park runs popular campgrounds around Bear Creek and Storm Creek Lakes. In fall (which means November here), the deciduous trees put on a good show of color. The park sees fewer visitors during the peak of summer heat, but gets pretty busy in spring and fall, especially on weekends.

HIGHLIGHTS

Stop into the visitor center to get oriented to the park, ask a few questions, and read the exhibits about the human and natural history of the area. The only formal hiking trail is Bear Creek Nature Trail, on the southwest side of Bear Creek Lake. Leave the paved road behind and head south on Lee Road 239. Along the way, you'll pass the road to a boat ramp on the St. Francis River (good for putting in a canoe or kayak) and Beaver Pond, which is a lovely cypress swamp.

A little farther down the road (1.4 miles after turning from Highway 44), St. Francis Overlook offers a chance to roam around the confluence of the two rivers—the St. Francis and the Mississippi. There are places to park just above the confluence as well as a little farther back if the road is too muddy to drive (like it was when I visited). From the end of the road, it's a short walk down to the confluence. If the rivers aren't too high, a sandbar emerges where they meet, which is fun to explore. The views from above the confluence are also stellar.

CONTACT

St. Francis National Forest
605 W. Main (office)
Russellville, AR 72801
(479) 280-8162

Mississippi River State Park
2955 Highway 44 (Visitor Center)
Marianna, AR 72360
(870) 295-4040

DIRECTIONS

From Marianna, take Martin Luther King Jr. Drive east. It veers south on the edge of town and becomes State Highway 44 and heads right to the visitor center. At the south end of Bear Creek Lake, Highway 44 ends, but you can continue through the rest of the park on well-maintained gravel roads. Lee Road 239 and Phillips Road 239 go past the areas highlighted previously and into Helena-West Helena.

HELENA RIVER PARK AND BUCK ISLAND WILDLIFE MANAGEMENT AREA

Mississippi River at Helena during a period of low water

HELENA RIVER PARK is an ideal place to stop for a good look at the main channel and appreciate the extent to which the river's height can change. At Helena-West Helena, the difference between the highest and lowest recorded crests is sixty-four feet!

HIGHLIGHTS

A boardwalk lined with interpretive signs extends from the parking lot to an observation deck with an unobstructed view of the river. The park offers places to picnic and a small area of bottomland hardwood forest around it.

If you have a boat with you, you can launch from the ramp and venture up to Buck Island Wildlife Management Area. It's about a mile upstream, so if you're paddling, stick close to shore to stay out of the strongest currents. The island's bottomland hardwood forests are regenerating, and at lower water levels beautiful sandbars spread out from the forest, including a gravel bar or two. Several miles of hiking trails wind through the woods, the beaches are great for lounging and swimming, and you can even camp here, although the only amenities (besides the river and woods) are the ones you bring with you.

CONTACT

Helena River Park
 (870) 406-6128
Buck Island WMA
 (877) 734-4581

DIRECTIONS

Helena River Park is at the north end of downtown Helena. Turn right on Perry Street, then right onto Cunningham Road to reach it. To get to Buck Island, you'll need a boat. You can put in at the ramp at Helena River Park and head upstream. If you're paddling, assume it will take about an hour.

DELTA HERITAGE TRAIL STATE PARK

Delta Heritage Trail

THE OLD UNION Pacific corridor through eastern Arkansas is now the Delta Heritage Trail State Park, a flat, crushed-gravel trail for biking and hiking. When the project is complete, the trail will run eighty-four miles from Helena-West Helena to Arkansas City, much of it through floodplain and bottomland hardwood forest and across the White and Arkansas Rivers. Two sections are ready for your bike (or legs) right now. Rows of shade trees line some parts of the trail, whereas others are in full sun.

There are campsites at the Barton Visitor Center and around Arkansas City, but most people currently ride the trail for day trips. The best place to find a room is in Helena-West Helena. You can rent bicycles at the Barton trailhead.

HIGHLIGHTS

The northern section of the trail runs nearly twenty-one miles from Lexa (just outside Helena-West Helena) to Elaine and includes trailheads at Lexa, Barton, Lick Creek, Lake View, and Elaine. The southern route covers twenty-four miles from Arkansas City to Watson, with a trailhead in between at Rohwer, the site of a Japanese internment camp during World War II. Fourteen miles of the southern route run on top of the Mississippi River levee (which is shared with automobile traffic).

CONTACT

Delta Heritage Trail State Park
5539 US Highway 49
Helena-West Helena, AR 73290
(870) 572-2352

DIRECTIONS

The park office is at the Barton Trailhead (5539 US Highway 49). Download a geo-referenced trail map from the state park website.

ARKANSAS POST NATIONAL MEMORIAL AND ARKANSAS POST MUSEUM STATE PARK

Wetlands at Arkansas Post

THE AREA NEAR the confluence of the Arkansas and Mississippi Rivers has long attracted people to live there. Mississippian people thrived in dozens of villages in the area for hundreds of years, as had many other cultures before them. When Europeans arrived in the seventeenth century, the Quapaw People lived in several villages near the confluence.

Henri de Tonti built a small fort in 1686, which started a couple of centuries of attempts by Euro-Americans to establish communities in the area. The community relocated many times as residents searched for ground high enough to escape flooding from the Arkansas and Mississippi Rivers. For a while, a few hundred people lived at Arkansas Post, including enslaved Black people, and the village served as the first capital of Arkansas Territory. Many, though, found the heat, humidity, bugs, and flooding difficult to cope with. In 1727, Father Paul du Poisson wrote, "But the greatest torture—without which every thing else would have been only a recreation, but which passes all belief, and could never be imagined in France unless it had been experienced—is the mosquitoes, the cruel persecution of the mosquitoes."

HIGHLIGHTS

You can learn the history of the area at two sites. The US Park Service manages Arkansas Post National Memorial, and the state of Arkansas manages Arkansas Post Museum State Park a few miles away. Apart from the historic markers and exhibits, the sites also offer a look at the environmental context. Wetlands surround the National Memorial, and teem with birds and other wildlife. I've watched armadillos root around the grounds as well as multiple species of waterfowl in the adjacent wetlands. A walkway leads to an overlook with a view of the Arkansas River, with its bottomland forests and sandbars. The state park is restoring several acres of the native prairie. (Arkansas Post was at the southern end of the Grand Prairie.)

CONTACT

Arkansas Post National Memorial
1741 Old Post Road
Gillett, AR 72055
(870) 548-2207

Arkansas Post Museum State Park
5530 US Highway 165 South
Gillett, AR 72055
(870) 548-2634

DIRECTIONS

The state park sits at the intersection of US Highway 165 and State Highway 169 about seven miles south of the town of Gillett. To reach the national memorial, go east on State Highway 169 for two miles to the entrance.

FREDDIE BLACK CHOCTAW ISLAND WILDLIFE MANAGEMENT AREA

Choctaw Island

FREDDIE BLACK CHOCTAW Island Wildlife Management Area offers plenty of space to get lost in the river's world. The east unit sprawls over seven thousand acres of batture territory, with some portions on the mainland and the rest on Choctaw Island. Dense bottomland hardwood forest covers much of the area, but you'll also find lakes, ponds, and other assorted wetlands, plus sandbars at some river levels. The mix of habitats attracts a lot of birds, many of which stick around all year.

The area is definitely off the beaten path, so you may not see many other people, especially during the week. And you probably won't have cell service. The WMA maintains trails, a few primitive campsites, and a boat launch into a backwater channel between the mainland and the island.

HIGHLIGHTS

The Mississippi River Trail (2.8 miles) parallels the river and loops into the forest. Access it from Thane Road just past the turnoff to the boat ramp. The Levee Trail (3.4 miles) passes through a mature bottomland forest. Both are great places for bird-watching and, occasionally, for spotting other wildlife.

The boat ramp provides access to a secondary channel between the mainland and Choctaw Island. At lower water levels, you'll find a complex of sandbars visible from the boat ramp. If you have a boat with you, take the quick trip over to the willow-lined island. It's a delightful place to explore, with thick forests and sandy beaches. You could kill a lot of time poking around the gravel bars and checking out driftwood and the hidden spaces in the forest.

CONTACT

Freddie Black Choctaw Island Wildlife Management Area
(833) 363-7638

DIRECTIONS

The WMA is next to Arkansas City, about eleven miles east of US Highway 65 along State Highway 4. You can enter the WMA from either Sprague Street or President Street. Drive over the levee and follow the road into the WMA. If you brought a boat and want to paddle to the island, enter the WMA from President Street, which becomes Thane Road in the park, and follow the signs to the boat ramp.

LAKE CHICOT STATE PARK

Lake Chicot

IN SOUTHEAST ARKANSAS, the Mississippi River left behind a remnant of its old channel, an oxbow lake that is the largest of its kind in the United States. The lake formed about five hundred years ago after the Mississippi cut a fresh path and abandoned its old channel. The oxbow lake it left behind is nearly a mile wide in places and twenty-two miles long. Clay soils shape the outside bank, which rises high above the water; the deepest parts of the lake run along this bank. On the opposite side, the sandy inner bank slopes gradually toward the water. You'll even find a small cypress swamp in one area. It's a good place to relax

for a night or two to enjoy the scenery and birds. The park maintains a campground and rents cabins, and nearby Chicot County Park also maintains a campground.

HIGHLIGHTS

Tour the visitor center for exhibits on the human and environmental history of the lake. Park staff maintain a one-mile hiking trail through a bottomland forest, plus places to picnic. You'll also find beaches on the lake and a boat ramp, and the park rents kayaks and fishing boats.

Horseshoe Lake, an oxbow, from the air

Oxbow Lakes

Their characteristic crescent shape gives them away. Oxbow lakes form when meandering rivers get the itch to explore fresh territory and dig out a new channel in favor of an old one. The former channel gets cut off from the flow of freshwater, except during periods of high water. The new lake often evolves into a swamp or bog. Pulses of high water bring a refreshing burst of nutrients and clear out some of the accumulated detritus. During those periods when they reconnect with the river, these lakes also provide critical breeding habitat for species such as pallid sturgeon. Even when they aren't connected directly to the river, they provide habitat (and drinking water) for birds, mammals, and many other creatures. Today's levees have cut off the flow of water to many of the oxbow lakes along the Mississippi, and they are slowly filling in. They are also suffering from declining water quality, as fertilizers from nearby farms run off into them.

CONTACT

Lake Chicot State Park
2542 Highway 257
Lake Village, AR 71653
(870) 265-5480

DIRECTIONS

From Lake Village, follow State Highway 144 for seven miles to the park entrance.

MISSISSIPPI

GETTING NEAR THE Mississippi River is a bit of a challenge in the state that takes its name from the Big River. Much of the land is privately owned. Much of the rest is just darned hard to reach without a boat, although a few boat ramps offer a glimpse of the main channel. Agricultural fields cover much of the delta today, but as you drive around, you'll pass "ghost swamps," little fingers of bayous and streams that were once surrounded by dense forest.

Still, the places that are accessible are wonderful. Only a couple of them are in the batture (between the levees), so I've included a few places away from the river that offer a look at historic delta habitats. Most of these places will be most rewarding to visit from November to March when migrating birds settle in. Summers are hot and humid and not the best time for a long hike. Even though the land lies about as flat as land can, you'll find terrific views of the river from the top of the loess

bluffs at Vicksburg Tourist Center. The views are even better at Natchez, where you can saunter along the bluff next to the river and slowly savor the views of the main channel.

If you're looking for a place to use as a base and settle in for a couple of days, Clarksdale and Greenville work well for the northern and middle sections along the river, whereas Vicksburg and Natchez are good choices farther south.

The Mississippi often rises in January and can reach flood stage shortly after that. Some of the places in this guide flood regularly, so it's a good idea to check river levels before you go if you have your heart set on visiting them. When you visit a Mississippi Wildlife Management Area, fill out the top half of the permit at the self-clearing station (there's no fee), then drop the other half into the box at the station when you leave. Most don't maintain hiking trails, but you are welcome to walk along the ATV trails.

TUNICA COUNTY RIVER PARK

A HIDDEN GEM among the towers of riverfront casinos, Tunica County River Park offers a rare close encounter with the Mississippi River in Mississippi.

HIGHLIGHTS

The featured attraction is the modern museum and aquarium next to the river, but the views of the river from the walkways and observation deck are stellar. From the observation deck, it's easier to appreciate the wide variations in the river's height from year to year (or season to season), which can be as extreme as fifty feet. After enjoying the views, explore the gardens and take a walk around the 3.1-mile trail that circulates through the bottomland hardwood forest in the batture (on the river side of the levee). The museum features a mix of permanent and temporary exhibits, but all center on

the Mississippi River. Some cover human history, from the mound-building cultures to plantation agriculture to today. The small aquarium features native fish and turtles.

CONTACT

Tunica County River Park
1 RiverPark Drive
Tunica Resorts, MS 38664
(662) 357-0050

DIRECTIONS

From US Highway 61 go west on Casino Strip Resort Boulevard, then turn right on Fitzgerald Boulevard, and veer left onto Lucky Lane. Turn left on RiverPark Drive to reach the parking area.

GREAT RIVER ROAD STATE PARK/RIVERFRONT WILDLIFE MANAGEMENT AREA

Sandbar at Great River Road State Park

ROSEDALE ISN'T THE Mississippi River hub it was in the nineteenth century, but it offers one of the best places to get near the river in the northern half of the state, thanks to two adjacent public properties: Great River Road State Park and Riverfront Wildlife Management Area. Between them, they protect three miles of Mississippi River shoreline and hundreds of acres of bottomland hardwood forest.

HIGHLIGHTS

Big floods in the 2010s limited access to these areas for a while, but they are open again and the trails are slowly being restored. A fishing pier at the state park's oxbow lake is a good place to watch for wildlife, birds especially.

The main attraction at the state park is access to the giant sandbars that form as the river drops in summer. They are enormous, up to one-half mile wide, and offer a mix of textures from fine sand to gravel. It's one of the few places along the Lower Mississippi with public access where it's possible to walk from land onto a sandbar. If you're going to hike on the sandbar, wear a hat and bring water as the sun can be intense and there's nowhere to hide from it. To reach the sandbar, drive the park road past the fishing pier and across a bridge. Turn right at the first road and look for a place to park. When you get out of the car, look for a narrow dirt road with deep tire tracks and follow it to the river and the sandbar.

If you just want a view of the main channel in this area, drive to Terrene Landing. The views are good, especially at sunset.

CONTACT

Great River Road State Park
101 State Park Road
Rosedale, MS 38769
(662) 827-5436
Riverfront Wildlife Management Area
(662) 326-8029

DIRECTIONS

From Highway 1 in Rosedale, turn west on State Park Road to enter the park. When the road ends, you can park and walk into the WMA.

Terrene Landing is at the north end of Rosedale. Head north on Terrene Road, then west on Terrene Landing Road.

SKY LAKE WILDLIFE MANAGEMENT AREA

DENSE FORESTS AND cypress-tupelo swamps once covered the Mississippi Delta, but most of it was cleared and drained for cotton agriculture. At Sky Lake Wildlife Management Area, though, you can take a step back into that world. The WMA preserves one of the last remaining stands of old-growth cypress swamp in the world. Sky Lake was a distributary channel of the Mississippi River about 7,700 years ago and flowed with the river's water for nearly 3,000 years. Indigenous People made their homes in this area for thousands of years.

Sky Lake old-growth swamp

HIGHLIGHTS

A long boardwalk meanders through the swamp, past cypress trees hundreds of years old. The dense canopy shades the walk, offering welcome relief on the hottest of days, even though the air is still thick. Interpretive signs line the boardwalk, and multiple observation decks offer tempting places to stop, watch, and listen. It's the kind of place one could revisit at different times of year and have a unique experience each time.

CONTACT

Sky Lake Wildlife Management Area
1090 Simmons Road
Belzoni, MS 39038
(662) 335-2422

DIRECTIONS

Sky Lake WMA is northwest of Belzoni, about forty-five miles east of the Mississippi River. From Belzoni, head north on State Highway 7 for six and one-half miles, then turn left onto Kornegay Road, which becomes Four Mile Road. After three-quarters of a mile, turn left. When the road ends, turn right and drive three-quarters of a mile. The parking lot for the boardwalk is on the right.

DELTA NATIONAL FOREST AND SUNFLOWER WILDLIFE MANAGEMENT AREA

Blue Lake at Delta National Forest

IT'S EASY TO get lost among the trees in the sixty thousand acres managed as Delta National Forest and Sunflower Wildlife Management Area, a wide swath of bottomland hardwood forest intermixed with some wetlands. The area is managed as winter habitat for migrating waterfowl, for logging, and for recreation, including hunting. The forest service maintains fifty-seven primitive campsites that are spaced widely apart and feel pretty darn isolated.

HIGHLIGHTS

You'll find two recreation areas in the forest: Little Sunflower River and Blue Lake. Both include a few campsites and picnic tables. Little Sunflower also has a boat ramp to access the namesake Little Sunflower River. Blue Lake has a one-mile walking path through bottomland forest and next to cypress swamp (that isn't a lake and certainly isn't blue) that includes a few interpretive signs. It's an easy walk—and you may glimpse an alligator (don't let your dog swim in the water!).

CONTACT

Delta National Forest
68 Frontage Road
Rolling Fork, MS 39159
(662) 873-6256
Sunflower WMA
(662) 873-6958

DIRECTIONS

To get to Little Sunflower from Rolling Fork: Go south on US Highway 61 for eighteen miles, then left on Omega Road for a mile. Turn right on Dummyline Road; the entrance to the recreation area is 3.2 miles on the left.

To get to Blue Lake from Rolling Fork: From the intersection of US Highway 61 and State Highway 16, go east on State Highway 16 for 6.8 miles. Turn right on the gravel road and drive three miles; turn left to enter the recreation area.

SHIPLAND WILDLIFE MANAGEMENT AREA

Backwaters at Shipland WMA

SHIPLAND WILDLIFE Management Area offers another chance to go deep into a bottomland hardwood forest next to the main channel of the Mississippi River. Getting to the WMA includes a short drive on top of a levee, which is kinda fun, and provides a visceral experience of the immensity and height of the structure. Shipland WMA occupies a beautiful, isolated area in the batture, so it floods regularly. If you'd like to visit, check in advance to make sure it's open. When the roads are muddy, you may prefer driving a four-wheel-drive vehicle to navigate them.

HIGHLIGHTS

There are a few places where it's possible to get to the river and maybe even a sandbar (at some river levels) after a short walk. The easiest is from a clearing on the right that is 0.7 mile from the permit station; look for an open area where you can park. (If you reach the shed, you've gone too far.) Walk ahead, then follow the trail to the left to get to a backwater habitat. If you continue walking forward instead of turning left, the trail parallels the back channel through the forest. There's much more to explore beyond that, so feel free to wander.

CONTACT

Shipland Wildlife Management Area

(662) 873-6958

DIRECTIONS

Shipland WMA is a fifty-minute drive from Vicksburg. Take US Highway 61 north across the Yazoo River. At Onward, go north on State Highway 1 for twelve miles. Turn left at the sign for the WMA, then go up onto the levee and drive for 1.2 miles. Turn left and follow the road into the WMA.

MAHANNAH WILDLIFE MANAGEMENT AREA

JUST DOWN THE road from Shipland WMA, Mahannah Wildlife Management Area offers an entirely different experience. The land was intensively farmed until recently, so the state is now in the process of reestablishing hardwood forests with selective plantings. The state also manages several areas as wetlands for migrating waterfowl and has been quite successful at it. Thousands of birds take respite in the WMA in winter.

Bottomland forest at Mahannah WMA

HIGHLIGHTS

The park road runs seven miles (one way) through managed wetlands and bottomland hardwood forest, over a levee, then dead-ends at Buck Bayou. After it crosses the levee, the road enters a dense stand of old hardwood forest with some impressive oak trees. Mahannah WMA is a good place for a leisurely drive or a walk on the ATV trails, especially when a lot of waterfowl are present. The WMA is subject to flooding, so make sure it's open before you try to visit.

DIRECTIONS

From Vicksburg, go north on US Highway 61. After crossing the Yazoo River, turn west on Floweree Road and drive three miles to the sign for the WMA. Turn left on Anderson-Tully Road and drive two miles to the headquarters for the WMA, where you can fill out your day permit, then continue driving into the WMA.

CONTACT

Mahannah Wildlife Management Area
(601) 661-0294

ST. CATHERINE CREEK NATIONAL WILDLIFE REFUGE

Cypress swamp at St. Catherine NWR

ST. CATHERINE CREEK National Wildlife Refuge is another terrific place, and it offers a pleasing mix of habitats that includes bottomland hardwood forest, cypress swamp, and managed wetlands, with bits of prairie and upland forest mixed in here and there. The refuge was established in 1990 to conserve habitat in this dynamic area in the Mississippi River floodplain. The area remains connected to the river, so the refuge property floods most years from late winter through spring.

HIGHLIGHTS

The visitor center is a good place to get oriented to the refuge and to check out the displays on native plants and animals.

The entire Magnolia Trail runs 4.1 miles from the visitor center and back. There's a separate trailhead and parking lot for the southern portion of the trail. The south Magnolia Trail begins with a short walk through a prairie lined with partridge pea, false foxglove, and other prairie plants, then enters a dense bottomland hardwood forest. Orb weaver spiders are abundant by summer and spin their webs across the trail in some places. When the elevation drops a few inches, the forest disappears into cypress swamp.

The Swamp and Sibley Impoundments are a collection of managed wetlands that attract a lot of birds; there are places to pull over and observe.

The road to Gilliard Lake ends at a striking cypress swamp. You'll find a boat ramp there, if you'd like to put in and paddle around. A few alligators inhabit the swamp, so don't let your dog go for a swim.

CONTACT

St. Catherine Creek National Wildlife Refuge
21 Pintail Lane
Natchez, MS 39120
(601) 442-6696

DIRECTIONS

From Natchez, go south on US Highway 61 to York Road (about eleven miles from the south part of town). Turn right and drive two miles to Pintail Lane. The visitor center is one-quarter mile on the left.

Orb Weavers

On a late summer hike along an infrequently hiked trail through a bottomland forest, spiderwebs periodically spanned the trail and blocked my path. These weren't just any spiders: They were big, about the size of the palm of my hand, and they lurked in the middle of webs that stretched four feet or more across. I was pretty sure they were orb weavers—entirely harmless and not at all aggressive—but the sheer number—and size—of them creeped me out. Those southern forests sure grow some enormous spiders!

So, naturally, I dug into researching orb weavers to settle my anxieties about them. Orb weavers are a diverse and ancient group of spiders. Scientists have identified nearly three thousand species, and the oldest one (*Mesozygiella dunlopi*) probably emerged 150 million years ago. Their bodies are often brightly colored, and they come in many shapes and sizes, from the palm-size ones with spiky legs that I maneuvered around to thumbnail-size creatures with geometrically shaped armor.

Orb weavers are silk artists. They spin a new web nearly every day, starting the process by shooting a string of silk into the wind. Once the string attaches to another object, the spider crawls to the middle and drops another line of silk to form a Y shape, then goes round and round to finish the web. When prey gets snagged in the threads (usually insects, but they have been observed eating small frogs and hummingbirds unlucky enough to get caught in their web), they paralyze it with a quick bite, then encase it in silk. Once their prey is dead, they vomit digestive juices on the body, then chew and suck it dry.

By late summer, they have grown as big as they are going to get and turn their attention to mating. Male orb weavers don't spend much time in a web. Instead, they prowl around looking for a mate. All of those orb weavers I encountered were probably females. When a pair gets busy mating, it is usually the end of the line for the male. If they copulate for five seconds or less, the male might get away and survive to mate again. However, if the pair copulates for ten seconds—which gives the male a much better chance to pass on his genes—the male is a goner. The female will eat him once they're finished. Female orb weavers lay hundreds of eggs, then they die. The little ones emerge in spring and start the process all over again.

As to my anxieties, they are unnecessary. Orb weavers aren't the least bit aggressive (unless you're an insect or small frog or unlucky hummingbird). They flee when threatened. The only time people get bit (their bite stings but isn't venomous) is when someone tries to handle one, which I will never do.

Orb weaver

CLARK CREEK STATE PARK

Waterfall at Clark Creek

SOUTH OF NATCHEZ, loess hills stretch a few miles east of the Mississippi River, built up by millennia of winds that picked up fine sediments from across the river. Clark Creek sits atop some of those hills, and it is a gorgeous place, with rolling hills and steep valleys. Several waterfalls flow down and over the hills, even during relatively dry times of year. A mix of deciduous and pine trees populates the upland forests, including beech, magnolia, witch hazel, and even some sugar maple. There's a modest fee to enter the park, and it is usually closed on Tuesdays and Wednesdays.

HIGHLIGHTS

A series of trails makes it easy to explore the area, but given the number of hills, you should be in decent shape if you're going to spend more than a little time hiking around. The trails near the parking lot are wide and well tended. When you start from the pay station, the trail follows a narrow, forested ridge with sharp drops on each side, then descends to a creek before ascending another hill. A narrower and less tended trail winds for about two and one-half miles around the perimeter of the property. Pay attention to where you're going, as it is easy to lose your bearings. It's a beautiful place to spend a couple of hours.

CONTACT

Clark Creek State Park
366 Fort Adams Pond Road
Woodville, MS 39669
(601) 888-6040

DIRECTIONS

From Natchez, the drive takes about fifty minutes. Follow US Highway 61 south for thirty-three miles (from the south end of town). Turn right (west) on Main Street in Woodville. After a mile, turn left on Pinckneyville Road and drive for about thirteen miles to Fort Adams Pond Road. Turn right and follow the road to the parking lot.

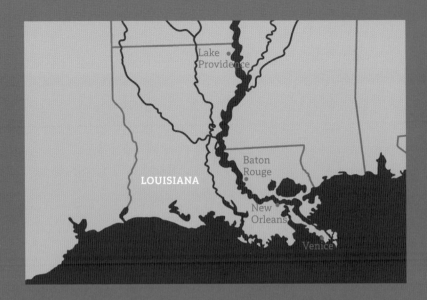

LOUISIANA

THE MISSISSIPPI REACHES its end in Louisiana after passing through a couple hundred miles of land it built in the last seven thousand years. Water is central to life in Louisiana. Louisianans are among the top ten in boat ownership in the United States, and fishing is a top recreational activity, even for those who don't own boats. When people aren't out on the water, they are fighting to keep it away from their homes and businesses.

The Mississippi River has shaped (and continues to shape) much of the state, but what we mean by the "Mississippi River" gets a lot murkier as one travels south in Louisiana. The Big River slows downs and spreads out. Small channels branch off to reach the Gulf of Mexico on their own (channels that are called distributaries). For this guide, I'm sticking mostly to the main channel, with an occasional detour to nearby bayous, distributaries, or remnants of channels the Mississippi River once followed.

Above Baton Rouge, there are still a lot of quiet places to enjoy the river's world, but those places are a little harder to find in the industrial corridor from Baton Rouge to New Orleans. The Great River Road ends at Venice, so you'll need a boat to explore the very end of the river. It's possible to paddle in a canoe or kayak to some places downriver of Venice, but it's probably best to plan a multiday trip

The end of the road at Venice, Louisiana

with camping in remote areas. The paddle back upriver will be easier if you stick close to shore where the current isn't much of a factor. If you aren't interested in paddling but want to get to the end of the river, check at the local marinas to hire a private boat tour.

Baton Rouge and New Orleans offer the greatest range of options for lodging and dining. If you're going to stay in New Orleans for a few days (and why wouldn't you?), consider bicycling around town instead of driving. Accommodations get harder to find downriver of New Orleans.

Louisiana gets a lot of rain so the trails are often muddy. In many places, the hiking trails are also rather short, although you are welcome to walk the ATV trails. If you're going to visit one of the state's wildlife management areas (WMAs), stop at the clearance station to fill out a brief check-in form, then complete the lower half to check out when you leave. Most state parks charge a small entrance fee (per person).

To get the absolute most from a visit to the river's world in Louisiana, you'll want to get in a boat. If you bring your own, you'll find plenty of places to use it. If you don't have a boat with you, many tour operators offer experiences on the water that range from leisurely kayak explorations to amped-up airboat excursions.

TENSAS RIVER NATIONAL WILDLIFE REFUGE

TENSAS RIVER NATIONAL

Wildlife Refuge protects one of the largest remaining patches of bottomland hardwood forest in the Lower Mississippi River floodplain—more than seventy thousand acres. The refuge sprawls in the flatlands between the Red and Mississippi Rivers and offers some stellar opportunities to experience the world of the Lower Mississippi and to see some wildlife.

The land was privately owned until 1980. In the early part of the twentieth century, the Singer Corporation cut down trees from this area to build cabinets for its sewing machines. The Chicago Mill and Lumber Company later took over the property and continued to harvest the area's big trees. The federal government purchased the land in 1980 and established the refuge. Today, the dense forest, oxbow lakes, and swamps provide suitable habitat for alligators, black bear, bobcat, deer, waterfowl, and wild turkey.

Palmettos at Tensas River NWR

HIGHLIGHTS

The boardwalk behind the visitor center passes through a bottomland hardwood forest abundant with palmetto and a patch of cypress swamp and ends at an overlook. You may see armadillos, birds such as black vultures, and orb weaver spiders.

If you want to observe from a distance, Greenlea Wildlife Loop circles three miles around an open field and through a patch of bottomland hardwood forest. Birds are often abundant, and late August is a good time to watch for bears, as they work their way down the sides of the road to pick ripe muscadine grapes.

The Rainey Lake Loop Trail winds four miles through one of the most scenic parts of the refuge. The beautiful, elongated lake provides homes for alligators, waterfowl, and other birds. One short branch of the trail leads to a blind deep in a cypress swamp where egrets have set up a rookery. They are active from late spring into early summer. The easiest place to access the trail is from the small parking area near the beginning of the Greanlea Wildlife Loop. You can also launch a canoe or kayak from the fishing pier on Rainey Lake. Just watch your step, as alligators may be near. The refuge also maintains miles and miles of ATV trails that visitors are welcome to wander.

CONTACT

Tensas River National Wildlife Refuge

    2312 Quebec Road

    Tallulah, LA 71282

    (318) 574-2664

DIRECTIONS

Don't rely on GPS or online maps. From Tallulah, go west on US 80 for eight miles to Quebec Road. From there, it's about eleven miles to the visitor center, Greanlea Wildlife Loop, and hiking trails.

CAT ISLAND NATIONAL WILDLIFE REFUGE

CAT ISLAND NATIONAL Wildlife Refuge is off the beaten path but well worth the detour. Located in the batture—the area between the levees—the refuge remains connected to the ebbs and flows of the Mississippi and is, therefore, still shaped and reshaped by the river. The refuge protects ten thousand acres of bottomland hardwood forest, cypress swamps, and other wetlands. The area floods regularly, so it's a good idea to call ahead or check the website to make sure it is open. The gravel road is fine for most vehicles most of the time, but if it's been wet, parts of the road may be a challenge to maneuver through without four-wheel drive. There is no visitor center or services, and cell service is spotty.

Ancient cypress tree at Cat Island

HIGHLIGHTS

If you have limited time, just take a leisurely drive along the refuge road. You can pull over in many places to sit and watch (birds are often abundant). If you have a few extra minutes, hike the Big Cypress Trail to see one of the largest and oldest cypress trees in the United States: eighty-three feet tall, fifty-four feet around, and at least one thousand years old. At the end of the refuge road, the Riverside ATV trail runs two miles, some of which is along the main channel of the Mississippi.

CONTACT

Cat Island National Wildlife Refuge
(985) 882-2000

DIRECTIONS

From St. Francisville, take US Highway 61 north about a mile to Charlotte Armstrong Drive and go left (west) for one-quarter mile. Take a left on Airport Road (County Road 5) and follow it for a mile to Creek Road (County Road 225). Turn right and follow Creek Road into the refuge.

WADDILL WILDLIFE REFUGE

Comite River at Waddill Wildlife Refuge

WADDILL WILDLIFE REFUGE is a quiet place on the edge of urban Baton Rouge. The refuge is closed a couple of days a week, so confirm their hours in advance if you are planning to visit. It's easy to pass an hour wandering the refuge, maybe a little longer if you stick around for a picnic lunch.

HIGHLIGHTS

The fishing holes are popular, and wide hiking paths through a bottomland hardwood forest crisscross the property. One trail leads to the willow-lined Comite River, which is a short walk from the parking lot. Some paths have slight elevation changes and pass through areas where pulses of high water have carved up the loess soil.

CONTACT

Waddill Wildlife Refuge
4142 North Flannery Road
Baton Rouge, LA 70814
(225) 274-8192

DIRECTIONS

From downtown Baton Rouge, take Florida Street (Business US 190) for nine miles to Flannery Road. Turn left (north); the entrance is about two miles on the right.

DOWNTOWN BATON ROUGE

Mississippi River from Louisiana State Capitol in Baton Rouge

BATON ROUGE IS the upriver end of a busy port complex that runs all the way to the Gulf of Mexico. Although much of the riverfront is industrial, there are still good reasons to stop and take in views of the river's main channel (and the busy shipping traffic).

HIGHLIGHTS

From downtown, an observation deck extends into the river, plus you'll find plazas for public events, walking trails, and museums.

For a higher perspective, head to the Louisiana State Capitol (900 North 3rd Street), the Art Deco tower championed by Huey Long when he was governor. Take the elevator to the observation deck on the 27th floor. The views of the river and floodplain are unbeatable. There is no fee, and there is plenty of free parking around the capitol. The observation deck is usually open from 8 a.m. to 4 p.m. Monday through Friday, but confirm the hours before you go: (225) 342-7317.

FONTAINEBLEAU STATE PARK

HUGGING THE NORTHEAST shore of Lake Pontchartrain, Fontainebleau State Park is a lovely place to enjoy the wetlands and woods that were once common around the lake. In the early nineteenth century, Bernard de Marigny de Mandeville built a sugar plantation on the site and named it Fontainebleau after a well-known forest in Paris. Marigny, unfortunately, died in poverty in 1868 after gambling away his fortune. The land became a state park in 1942 and today offers a mix of historic sites and recreation opportunities. Signs throughout the park mark the sugar mill's site and pay homage to the enslaved men, women, and children who worked on the plantation. Another marker outlines the history of Indigenous People who lived in the area for thousands of years before Euro-Americans moved in. The park maintains a large campground.

Note: Louisiana charges a modest fee (per person) to enter its state parks; children three years old and younger and adults aged sixty-two and older enter free.

HIGHLIGHTS

Live oaks draped with Spanish moss line the roads and walkways in the park, especially close to Lake Pontchartrain. There's an inviting beach on the lake, and an observation deck with good views of the lake and the causeway that connects Pontchartrain's north and south shores. An atmospheric trail runs 4.8 miles through the park's bottomland forest and swamps. The trail is wide and covered with crushed limestone, making it easy for both walking and biking.

The Tammany Trace, a thirty-one-mile paved trail between Slidell and Covington, runs through the north end of the park.

CONTACT

Fontainebleau State Park
62883 Highway 1089
Mandeville, LA 70448
(985) 624-4443

DIRECTIONS

From Mandeville, go east on US Highway 190 for two miles to the park entrance.

Spanish moss hanging from a live oak

Spanish Moss

Is there a more iconic image of the American South than Spanish moss draped over the limbs of a live oak tree? The plant thrives in the South's heat and humidity and seems to prefer live oaks and bald cypress over most other trees.

Spanish moss is often mistaken for a parasite. It's not. It is an epiphyte, a plant that extracts the nutrients and water needed to survive directly from the air. Stems of Spanish moss dangle in shapes that resemble a long beard (shapes that remind me of the beards on the men in the rock band ZZ Top). If you look closely at a stem, you'll see the scales—they look like fine hairs—that pull in nutrients and water. A single stem can grow as long as twenty-five feet. Spanish moss practically creates its own ecosystem. A lot of insects (ticks, spiders, mites) find the moss an accommodating place to live, as do rat snakes and some bats.

Native Americans harvested Spanish moss for generations, using it for insulation—but only after they had boiled it to kill the insects. That lesson escaped the attention of many Euro-Americans when they began using Spanish moss to stuff their pillows and beds. Sure, they dried it out before using it, but every few weeks they had to remove the stuffing and beat the hell out of it to kill the bugs that had returned. In the early twentieth century, car and furniture manufacturers harvested Spanish moss for padding, including Henry Ford, who used it in his Model Ts.

BIG BRANCH MARSH NATIONAL WILDLIFE REFUGE

BIG BRANCH MARSH National Wildlife Refuge offers contrasting experiences along the northeast shore of Lake Pontchartrain, from the well-tended pollinator garden and camellias around the visitor center to the native marshes, bottomland forest, bayous, and pine savanna more typical of the ecosystems that sustained Indigenous People in the area for thousands of years. The refuge headquarters occupy the former site of Bayou Gardens, a public garden founded in 1950 by former Governor Richard W. Leche, who had purchased the property five years earlier after serving five years in prison for stealing federal funds. Bayou Gardens was famous for its azaleas and four hundred varieties of camellias, many of which are still blooming today around the visitor center. The Redemptorist order purchased the property in 1956, where they ran retreats and a seminary. The federal refuge was created in 1994.

HIGHLIGHTS

Nearly two miles of paths surround the visitor center (housed in the former Redemptorist chapel) and wind through the old garden beds. Camellias are mixed in throughout, but the biggest cluster is along the Camellia (Yellow) Trail. They bloom from November through winter.

Boy Scout Road Trail offers a less curated experience. The trail begins with a half-mile stroll through a marsh on a boardwalk marked with interpretive signs. When the boardwalk ends, the trail continues for about four miles through pine savanna and marsh, ending at Bayou Lacombe. The trail also passes a landform called a chenier, which is a sandy ridge built up by waves and typically flanked by mudflats or swamps. In Big Branch Marsh, clusters of oak trees grow on top of the cheniers.

CONTACT

Big Branch Marsh National Wildlife Refuge Visitor Center
61389 Highway 434
Lacombe, LA 70445
(985) 882-2000

DIRECTIONS

The refuge visitor center is two miles south of Interstate 12 on Highway 434 (take Exit 74). To reach Boy Scout Road Trail from the visitor center, head south on Highway 434 to US Highway 190, then turn left (east). After two miles, turn right on South Oaklawn Drive. Turn left on Lacombe Harbor Lane, then left on Grand Avenue, which becomes Paquet Road. When you get to Boy Scout Road, turn right.

MANCHAC WILDLIFE MANAGEMENT AREA

WEST OF NEW Orleans, the area between the big lakes (Maurepas and Pontchartrain) is wet and relatively wild. Most of the original cypress swamp at Manchac has long since been logged, so the remaining areas are a mix of regenerating cypress-tupelo swamp and marshes. It's an easy place to spot alligators and many species of birds. Bulltongue and palmetto are common plants under the mostly open canopy. Water levels vary depending upon the direction of the wind, which can push water out of Manchac Swamp or into it from Lake Pontchartrain.

Kayaking in Manchac Swamp

HIGHLIGHTS

Several companies offer guided kayak swamp tours. The pace is typically lazy and you don't need any kayaking experience (although it helps). You can also paddle around on your own, but if you do, make sure you keep track of the path you're taking so you don't need to call 911 for help finding your way back.

If you're driving to or from the put-in, consider stopping to walk a short hiking trail on the west side of Lake Pontchartrain that is part of the Maurepas Wildlife Management Area. The trail passes through dense swamp thick with willows and tupelo. Louisiana black bear are sometimes around. Access the hiking trail from Old US Highway 51 about two miles north of its exit from Interstate 10 and about one-half mile north of Peavine Road.

CONTACT

Manchac Wildlife Management Area
  (985) 543-4777

DIRECTIONS

If you booked a kayak swamp tour, your guides almost certainly offer transportation to the put-in site from New Orleans (for an extra fee). If you brought your own boat, there's a ramp along Old Highway 51 about five miles north of the Interstate 10 exit; it'll be on the left.

AUDUBON PARK AND THE FLY

The Mississippi River from The Fly

ONE OF THE great urban green spaces in the country, Audubon Park is a popular place to walk, jog, bike, and just hang out.

HIGHLIGHTS

To hang out next to the Mississippi, head to the southwest end of the park, an area called Riverview, or The Fly (after a butterfly-shaped shelter that stood here from the 1960s to the 1980s). The ground rises to about levee height and features soccer fields, picnic tables, and open spaces to watch the river flow and big boats pass by.

Famous for its rows of live oaks and its zoo, the park is also home to a unique urban rookery on Ochsner Island (better known as Bird Island) that provides breeding space for egrets, herons, and other birds.

CONTACT

Audubon Park and The Fly
6500 Magazine Street
New Orleans, LA 70118
(504) 861-2537

DIRECTIONS

Audubon Park is located in the city's Uptown neighborhood. It's about a fifteen-minute drive from the French Quarter. If you're driving, you can get to The Fly by following Magazine Street through the park to West Avenue, which becomes River Drive. Turn left and follow the one-way road around to The Fly, where you'll find plenty of parking. The St. Charles Avenue streetcar stops near the park, which is a more pleasant way to get there and back, if you ask me. From the streetcar stop, you can hop on a shuttle to get you to the zoo and closer to The Fly.

COUTURIE FOREST
AT CITY PARK

NEW ORLEANS FEATURES another unexpected natural space: dense, lush woods in the middle of the city called Couturie Forest that offers a refreshing dose of quiet in a typically noisy place.

HIGHLIGHTS

Located in another fantastic urban park, New Orleans City Park, Couturie Forest features sixty acres of bottomland hardwood forest and wetlands. It's a haven for birds and bird lovers. A maze of trails crisscrosses the forest, including a few that go around the city's highest point, a mound built from leftover construction material that is known as Laborde Mountain, which rises an astonishing forty-three feet above sea level.

City Park offers much more than Couturie Forest. Stay for a while and visit the botanical garden, the children's amusement park known as Carousel Gardens, the New Orleans Museum of Art, Besthoff Sculpture Garden, or play mini-golf, adult-size golf, picnic, fish, or just people watch.

Couturie Forest at City Park

CONTACT

Couturie Forest at City Park
1009 Harrison Avenue
New Orleans, LA 70124
(504) 482-4888

DIRECTIONS

The parking lot and entrance to Couturie Forest are along Harrison Street, just west of the middle of City Park. It's about a fifteen-minute drive from the French Quarter or a slightly longer bike ride along the Lafitte Greenway. Or, you can take the Canal Street streetcar (the City Park/Museum route).

NEW ORLEANS RIVERFRONT

WHARVES AND WAREHOUSES

lined New Orleans' Mississippi riverfront until fairly recently, but today much of that space has opened up. It's now easier than ever to walk next to the main river channel, where you can get a good sense of just how enormous it is.

HIGHLIGHTS

From the aquarium to the French Market, a mile-long elevated path called the Moonwalk (named after former mayor Maurice "Moon" Landrieu) parallels the river, filled with sculpture, historical markers, and gardens. Near the aquarium, Woldenberg Park's green space invites slowing down.

CONTACT

New Orleans & Company
2020 St. Charles Avenue
New Orleans, LA 70130
(800) 672-6124

DIRECTIONS

There are multiple places to access the Moonwalk, including from the end of most of the streets that terminate at the river.

CRESCENT PARK

Mississippi River from Crescent Park

THE NEWEST ADDITION to the public riverfront spaces, Crescent Park begins just past the French Quarter and the end of the Riverfront streetcar line. And what a wonderful urban space it is! Some parts are quiet enough to hear birds singing, and all along the walk, you'll find dramatic views of New Orleans, the river, and the port.

HIGHLIGHTS

From the upriver entrance—a tall iron staircase over railroad tracks—you enter an open warehouse, the Mandeville Shed, which hosts events throughout the year. A 1.4-mile walking path continues downriver, past willow stands growing amidst industrial ruins. You'll find multiple irresistible places to stop and enjoy the sights.

CONTACT

Crescent Park
 (504) 636-6400

DIRECTIONS

There are three entrances to the park. You can enter from a walkway over the railroad tracks that is two blocks downriver of the French Market along North Peters Street. Continuing downriver, there's an entrance from Chartres Street between Piety and Desire Streets and another at the downriver terminus of the park off Chartres near Bartholomew Street.

LAFITTE GREENWAY

HIGHLIGHTS

The Greenway is a popular place for biking, walking, and public events. It offers space to hang out and relax—and it's all dressed up with impressive works of art. In one area, volunteers are replanting a stand of cypress trees.

CONTACT

Friends of Lafitte Greenway
(504) 462-0645

THE LAFITTE GREENWAY runs 2.6 miles from the French Quarter almost to City Park, a lovely parkway created from abandoned railroad tracks after Hurricane Katrina to improve stormwater management and for other public benefits.

DIRECTIONS

The greenway parallels Lafitte Avenue, then continues northwest between Conti and Toulouse Streets. There are multiple points along the way to get on the trail. You'll find one trailhead near the French Quarter on Basin Street just west of Louis Armstrong Park. At the other end of the greenway, near City Park, there's a trailhead at St. Louis and North Alexander Streets.

WOODLANDS PRESERVE

ON THE WEST bank, near another big bend in the Mississippi known as English Turn, Woodlands Conservancy manages 649 acres of bottomland hardwood forest known as the Woodlands Preserve. Thirteen miles of hiking trails snake their way through the woods, some of which are reserved for equestrian use. The forest provides habitat for birds, swamp rabbits, and other life. You may spot an alligator in the canal. The trails are open to the public daily from dawn to dusk, and some come with a surprise.

HIGHLIGHTS

The Upland Trail is an easy 1.1-mile walk along a ridge and a canal, through forest and a meadow before returning to the parking lot. Native trees line the trail, including live oak, water tupelo, swamp red maple, hackberry, and elderberry.

The Bottomland Trail runs 2.2 miles through forest; there are separate but parallel trails for hikers and for horseback riders. There's a surprise at the end of the Bottomland Trail: several concrete shelters that the US government built to store ammunition during World War II. The Naval Ammunition Depot in Minden, Louisiana, produced ammunition that it transported by rail to these shelters, then shipped to American forces in the Pacific via the Mississippi River. You can take a longer hike (another two miles) by following the North Trail near the ammo depots. If you hike the entire Bottomland Trail, Depot Loop, and North Loop, the total distance is 5.5 miles.

CONTACT

Woodlands Conservancy
449 F. Edward Hebert Boulevard
Belle Chase, LA 70037
(504) 443-4000

DIRECTIONS

From New Orleans, cross the Mississippi River on the Crescent City Connection (US Highway 90 Business), then exit at General De Gaulle Drive (Highway 407) and go east. After 2.9 miles, go left at the traffic circle onto Highway 406 and under the bridge. After one-half mile, turn left onto F. Edward Hebert Boulevard. After another one-half mile, turn left into the driveway and follow the gravel road until it ends at a parking area.

BAYOU SAUVAGE URBAN NATIONAL WILDLIFE REFUGE

Bayou Sauvage marsh

AT THE EASTERN edge of the city—but still within New Orleans' city limits—Bayou Sauvage offers another way to exchange the hustle and bustle of the city for bird-watching and wildlife spotting. The twenty-three-thousand-acre refuge includes a mix of ecosystems, but is mostly freshwater and brackish marshes, with some bayou and a small patch of bottomland hardwood forest along the few sections of natural levee. The area is part of the old St. Bernard lobe, land built by an old distributary channel of the Mississippi River at the end of the Gulf of Mexico between 2,800 and 1,000 years ago. The refuge attracts tens of thousands of geese and ducks each winter, and provides full-time habitats for alligators, bobcats, deer,

raccoons, and much more. The refuge is still recovering from damage caused by Hurricane Katrina. The high winds and intrusion of salt water destroyed most of the refuge's trees and large swaths of freshwater and brackish marshes. Since 2008, the refuge has been replanting cypress, hackberry, live oak, and other trees to reestablish forest habitat.

HIGHLIGHTS

There are two places to walk around the refuge's marshes, both of which follow boardwalk trails. The Ridge Trail loops for two-thirds of a mile through bottomland forest and marsh, and includes multiple interpretive signs. The Joe Madere Marsh Trail is a shorter boardwalk that leads to an expansive view of a marsh. Along US Highway 11, there's a boat ramp on the left (west) side of the road with a viewing platform. It's a good place to put in a canoe or kayak and paddle to Lakes Maisson and Antoine.

CONTACT

Bayou Sauvage Urban National Wildlife Refuge
17160 Chef Menteur Highway
New Orleans, LA 70129
(985) 882-2000

DIRECTIONS

The Ridge Trail is located on US 90 four miles east of the Interstate 510/US 90 junction; the parking lot is on the left. The Marsh Trail parking lot is another 0.3 mile east on the right side of the road. To reach the boat ramp, head north on US Highway 11 for three miles from US Highway 90; the ramp is on the right side of the road.

JEAN LAFITTE NATIONAL HISTORICAL PARK AND PRESERVE

Jean Lafitte hiking trail

AN EASY DRIVE from New Orleans, the Barataria Preserve at Jean Lafitte National Historical Park and Preserve is charming and seductive. The Barataria Preserve is part of the St. Bernard lobe built by the Mississippi River between 2,800 and 1,000 years ago. Bayou des Familles, which runs through the preserve, was once a major distributary channel for the Mississippi. The natural levees along its banks provide solid ground for rows of oak trees.

Cypress-tupelo swamps are common in the preserve, as are marshes, bayous, and bottomland hardwood forest. The plants that grow in the preserve vary with subtle changes in elevation. Just a foot difference might turn cypress swamp into marsh, for example. In the preserve, you'll also find a type of marsh known as a flotant, basically, a floating mass of organic peat with grasses on top.

HIGHLIGHTS

Stop into the visitor center for a good orientation to the area, then walk the boardwalk trail that winds through the swamp and marsh behind the building.

Bayou Coquille is a peaceful walk on a well-maintained trail that passes through cypress swamp, bottomland forest, and brackish marsh in less than a mile (one way). It's not unusual to spot alligators and cottonmouth snakes as well as a variety of plant life. The high ground at the start of the trail is a shell midden, basically a hill of clamshells that served as architectural foundations and, sometimes, as ceremonial center for Indigenous People of the area. The Palmetto Trail runs a mile through palmetto-rich forest and connects the visitor center with the Bayou Coquille parking lot.

If you want to paddle around the preserve's streams, call ahead to find out which ones are currently accessible: (504) 689-3690, extension 10. Several companies offer leisurely tours of the Barataria Swamp in slow boats or fast (air) boats. Many emphasize alligator spotting over everything else, but still get you out in the middle of the swamp, where you will probably also see birds and other wildlife.

Alligators

The story of American alligators is a hopeful account of what's possible when we adopt a more thoughtful and respectful relationship with the rest of life on the planet. By the 1950s, alligators were in deep trouble due to excessive hunting and habitat destruction. In 1967, the federal government listed them as endangered (under a program that preceded the Endangered Species Act), and state and federal governments cooperated to enforce habitat preservation and strict limits on hunting. In the late 1980s, authorities declared alligators fully recovered. We still hunt them today, but in a specific season only and with a cap on the number that can be killed.

American alligators are one of the last surviving relatives of dinosaurs; the earliest alligators emerged eighty to one hundred million years ago. They are cousins to crocodiles, but American alligators have a wider and rounder snout.

Adult males range from eleven to fifteen feet long and can weigh up to a thousand pounds; females are only slightly smaller. Alligators like it wet, inhabiting swamps, rivers, and lakes, and have a strong preference for freshwater. Along the Mississippi River, alligators live as far north as central Mississippi and Arkansas.

About eighty teeth line their jaws, and they have an extremely powerful bite, strong enough to penetrate a turtle shell. Their teeth are better suited for gripping rather than shredding, though, and the muscles that open their jaws are surprisingly weak. A strong grip or tape around the jaw is good enough to clamp their jaws shut.

Alligators are top predators, so they eat whatever they want: turtles, mammals (especially muskrats and raccoons), birds; nonnative nutria are among their favorites. Sometimes, they even snack on fruit, such as elderberries and native grapes. They will also use lures to attract birds, perhaps a few sticks or branches that look tempting for nest building. They hunt in the water and on land, sometimes wandering a hundred feet or more from the water. On land, they can sprint up to thirty-five miles an hour, although they tire quickly.

When the weather turns cold, they dig into a bank or under a tree for insulation and slow their biological functions, but they usually stick their snouts just above the waterline to breathe fresh air. During mating season in spring, male alligators attract females by producing a low, rolling groan that shoots short sprays of water up a few inches. It's a fun show to watch.

Alligators are rarely aggressive, but they will strike if provoked. Keep your distance, especially if you see a nest. And never, ever feed them. Doing so erodes the natural wariness they have of humans and associates us with eating, which isn't a good thing.

Swamp tour of Barataria Bay

CONTACT

Jean Lafitte National Historical Park and Preserve

6588 Barataria Boulevard
Marrero, LA 70072
(504) 689-3690

DIRECTIONS

The Barataria Preserve is about a twenty-five-minute drive from the French Quarter. Take the Crescent Connection across the Mississippi (US 90 Business). Exit at Louisiana Highway 45/Barataria Boulevard and follow it for three miles. Turn left on Leo Kerner Parkway/Louisiana Highway 3134 for five miles to Louisiana 45. Turn right. The refuge visitor center is a mile on the left.

ELMER'S ISLAND WILDLIFE REFUGE

Elmer's Island

THERE'S MORE THAN one "end of the road" community south of New Orleans and although each has its merits, I recommend following Highway 1 south of New Orleans along Bayou Lafourche, a distributary channel of the Mississippi River, to Grand Isle. The road passes through small towns, then exits the levee protection after Golden Meadow, and the landscape changes to seascape with dots of saltwater marshes breaking up the water, bits of land built between 1,600 and 600 years ago when the Mississippi's Lafourche Delta was still depositing sediment. Saltwater marshes line a road that rises high above the water; bridges are visible for miles before you cross them. From late fall to early spring, these coastal waters teem with birds.

HIGHLIGHTS

At Grand Isle you'll find 1,100-acre Elmer's Island Wildlife Refuge, a bit of paradise at the edge of the continent. Coastal marshes fill the interior, and wide sandy beaches that stretch to the horizon invite slow strolls. The refuge is a popular place to fish and relax on weekends, but the beach itself is so big it rarely feels crowded. During migration season, the island provides sanctuary to many species of birds, including piping plovers, frigate birds, and egrets. Occasional shuttles provide transportation from the parking lot to wherever you'd like to go on the beach.

The community of Grand Isle stretches on from Elmer's Island for about ten more miles, a drive that you may as well take since you've come this far. The community has a few places to eat and sleep and more beach access—a quiet escape at the end of the world.

Where the road ends at Grand Isle

CONTACT

Elmer's Island Wildlife Refuge
(504) 286-4041

DIRECTIONS

Turn right one-half mile after passing the colorful Grand Isle sign. You'll see a check-in station next to the dirt road.

THE END OF THE RIVER

Brown pelican

ABOUT ONE HUNDRED miles downriver of New Orleans, the Mississippi River enters Head of Passes and the river splits into smaller channels. Many areas around Head of Passes are now protected as conservation areas.

HIGHLIGHTS

Just southeast of Venice, Louisiana, Delta National Wildlife Refuge provides winter habitat for thousands of migrating waterfowl, and its waters and marshes teem with shrimp, fish, and crab. Several species of shorebirds and wading birds make their homes in the refuge year-round, taking advantage of the extensive mudflats and shallow waters.

Breton National Wildlife Refuge protects a sixty-mile-long crescent along the Breton and Chandeleur Islands, the fading remnants of land built by the Mississippi as part of the St. Bernard Delta lobe a couple thousand years ago. Seagrass meadows and mangrove stands occupy portions of these barrier islands, which provide important habitat for brown pelicans as well as brown and white shrimp, spotted sea trout, red drum, loggerhead sea turtles, and Kemp's ridley sea turtles. The two federal refuges are open for day use only and don't offer any services.

Downriver of Venice, Louisiana's Pass-a-Loutre Wildlife Management Area covers 115,000 acres of marshes of varying salinity, some of which have been declining after hurricane damage. Invasive mealy worms have been taking a toll on the roseau cane that is widespread in these marshes. The WMA includes a few remote campsites.

CONTACT
Delta NWR
  (985) 882-2000
Breton NWR
  (985) 882-2000
Pass-a-Loutre WMA
  (337) 735-8667

DIRECTIONS
The road ends at Venice, so if you want to get to these refuges at the end of the Mississippi River, you'll need a boat. There is no regular service, but you can hire a charter boat at one of Venice's marinas.

ACKNOWLEDGMENTS

I know we're at a place in the United States where it's common to say that we've lost faith in our basic institutions. Don't count me among that group. I can't speak to the viability of every American institution, but I've been lucky enough to spend a lot of time in the last dozen or so years visiting places that are being conserved for wildlife and future generations of humans.

Visiting with the rangers, staff, and volunteers who look after these places always reassures me. Sure, many don't get the funding they could use but, in every one of them, dedicated people tend to them, watch over them, and share their love of those places with others. Our public lands and conservation areas are in good hands.

This book is in your hands now because so many people at those conservation areas took the time to answer my silly questions and show me around. Literally, dozens of rangers and volunteers all along the Mississippi River shared their expertise with me. Among those who showed exceptional patience and grace were Connie Cox at Itasca State Park, Julie Ray at T.O. Fuller State Park, and Jack and Elizabeth Coleman in Rosedale, Mississippi. I'm also indebted to the sages of the river, those dedicated people who spend big chunks of their lives living and guiding on the Mississippi, especially Terry Larson, Mike Clark, and John Ruskey. For a couple of years, Ken Lubinski has patiently answered my many questions and given me answers I could understand. I'm also grateful to Mary Harner and Gregory Pec from University of Nebraska at Kearney for taking time to talk with me. And thanks to everyone who is a part of the Mississippi River Network, a coalition of organizations working to make the river better for all. Over the years, so many of you have shared your expertise with me, and I am deeply appreciative.

Two books inspired me to go deeper into understanding the river's world: *Immortal River* by Calvin Fremling and *The Last River Rat* by Kenny Salwey. If you've never read them, go get a copy. Now.

As always, I couldn't have finished a project this without a lot of support from friends and family. My love and thanks to all of you, but especially to my husband, John.

PHOTOGRAPHY AND ILLUSTRATION CREDITS

INDEX

Shawn McDaniel

ABOUT THE AUTHOR

DEAN KLINKENBERG is a St. Louis-based writer. Since leaving his career as an academic psychologist, he has focused much of his writing and research on the Mississippi River. He has driven virtually all of the Great River Road, hiked and canoed the river on multiday expeditions, and cruised on the *American Queen* steamboat as a guest lecturer. His other books include the Frank Dodge mysteries, which explore another side of the river's world. He also served as contributing editor for *Big River Magazine*. His writing has appeared in *Smithsonian*, *The National*, the *Star Tribune*, and the *St. Louis Post-Dispatch*. Dean is a longtime partner in the Mississippi River Network (MRN), a coalition of organizations advocating for healthy and resilient river ecosystems.